FOREWORD

"Newly risen, how brightly you shine."

I hope this book will give you, the student, opportunities to flourish i ....xtbooks don't allow. I have kept you in mind for every page of this book and tried to make it as interesting and varied as I could. My greatest wish for you is that you will learn three vital lessons by using this book:

1) There is no such thing as an 'intelligent' person in the way that people refer to it. There are 8 forms of intelligence. You will get the opportunity to see which ones you are strongest and weakest at. Everyone has degrees of these intelligences in larger or smaller amounts and so do you. The 9th intelligence is an awareness of your place in the world. If this book helps you to see that, I have done *my* job. If you develop a lifelong passion for learning, then you will be the richest person in your class and your teachers are fabulous at *their* job!

2) Every successful person has a plan. In the words of Professor John M. Richardson**: "When it comes to the future, there are three kinds of people: those who let it happen, those who make it happen, and those who wonder what happened."** The hope is that you will use the Life Map in the book as a compass towards your future success. Working towards your goals and ambitions in a small way every day is better than making out a great plan and leaving it in a corner for months on end.

3) 'Blue-sky thinking' has a different definition depending on which dictionary you check. My favourite is that you picture yourself as being successful in the future. Ask yourself how that came about and work back through the good choices you made in life. Then carry out those successful choices every day in school. Smoking a cigarette today can cost you a lot of health problems and money in the future, so don't do it. Making friends with everyone may pay off down the line, however. Be nice to others and be the change you would like to see in others. Blue-sky thinking also means that you dare to think in a way others can't or won't. Don't be afraid to be unique as you *are* unique. Use your talents to be dynamic, creative and willing to learn. If you can do that: **"Yours is the earth and everything that's in it."**

Rudyard Kipling

And always remember: wisdom that comes early has deeper roots. The quote at the top of the page means anyone can have a new beginning if they choose it. Use the privilege of an education to make the best version of you possible. I wish you the very best of fortune and hope that you enjoy reading this book as much as I enjoyed writing it for you.

TABLE OF CONTENTS

INTRODUCTION

You are walking on the beach. You see a blind man falling and you help him.

"Are you all right, sir?" you ask him.

"Thank you. I'm fine," he says. "Could you describe everything you can see from the horizon in for me? I feel comfortable with patterns and that is how I like open spaces to be described. I can hear, feel, smell and taste better than most. If you do this for me, I will give you *my* impressions of the beach."

"I will try my best," you answer. Then you begin.

"The horizon is a like a plumb line of silver."

"Very good," he said. "What colour silver?"

"It is skyline-silver."

"What does it look like?" he questioned.

You can see that he is a demanding person. You decide to give him all the detail he needs to get a mental map of the scene.

"It looks like a long thread. There is a lighthouse on the horizon also. It has midnight-black hoops and it soars up into the air. Far out to sea, there are some seagulls. They are circling and gliding in the air and they are wolf-white. It looks like they are hunting for fish. Beneath them, there are some fishing boats. They are bobbing and dipping in the waves. The fishing nets are glistening in the sea-light. I can see dolphins leaping into the air and they seem to be a cold, steel-grey.

Closer to the shore, the waves are tumbling onto the beach. The sea is chemical-blue and the wave crests are milk-white. The shape of the beach is like a horseshoe and it is gleaming as golden as melted treasure. Children are building sand castles and slapping the sand with their spades. There are tourists walking about with leather-brown faces. They all look as fit as trout and they are laughing a lot. The coconut trees on the edge of the beach are lush and Eden-green. There's a barbecue grill just up ahead of us and the coals are glowing molten-red."

"Thanks very much. You're a very good narrator. You tell a good story with excellent detail."

"You are very welcome," you tell him. You're very proud of yourself. You have learned something very valuable also. It is easier to use patterns of description when you are starting out as a narrator. In this case, it was easy to start with the horizon and work in towards the beach. You promise yourself that you must use this technique more often.

"However, you never answered my question fully," he says.

"I'm sorry. I thought I had." You are very annoyed with yourself now.

"What's in the blue sky?'" he asks. You look up at its vastness. Then you start all over again.

Date: __/__/__	Title: **DESCRIBING A BEACH: 1st GRID**	Lesson number:

Latin phrase: Sapere aude.

Definition: D_re/t_ /b_/wi_e.

Meaning: _____

_____

Spelling revision	New words	Dictionary definitions, corrections and synonyms.
	P45	pneumonoultramicroscopicsilicovolcanoconiosis
	pneumono	
	ultra	meaning extremely or a lot of (from Latin)
	microscopic	
	silico	
	volcano	
	coniosis	

You are walking on the beach on a sunny day. What's in the sky?

1 POINT	2 POINTS	3 POINTS	4 POINTS
cl_u_s	a b_rd	se_g_lls	f_o_k/att_c_i_g/you
the/s_n	an/a_r_pl_ne	a k_te	a_rpl_ne with l_t_ers

5 POINTS	6 POINTS	7 POINTS	8 POINTS
the s_a_s	t_u_d_r_l_u_s	a h_n_g_i_er	t_rn/c_r_or_nt/r_v_n
the mo_n	a /n_med /s_ar	a p_r_ch_te	sw_n/h_r_i_g_g_ll

9 POINTS	9 POINTS	10 POINTS	10 POINTS
nothing-you're b_i_d	a/t_una_i /w_ve	a/bo_y/f_ll_ng	any/bl_e_/ad_e_ti_e
w_r_d/en_i_g/co_et	n_cle_r/m_shr_om	an/a_i_n/sp_ce_ra_t	

super student ideas

POINTS SCORE

0-50 good first try	51-100 well done	101-130 very good	131-148 excellent

A full stop closes a sentence. This means readers can understand your sentences properly.
Do you think this a good idea? List three reasons why on the next page.
"Always aim for the moon: even if you miss, you'll land among the stars." W. Clement Stone

1. I should use full stops because _____.

2. I should use full stops because_____.

3. I should use full stops because_____.

RULES FOR FULL STOPS

a) Use a full stop at the end of a sentence.

b) Use a full stop for abbreviations (i.e. a word that is shortened by using letters).

c) You may or may not decide to use a full stop for contractions. A contraction is where the word is shortened by omitting letters. It is probably better to use a full stop with these to avoid confusion. Examples include *Dr.* (Dr) for doctor or *qt.* (qt) for quart.

COMMON ABBREVIATIONS

Latin terms:

1. i.e. means **id est**. This is **that is to say** in English.

2. etc. means **et cetera**. This is **and so on** in English.

3. et al. means **et alii.** This is **and others** in English.

4. A.M means **ante meridiem**. This is **before noon** in English.

5. P.M means **post meridiem**. This is **after noon** in English.

Tick the correct abbreviations and correct any spelling errors:

1. I went to the beech early (i.e. / etc. / et al. I went at 7a.m. / p.m.).

2. I bought a lot of vegatables for the barbaque: mushrooms, onions (i.e. / etc. / et al.).

3. John and Helen (i.e. /etc. / et al.) all came with us to the beach

Find out these abbreviations: Military rank. Fill in the spellings.

1. ex. / e.g.   1. Pvt =   6. Maj. =

2. ibid. / lb.   2. Cpl =   7. Lt. Col. =

3. N.B. / P.S.   3. Sgt =   8. Col. =

4. R.I.P / R.S.V.P   4. Lt =   9. Lt. Gen. =

5. S.O.S / a.k.a.   5. Capt. =   10. Gen. =

Date: __/__/__	Title: **DESCRIBING A BEACH: 2nd GRID**	Lesson number:

Latin phrase: Iucundum est narrare sua mala

Definition: A/pr_bl_m/s_ar_d/i_/a/pr_bl_m/h_lv_d.

Meaning: _____

_____

Spelling revision	New words	Dictionary definitions, corrections, and synonyms.
P45		p_e_m_n_ul_t_m_cr_sc_p_cs_l_cov_lc_n_c_n_osis
pne_m_no	im_ge	
u_t_a	pe_ma/t_n	
m_cr_sc_p_c	sp_in_li_g	
s_li_o	bra_i_g	
v_l_ano	l_lli_g	
con_o_is	pl_mb/li_e	

images for the seaside

1 POINT	2 POINTS	3 POINTS	4 POINTS
chi_dr_n /pl_ying	d_nk_ys/bra_i_g	si_zl_ng /b_rb_cues	ya_h_s /l_lli_g
bo_ts /b_b_ing	pe_ma/t_n/to_ri_ts	p_ll_rs of s_nsh_ne	pl_mb /li_e /ho_i_on

sky colour

b_tte_f_y-blue	c_ckt_il-blue	br_ch_re-blue	J_ru_a_em-blue
j_w_l-blue	ne_n-blue	e_ec_ric-blue	B_r_u_a-blue

calm sea sounds

the sp_in_li_g/waves	the g_rg_ing waves	the e_bi_g tide	m_rm_r_ng sea
s_a /so_g of waves	the hu_m_ng sea	the tr_mb_i_g sea	g_n_ly /e_h_li_g

POINTS SCORE

0-10 good first try	11-29 well done	30-50 very good	51-60 excellent

"Success is no accident. It is hard work, perseverance, learning, studying, sacrifice and most of all, love of what you are doing or learning to do."   **Pele**

Which quality mentioned is the most important in achieving success, in your opinion? Why?

A capital letter starts a new sentence. This means readers know where one sentence starts and another begins.

Do you think you should use capital letters in your writing? List three reasons why.

1. I should use capital letters because_____.

2. I should use capital letters because_____.

3. I should use capital letters because_____.

10 guidelines for capital letters

1. use a capital letter for the **first word of a sentence**. change both these sentences!

2. Use a capital for the **pronoun 'I'** as you are the most important person in the world!

3. Use it for **your** mother and father but not for other people's.

Ex's: a) I heard **M**om say that **D**ad was a goldfish in another life.

   b) **Your m**other and **f**ather have great manners.

4. Use a capital for **proper nouns** (i.e. Christian names and surnames, characters in books and films et cetera and organisations). Capitalise the following if you think it necessary:

a) john murphy is my neighbour

b) the gruffalo's don't scare me anymore

c) the simpsons are an American family on television

5. Use a capital for **titles** that come before a name (e.g. President Obama).

6. Use a capital for **days, months** and **holidays** but **not** seasons (e.g. **autumn**).

7. Use a capital for **religious** gods and books (e.g. the Koran/ Qur'an).

8. Use a capital for all **nationalities, languages, ethnic groups** and **religions** (e.g. Irish).

9. Use a capital for **historical events** and **periods** (e.g. the Middle Ages).

10. Use a capital for **acronyms** like UN (i.e. letters that represent a group or organisation).

Date: __/__/__	Title: **DESCRIBING A BEACH: 3rd GRID**	Lesson number:

Latin phrase: Tarde venientibus ossa.

Definition: For/th_se/wh_/ar_ive/l_te, on_y/the/b_nes.

Meaning: _____

_____

Spelling revision	New words	Dictionary definitions, corrections, and synonyms.
b_rb_c_es	b_es_ax	
lol_i_g	o_e	
p_r_at_ns	ear_hsh_ne	
lago_n	m_lten	
bro_h_re	a_c	
g_r_l_ng	sic_le	
cres_en_	scyt_e	

colour of the sand

1 POINT	2 POINTS	3 POINTS	4 POINTS
po_der-white	st_rbe_m-gold	wh_leb_ne-white	m_lten-gold
o_st_r-white	b_es_ax-gold	o_e-gold	ear_hsh_ne-gold

shape of the beach in metaphors

an/a_c	a/ho_k	sic_le/shaped	a h_lf/mo_n
a/b_w	a/ho_sesh_e	scyt_e/shaped	a cr_sc_nt/mo_n

physical sensations

skin/ti_gl_ng	parc_ed/t_ro_t	feet like h_t/co_ls	stab_ed by s_n/spea_s
skin/b_rn_ng	deh_dr_ted	face like G_e_k/fi_e	scr_p_d by sa_dpa_er

POINTS SCORE

0-10 good first try	11-29 well done	30-50 very good	51-60 excellent

Writing sentences in point form helps to structure your work clearly and is easy to read.

Do you think it is sometimes better to write in this way as a student of English? List three reasons why in your copy book.

WRITING A STORY IN POINTS

1. I walked on the ear_hs_i_e-gold beach.	COLOUR
2. It was pi_l_w soft.	TEXTURE
3. The song of the sea was a hus_ed /m_rm_r.	SOUND
4. It was a sc_t_e shaped beach.	SHAPE
5. The crests of the waves were r_l_ing like a line of ho_s_s.	ACTION
6. P_l_ars of su_s_i_e moved across the w_t_r.	IMAGE
7. The clouds in the sky were e_f-mist white.	METAPHOR
8. My face felt like it was sta_b_d by sun sp_a_s.	SENSATION
9. There was a smell the ar_ma of br_ne was in the sea air.	SMELL
10. I ate a ch_rc_al_d tuna st_ak and it was delicious.	TASTE

Now write two more stories in bullet point by choosing from a selection of these words.

1. COLOUR	(o_e-gold/ m_lt_n -gold/ sta_be_m-gold)
2. TEXTURE	(co_t_n soft/ do_ny soft/ ei_er soft)
3. SOUND	(g_rg_ing sea/ h_m_ing sea/ eb_i_g sea)
4. SHAPE	(an a_c/ a h_l_ mo_n/ a ho_s_s_oe)
5. ACTION	(tum_l_ng waves/ casc_d_ng waves/ cu_l_ng waves)
6. IMAGE	(seag_l_s di_e bo_b_ng/ c_c_n_t tre_s sw_y_ng/ boats bo_b_ng)
7. METAPHOR	(pil_a_s of s_nsh_ne/ str_a_s of li_ht/ lan_er_s of light)
8. SENSATION	(skin tin_l_ng/ par_h_d th_o_t/ skin bu_n_ng)
9. SMELL	(oi_y/ f_s_y/ sa_ty)
10. TASTE	(spi_y ch_c_en/ yu_my h_t d_gs/ fl_me gr_l_ed me_t)

Did you know? There are 8 types of intelligence. One of them is an appreciation of nature. The others are: bodily, people, inner self, language, logic, musical and spatial. These will be discussed later in the book. The 9th intelligence is having an awareness of your place in the world. Do you agree that a lifelong love of learning may be the 10th intelligence?

Punctuate the following and correct the 10 misspellings by rewriting it in a copy book.

If you have food in your frige, clothes on your back, a roof over your head and a place to sleep, you are richer than 75% of the world If you have money in the bank, money in your walet and some spare change, you are among the top 8% of the worlds' welthy If you woke up this morning with more helth than illness, you are more blessed than the milion people who will not survive this week If you have never experinced the danger of battle, the agany of imprisonment or torthure or the horrible pangs of starvation, you are luckier than 500 million people alive and suffering If you can read this mesage, you are more fortinate than the 3 billion people in the world today who cannot read at all

Questions:

1. Do you think all of this is true or just some of it? Why? Why not?

2. Does anything about this surprise or shock you? Why? Why not?

3. If you could help with one of the problems above, what would it be, and why?

4. Can you think of anyone in your community who might have some of these problems? How can you help that person or is it someone else's responsibility?

5. How important is it to appreciate a good education?

15 BLUES COLOUR SEARCH: CIRCLE THE LETTERS

a	q	k	p	l	a	g	o	o	n
m	p	n	b	k	x	r	l	k	o
o	c	e	i	w	p	t	j	a	m
b	r	o	c	h	u	r	e	r	e
j	a	n	e	y	i	e	r	p	l
d	f	i	l	a	k	e	u	b	e
p	w	v	o	j	d	l	s	u	c
w	b	e	r	m	u	d	a	t	t
c	o	c	k	t	a	i	l	t	r
o	m	t	g	a	q	j	e	e	i
g	a	l	a	x	y	f	m	r	c
s	p	o	w	d	e	r	o	f	h
i	s	e	h	b	s	x	p	l	o
d	z	j	e	w	e	l	e	y	i
z	e	u	s	n	m	t	e	a	l

Did you know? The original name for a butterfly was a flutter-by! Check it out on Google.

RIDDLE # 1: How many of each animal did Moses take on the ark?

"To err is human; to forgive, divine."   **Alexander Pope**

Date: __/__/__	Title: **DESCRIBING A BEACH: 4th GRID**	Lesson number:

Latin phrase: Abyssus abyssum invocat.

Definition: De_p/th_nk_ng/lea_s/to/de_p/und_rst_n_ing.

Meaning: _____

_____

Spelling revision	New words	Dictionary definitions, corrections, and synonyms.
be_sw_x	sim_le	comparing two things using as or like
o_e	d_me	
e_r_hsh_n_	meta_h_r	comparing two things without using as or like
m_lt_n	fle_ce	
ar_	anv_l	
si_k_e	med_lli_n	
s_yt_e	Tit_n	

describing the size of a sea sky

1 POINT	2 POINTS	3 POINTS	4 POINTS
the swe_p of sky	the ar_h of sky	the une_di_g sky	the inf_n_te sky
the d_me of sky	the sp_n of sky	the end_e_s sky	the cat_edr_l of sky

sim_les describing clouds

like fa_ry/sm_ke	like puf_bal_s	like fle_ce	like a_ry/anvi_s
like e_f-mist	like pu_fy/plat_s	like flu_fy/c_tt_n	like he_ve_ly/ho_ds

meta_h_rs for the sun

a fi_ry ball in the s_y	a g_ld_n/glo_e	God's da_st_r	a glo_i_g/med_lli_n
a gl_wi_g/o_b	G_d's/g_ld_n/e_e	God's/m_rni_g/star	Tit_n's/fie_y/w_e_l

magical words grid

bl_ss-blue	div_n_	the soug_ing sea	ult_am_r_ne-bl_e
sta_ry	the luc_d light	the sor_er_ of the s_a	spe_lbi_ding

POINTS SCORE

0-20 good first try	21-49 well done	50-69 very good	70-80 excellent

Did you know? One of the best metaphors for water is 'Adam's Ale'. That's because it was the only drink available to Adam in the Garden of Eden. Others call it 'the elixir of life'. The earliest reference to it is from William Prynne in 1643:

"They have beene shut up in prisons and dungeons…..allowed onely a poore pittance of Adam's Ale, and scarce a penny bread a day to support their lives."

Who do you think William Prynne was referring to? Do you feel sorry for these people?

The unusual words (dungeons, scarce, pittance etc.) are examples of **archaic** words. These are words that are no longer commonly used. Write the dictionary definition of 'archaic' and 'elixir' in your vocabulary notebook.

WHAT IS A METAPHOR?

A metaphor compares two things **without** using as or like. An easy way to remember it is that **metaphors** are **meat for** the bones of English!

A metaphor is **MEAT PHOR** the bones of English. It adds meat to the skeleton.

This is a metaphor because **the English language is being compared to a skeleton**.

This is also a metaphor because **metaphors are being compared to meat**.

Metaphors add 'sparkle' to a piece of writing and should be used as much as possible. Underneath are 10 examples of metaphors. Explain in your own words why they are metaphors. The first two are done for you.

1. The **sea** was **topaz**-blue. (Topaz is a beautiful, blue gemstone)

This is a metaphor because **the sea** is being compared to a blue **gemstone**.

2. Hawks are the Ferrari's of the sky.

This is a metaphor because **the hawks** are being compared to **Ferrari's**.

3. Rivers are the veins of the forest.

This is a metaphor because

4. i-phones are the new drug of the 21st century.

This is a metaphor because

5. She had bee-stung lips.

This is a metaphor because

6. Camels are the ships of the desert.

This is a metaphor because

8. Creativity is known as the 'third eye'.

This is a metaphor because

9. Branched lightning lit up the sky.

This is a metaphor because

10. Imagination is called the 'mind's eye'

This is a metaphor because

The grid below contains two ideas for a metaphor. Make a metaphor by using both of them in a sentence in your copybook. The first one might look like: **"Stars are the magicians' dust of the night sky."** The second one is easy also: **"He had seashell ears."** Then try to fill in the **FIRST IDEA/SECOND IDEA** column on the right. Ask your teacher to help you if you need it. Make up your own metaphors also.

MAKE A METAPHOR

FIRST IDEA	SECOND IDEA	FIRST IDEA	SECOND IDEA
St_rs	**are the ma_ici_ns' d_st of the sky.**	sky	the canv_s of the Gods
e_rs	**He had se_sh_ll ears.**	drugs	
A w_terf_ll	is the si_v_r /lo_m of the f_rest.	the moon	
T_it_er	is the t_l_p_o_e of the 21st c.	television	
The r_in	was i_e co_d.	mist	
K_o_led_e	is the sa_v_tion of m_nk_nd.	trees	
The s_y	was a clo_dsc_pe of c_l_u_s	the sun	
J_hn	is the al_h_ _m_le.	waves	
A mne_onic	is m_ntal Vel_ro.	darkness	
Po_l_n	is the mo_nd_st of the air.	sunbeam shape	
Ma_y	is the app_e of her tea_h_r's/e_e.	The cottage	
The dicton_ry	is the B_b_e of E_g_i_h.	fame	
Mo_nt_i_s	are ca_h_dr_ls of the s_yl_ne.	monster's eyes	
De_er_s	are a sau_a of h_a_.	rain	

"Impossible is just a big word thrown around by small men who find it easier to live in the world they've been given than to explore the power to change it. Impossible is not a fact. It is an opinion. Impossible is not a declaration. It's a dare. Impossible is potential. Impossible is temporary. Impossible is nothing." **Muhammad Ali**

Do you like this quote? Why? Why not? What does it tell you about his mind set?

How many metaphors can you spot?

Why not do a project on the life of Muhammad Ali? His quotes will entertain you!
You'll need to do a project on an issue or person of your choice soon. Start planning now!

REVISION FUN WITH CROSSWORDS: 100 YEARS ON

The crossword first appeared in the *New York World* on Dec 21, 1913. It was called 'word-cross' at first but a typo called it 'cross-word'. In Britain, many claimed that this new craze would unravel the social fabric of society. Housewives weren't doing their chores and people were doing them in church. Despite those hiccups, they're still here and they're still fun!

ACROSS

4 That is to say (2, 3)

5 Honey gold buzzing in your ear? (7)

7 Stop flying it! (4)

8 Shorter version of 'and others' (2, 2)

10 The long, low sigh of the sea (5)

12 Michelle is not the only First Lady! (3)

13 The shape of a dangerous beach (6)

14 A large ex-pans-e of sky (4)

16 The coldest blue of them all (3)

17 An old, arcane word. (7)

DOWN

1 A party to go to sleep at (10)

2 It causes huge waves (7)

3 Latin stems for influenza and one (8)

6 Breathing out gently (8)

8 To forgive is divine (3)

9 To shorten a word to its initials (7)

11 A gem of a blue colour (5)

13 A special intelligence (7)

14 So small it's a conjunction (2)

15 Clear of thought and colour (5)

WHAT IS A SIMILE?

A simile compares two things without using as or like. An easy way to remember it is:

"His smiles are **as** rare **as** rubies and **like** a lion's!"

This is a simile because it compares his smiles to rubies by using the word **'as'**.

It is also a simile because it compares his smiles to rubies by using the word **'like'**.

Similes add 'sunshine' to a piece of writing and should be used as much as possible. Underneath are 10 examples of similes. Explain in your own words why they are similes.

1. The moon's light was as silver as diamond flame.

This is a simile because the **moon's light** is compared to **diamond flame** using **'as'**.

2. Porridge is like rocket fuel for the body and mind.

This is a simile because

3. Her teeth were like a line of piano keys.

This is a simile because

4. The night was as cold as a phantom's soul.

This is a simile because

5. He has a voice like bottled thunder.

This is a simile because

6. Facebook is like a social crutch for some people.

This is a simile because

7. The morning dew glittered like a million, million fallen stars.

This is a simile because

8. Teachers are like the fountain of knowledge.

This is a simile because

9. Her voice was as clear as a crystal stream.

This is a simile because

10. Einstein was as wise as an owl.

This is a simile because

TURNING METAPHORS INTO SIMILES

Try to change the following metaphors into similes in your copybook:

1. The sea was a flat **sheet** of silver (i.e. the sea was **like** a …………………………).

2. The sky was a distant **ceiling** of blue (i.e. the sky was **like** a…………….......).

3. Seagulls are the **ballerinas** of the sky (i.e. the seagulls were **like**……………....).

SITTING ON THE BEACH AT NIGHT

In the grid beneath are phrases using similes (S) and metaphors (M). Write in an (S) or (M) after each one if you know what it is.

The phrases use only four of the senses to form a story: sight, sound, smell and sensation.

Write a story by using each phrase **going down the grid**. You should have 10 sentences by doing this but you should try to put in your own ideas also. Level 1 is the easiest and Level 3 is the most difficult to write.

LEVEL 1	LEVEL 2	LEVEL 3
a **feast** of stars in the sky (**M**)	a galaxy of stars overhead	a constellation of stars hung
like shiny dust (**S**)	like glitter on black velvet	like anvil sparks
n_g_t's/bl_ck/c_o_k closed	n_g_t's/in_y/ro_e covered all	night's da_k/s_ro_d appeared
as q_i_t as a c_u_ch	as q_i_t as a con_e_t	as s_ill as a to_b
the o_d-g_ld/m_on	the o_e-g_ld m_on	the m_l_en-gold m_on
the so_t so_g of the s_a	the g_n_le/o_e_a of the s_a	the h_s_ed/l_llab_ of the s_a
b_a_s of light on the water	s_ea_s of light on the water	l_n_es of light on the surface
w_nd felt like warm si_k	w_nd felt like warm s_t_n	w_nd felt like a veil of v_l_et
a so_p of smells	a b_ew of scents	a b_o_h of aromas
da_n/s_n like a gl_wi_g/o_b	s_n was God's g_ld_n/e_e	God's/m_r_ing st_r/ro_e

Did you know? The average person has a vocabulary of 5,000-7,000 words. Shakespeare used 31,534 different words when writing his plays and invented approx. 1,700. Get learning!

Riddle # 2: A clever prince is loved by his people but hated by his father. The father decides to get rid of him for once and for all. The misfortunate prince is accused of stealing a golden torc and he is sentenced to death. The people revolt when they see the injustice of it and the king has to make up a test of honesty that no one can escape from. The king parades the prince in front of the people on a raised, wooden platform so that everyone can see him from all sides. The prince doesn't have any clothes on so that he can't cheat the test. The king speaks:

"In this bag are two grapes. One is black and one is white. If my son takes out a white grape, he's innocent and will go free. If he removes a black grape, he's guilty and will be executed."

There are two black grapes in the bag, yet the clever prince walks free. How did he do it?

Punctuate the following by reading it once and correcting it in your copy book.

"when i was 5 years old, my mother told me that happiness was the key to life. when i went to school, they asked me what i wanted to be when i grew up i wrote down 'happy' they told me i didn't understand the assignment I told them they didn't understand life."

1. Who do you think said this: president barrack obama, john lennon or michael jordan?

2. Do you think that this is a good quote? Why? Why not?

3. What does it say about the student and what does it say about the teachers/questioners?

4. How do you think you can achieve happiness in your own life? Write down 5 things that make you happy and discuss them. Do fast foods and fizzy drinks make people happy?

5. The three people above worked harder at their job than any of their rivals. What is the lesson to be learned from this?

FILL IN THE BLANKS

1. The beach was ea_th_h_ne-gold.	COLOUR
2. We heard the sno_z_ sea lap gen_l_.	SOUND
3. We walked on a b_w of beach.	SHAPE/MOTION
4. Cyl_n_ers of light moved acro_s the sea.	METAPHOR
5. The other tou_i_ts were le_th_r-brown.	TANS
6. The horizon was thre_d_d with a border of silver.	HORIZON
7. Ch_ld_en were sq_ea_ing on the beach.	OTHER IMAGES
8. The sun to_s_ed our skin.	SENSATION
9. The sea air smelled of ch_or_ne.	SMELL
10. The sp_cy sa_sa_es in the burg_r bur_ed our tong_es.	TASTE

List the best six sentences you would pick from the above ten. Be careful, as there are six categories that you should try to put into every descriptive passage. Write down why in a copy book and then ask your teacher if he/she agrees.

Did you know? If you ever feel alone, alienated from other people or a bit down, all you have to do is type in 'Where the Hell is Matt 2012' into YouTube. You might begin to understand the world a bit more, your place in it and your potential to change it. Then type in the same for 2008 and 2006. It should at least make you smile.

RIDDLE # 3: You walk into a cold, dark room with a match. Inside are a candle, a woodstove and a heater. Which would you light first?

Blue-Sky Thinking

Date: __/__/__	Title: **DESCRIBING A BEACH: 5ᵗʰ GRID**	Lesson number:

Latin phrase: Oeulus animi index.

Definition: The/e_e/lo_k_/b_t/it/is/t_e/m_n/th_t/s_es.

Meaning: _____

_____

Spelling revision	New words	Dictionary definitions, corrections, and synonyms.
m_t_ph_r	sali_e	
d_m_	barb_cu_d	
p_nt_e_n	soo_hi_g	
fl_e_e	lul_i_g	
a_v_l	tan_y	
m_d_l_i_n	charco_l_d	
T_t_n	ke_p	

emotional sensations

1 POINT	2 POINTS	3 POINTS	4 POINTS
he_rt war_ing	sp_rit lif_ing	soul ref_es_ing	soul no_ris_ing
he_rt com_or_ing	sp_rit rai_i_g	soul soo_hi_g	soul lul_i_g

smells of the beach

oi_y	fi_hy	smell of k_lp	sali_e
sal_y	se_we_d	smell of bri_e	pelag_c

tastes of the beach

yum_y/h_t/do_s	spi_y/ch_c_en	fla_e/gri_l_d/me_t	siz_l_ng/ste_k
deli_io_s/bu_ge_s	barb_cu_d/sa_sa_es	co_l-fir_d/o_io_s	charco_l_d/tu_a

POINTS SCORE

0-10 good first try	11-29 well done	30-50 very good	51-60 excellent

A question mark lets you know that you are being asked a question. However, a lot of people never use them in text messages. Do you think, therefore, that they should be banned altogether from the English language? Discuss with your teacher and give three reasons why/why not.

18

USING THE MICRO WITH THE MACRO

Congratulations. You have completed one descriptive module and you will be moving onto another shortly. At this stage, you may have learned the value of patterns in English. They should help you to write with confidence and purpose. You don't have to be a slave to them, however. The best stories come from a child's imagination, not a textbook. Because of that, take a look at the grids below. They may help you to create a story using the **micro idea** instead of the **macro pattern**.

The word macro means 'large-scale'. You do not have to use the formula from the horizon in if you do not wish to. That is the macro pattern to help you start on the long journey of becoming a great writer, creative thinker and questioning student.

The word micro means 'extremely small'. The micro idea is just as valuable a technique. It is also called **laser-eyed attention to detail**. This is when you focus in on a small detail that very few others would have thought of. It could be an animal, a strange object or a character of some sort. Your story is launched from that point in. It usually leads students to a story that is rich, mysterious and unique. Forget the blind man. Forget the micro patterns. Forget the flipping dolphins. Fill in the grids and they may take you to a time or distant land you do not want to stop writing about.

You're walking on the beach when you spy a tidal pool or lagoon. What's in the pool?

1 POINT	sc_ttl_ng/cr_bs	t_rbo/ch_rg_d/sh_imp	n_ck_l-silver fi_h
5 POINTS	m_ss_ge in a b_tt_e	a Mi_len_i_m/c_ps_le	a/g_n_e's/la_p
5 POINTS	eng_av_d/g_ld_n/r_ng	a st_sh of R_m_n/co_ns	a tr_asu_e/ch_st
5 POINTS	t_u_a_i/wr_ck_ge with st_ange/ob_c_s	dr_ft_ood with an a__m h_ndcu_f_d to it	un_no_n/g_ant/s_a cre_tu_e
5 POINTS	un_xp_od_d WW2 bomb	in_adi_g/fr_gm_n from a foreign land	a bu_l/s_a_k/ci_cling a surfer

The difference between the first row (worth 1point) and the other 4 rows (worth 5 points each) is huge. If you were to ask every student in the country to describe what is in the pool, crabs and fish would be in a lot of answers. They might just end their story there also. Someone who can think of a **'story fizzer'** is an excellent student. Why not write a story using one of the objects mentioned in the 5 point grids? Ask yourself these questions:

1. **What** brought them here?

2. **Where** did they come from?

3. **When** did they get here? Is there something suspicious about them?

4. **Who** might have been responsible?

5. **Why** should you be careful?

6. **How** are they going to change your story or life?

INTERROGATIVE WORDS

An interrogative word is a word which normally starts a question. It is called an interrogative word because it comes from the word 'interrogation'. This means 'to question'. You have probably arrived home late sometime and a parent says loudly: "***Where*** were you?" Now you can say to that parent that they're very interrogative, though it is not recommended!

Interrogative word examples include:

1. What   4. Who

2. Where   5. Why

3. When   6. How

These are also the six questions that all English students should ask when writing a story. Journalists always try to follow this rule when writing an article.

Let's say a whale gets stranded on a beach. Re-arrange the interrogative words, add some more and write a short newspaper article on the whale story for your school newspaper. Consider the following:

Would you give the time and date of the incident first or the location?

Would you use 'who' for who was there or who caused the whale to beach?

Would you use 'how' for how many times this has occurred or for how the whale beached?

Try to be imaginative when you are posing questions. You will find that you are writing a very powerful story. Everyone will want to hear it.

PUNCTUATE THE FOLLOWING AND ANSWER/ GOOGLE THE QUESTIONS:

1. What colour would you put after the adjective 'tropical'

2. Where would you find kelp

3. when do whales appear off the coast of ireland is it in spring/summer or autumn/winter

4. Who and what is a 'hawker' on a beach

5. why is the sea blue

Did you know? Hedgehogs will avoid areas that smell of badgers. Badgers will eat hedgehogs if they can find them and hedgehogs will attack birds and eat them also. Do you find this cruel or do you accept that nature does not care about human feelings?

RIDDLE # 4: A woman walks into a restaurant and asks the manager for a glass of water. The manager aims a gun at her instead. The woman was pleased. She said thank you and left. Why was she pleased?

RECAP ON LESSON

Rewrite the following story by substituting the words/phrases underlined for different ones. Punctuate it where you think necessary also.

it was lava hot on a summer's day. I decided to go for a ramble on the beach with my friend, laura. When we got there the sky was an <u>endless dome</u> of <u>brochure-blue</u>. the clouds looked like <u>airy anvils</u> and drifted slowly.

The beach was shaped like a <u>sickle</u> and it felt feather soft. it was gleaming like melted gold. <u>donkeys were braying</u> in the distance and the horizon was a perfect plumb line of silver.

The soft <u>ballad</u> of the sea washed over us and we could hear the waves <u>singing</u>. <u>chords</u> of sunlight arrowed from the blue arch of the sky. Lots of tourists passed us sporting deep, <u>bronzed tans</u>.

are you hungry laura asked me as my stomach growled

yes i replied I could eat a hippopotamus

the sun beat down on us, making us <u>thirsty</u> as well

the smell of those <u>sizzling steaks</u> are making me famished as well she said lets go get some.

We bit into the steak and it was scrumptious.

it's the most divine steak ive ever tasted laura said.

We walked home as the sun set. it was like a <u>golden eye</u> in the sky getting dimmer. Just then we heard a whistling sound and a body dropped from the sky. It hit the sand with a mighty thump and was still. We looked at each other, horrified and stunned.

Do you think this is a good story? Why?

Do you agree that all descriptive writing passages should contain **colours, sounds** etc.?

What other categories should be put in all passages of descriptive writing?

Finish the story by telling us what happened next in 10-20 sentences. Try to put a twist in your story in order to surprise the reader.

RIDDLE # 5: It has been around for millions of years but it is only one month old. What is it?

Did you know? The lions of Njombe were the worst serial killers in history, killing over 1,500 people. A famed hunter called George Rushby was asked to kill them by the local tribe. Find out what happened next by looking up Google. Write a story about hunting man-eaters. You will see for yourself how tension and suspense are powerful tools in a story! You can read Jim Corbett's own experience of hunting man-eaters by typing in 'Man-Eaters of Kamaon' to: **archive.org**. It is a free, firsthand account by the greatest hunter of all time.

WRITING AN INFORMAL LETTER

There are two types of letter, formal and informal.

A formal letter is to someone you don't know very well.

An **in**formal (personal) letter is to someone you know for a long time or are very familiar with. To remember this, think of your **in**-laws. These are relatives by marriage. Pretend that you are married (yikes!) and that you have a brother-**in**-law, a sister-**in**-law and a mother-**in**-law. You don't have to know them very well or for very long, but they are still family. You would send these people an informal (in-laws') letter. Other people you might send an informal letter to include: a friend, a brother, an old classmate, your girlfriend/boyfriend etc.

Scott F. Fitzgerald was a famous author. This is an extract from a letter he sent to his 11-year –old child. It was printed in The New York Times for the public to read.

Read it once and see what you think of it.

LETTER FROM SCOTT F. FITZGERALD TO HIS CHILD

August 8, 19??

La Paix Rodgers' Forge,

Towson, Maryland.

Dear Pie:

Things to worry about:

Worry about courage

Worry about Cleanliness

Worry about efficiency

Worry about horsemanship

Worry about.......

Things not to worry about:

Don't worry about popular opinion

Don't worry about dolls

Don't worry about the past

Don't worry about the future

Don't worry about growing up

Don't worry about anyone getting ahead of you

Don't worry about triumph

Don't worry about failure unless it comes through your own fault

Don't worry about mosquitoes

Don't worry about flies

Don't worry about insects in general

Don't worry about parents

Don't worry about boys

Don't worry about disappointments

Don't worry about pleasures

Don't worry about satisfactions

Things to think about:

What am I really aiming at?

How good am I really in comparison to my contemporaries in regard to: a) Scholarship

b) Do I really understand about people and am I able to go along with them?

c) Am I trying to make my body a useful instrument or am I neglecting it?

With dearest love,

Daddy.

You have read it once. Now read it again carefully. Does this seem like an unusual letter to you? Why? Why not?

What do you think the best piece of advice is? Why did you pick that particular one?

Do you think Scott F. Fitzgerald was a good father? Write down your reasons why/why not.

What age and gender do you think the child is? Give some reasons for your choice.

The letter was written in the 20th century. What decade and year do you think it was?

You are 62 years of age. Write a letter to your 12-year-old son or daughter giving them advice on life. You might include how you have failed in certain areas and how you have been successful in others. Do you have any questions about this letter? Look up the full letter on Google to see what else it contained.

LETTER FROM FAMOUS AUTHOR TO HIMSELF

Bangor, ME 0441

June, 2010

Dear Me,

I'm writing to you from the year 2010, when I have reached the ridiculous age of sixty-two, in order to give you a piece of advice. It's simple, really, just five words: *stay away from recreational drugs*. You've got a lot of talent, and you're going to make a lot of people happy with your stories, but – unfortunate but true – you are also a junkie waiting to happen. If you don't heed this letter and change the future, at least ten good years of your life – from age 30-40 –are going to be a kind of dark eclipse where you disappoint a lot of people and fail to enjoy your own success. You will also come close to dying on several occasions. Do yourself a favour and enjoy a brighter, more productive world. Remember that, like love, resistance to temptation makes the heart grow stronger.

Stay clean.

Best regards,

_____?_____

Do you think this is a good letter? Write down the names of five famous authors and then Google the first sentence of the letter above to see if you got the name right.

Do you think it contains only one piece of advice? Can you see any more?

This letter puts the sender's address on the right hand side. This is the modern style of writing a letter. Hint: send**e**r and add**r**ess both contain the letter '**r**'.

Send**e**r's add**r**ess = always **r**ight. Is this a good mnemonic for the **right** hand side of the letter?

What age is the young man he is sending this letter to, in your opinion? Why?

What is the 'dark eclipse' a metaphor for, in your opinion? Do we all have a 'dark eclipse'?

LETTER FROM FAMOUS MAN TO HIS 11-YEAR-OLD SON

In 1915, Europe was just discovering how brutal and barbaric war can be. Millions of men were being sent to the frontlines to fight for their country. In the midst of all this horror, one man made a remarkable discovery in Berlin. This discovery (a.k.a. an epiphany) would change the way mankind thought about life forever……

Read the letter from this man in Berlin to his son in Zurich and guess who he is.

My dear son,

        Yesterday I received your dear letter and was very happy with it. I was already afraid you wouldn't write to me at all anymore. You told me when I was in Zurich, that it was awkward for you when I come to Zurich. Therefore I think it is better if we get together in a different place, where nobody will interfere with our comfort. I will in any case urge that each year we spend a whole month together, so that you will see that you have a father who is fond of you and who loves you. You can also learn many good and beautiful things from me, something another cannot as easily offer you. What I have achieved through such a lot of strenuous work shall not only be there for strangers but especially for my own boys. These days I have completed one of the most beautiful works of my life. When you are bigger, I will tell you about it.

I am very pleased that you find joy with the piano. This and carpentry are in my opinion for your age the best pursuits, better even than school. Because those are things which fit a young person such as you very well.

Mainly play the things on the piano which please you, even if the teacher does not assign them. That is the way to learn the most, that when you are doing something with such enjoyment that you don't notice that the time passes. I am sometimes so wrapped up in my work that I forget about the noon meal………..

                         Be with Tete kissed by your

                               Papa.

                         Regards to your Mama.

Fill in a Berlin address in the letter above.

Can you guess who wrote the letter? Do you think he was a caring and loving father? Why?

Write the letter that the 11-year-old boy sent to his father before this letter.

'Language register' is using different words and a different writing style depending on who you are writing to. Which of the 3 letters uses the best language register for a child, in your opinion? Why?

Who is the best father of the 3 men who wrote the letters? Give 3 reasons for your answer.

Do you agree with the advice he gives in the last paragraph? Why? Why not?

Did you know? The first handwritten letter is credited to Atossa, Queen of Persia, in 500b.c. Why not check the 20 countries that Persia was made up of? Its vastness might surprise you.

The grid below needs to be filled in. It is a grid for 'Describing a Forest'. Are you good enough to give the sounds, metaphors etc. needed for the grid? Try your best to complete it.

FOREST COLOURS		oak-brown	
FOREST SOUNDS			
FOREST IMAGES			twisted limbs of tree
ACTION IN FOREST			
METAPHORS	ribbons of moonlight		
SENSATION			cold mist on my face
SMELLS IN FOREST		honeysuckle	
FOREST TASTES	wild blackberries		

USING TEXTURE TO IMPROVE YOUR WRITING

The dictionary definition of texture: "The feel or appearance of a surface or substance."

A simpler definition is to describe it as **a sensation that comes from a specific image**. The grid below has the noun/image provided to describe soft and hard textures. Can you fill it in?

NOUN/IMAGE	**SOFT TEXTURE**	NOUN/IMAGE	**HARD TEXTURE**
do_gh	do_g_y	en_m_l	e_am_lled
e_der_own	like/e_der_own	f_i_t	f_in_y
fe_th_r	fe_th_ry	g_a_s	g_a_sy
fl_ec_	fl_e_y	gr_v_l	gr_ve_ly
fl_f_	fl_f_y	g_i_e	g_imy
goss_m_r	like/goss_m_r	gr_t	gr_t_y
s_t_n	s_t_n/so_t	l_at_er	l_at_ery
s_l_	s_l_y	m_t_l	m_t_llic
v_l_et	v_l_ety	s_o_e	s_ony
la_b's/w_o_	like la_bs' w_o_	s_ub_le	s_ub_ly

Now try to put a texture to the images below. Put in more than one if you can. You may find you have to use your imagination in order to do it.

For example, you might say that the moonlight felt like a veil of silk on your face or that the hailstones felt like glassy nails. Try to be as creative as possible with your answers.

soft sand	powdery	hard sand	
grass	like fleece	leaves	
hailstones		sleet	
sunlight		moonlight	
rocks		the wind	
snow		fog	
soft rain		flowers	
mist		tree bark	

THE IMPORTANCE OF DIET AND NUTRITION

Many people call it the 'head gym'. It is essential to your development as a student, yet so many neglect it. It is, of course, the human brain. Just like your body, it needs attention and nourishment in order to survive. In order for the brain to function properly, it needs proper rest, food and exercise. Paying it the proper respect will ensure you get rewards later in life as well as the present. Let's take a look at what some Irish Olympic athletes need to eat in order to keep both body and mind at peak condition. Pay attention to their daily routine also. Their sleeping patterns, early starts and physical workouts help the brain get the oxygen it needs.

Aileen Morrison: Triathlete.

"I'd get up in the morning at 4.55 a.m. and have something really light like a pancake with butter because I'm going to the pool to do a two-hour swim. While I'm at the pool I would take plenty of water with some sports drink.

When I get back home from there, I would eat porridge with blueberries, nuts and honey and then take a protein drink. From there it's out and about for three hours and I might have a bar on the bike. I'll stop at a café and have coffee and a big scone. I go home then for lunch which would be a toasted sandwich or a wrap with spinach and chicken or something like that. I'd have an apple at some stage throughout the day and a protein bar if I get peckish. I might have another lunch at 4 0' clock. This would be similar to the first one, or I might choose another coffee and scone.

Dinner would traditionally be meat and veg or stir fry. I also have chicken and salad or steak and salad a lot. I'll probably have a bowl of cereal before I go to bed and sometimes a chocolate treat also".

Are you surprised at the amount of food it takes to fuel Aileen's body and mind? Make a list in the grid of what she eats each day.

MEAL	A TRIATHLETE'S DAILY DIET:AILEEN MORRISON
breakfast	pancakes/butter/water/sports drink
breakfast	
snacks	
lunch	
snacks	
lunch	
dinner	
supper	
snacks	

Do you think it would be difficult to follow this routine every day? How would you find the motivation to attempt this? Is it because she is a 'special person', in your opinion?

Which of the meals above is best for a developing body and why, in your opinion? Look up Google for the benefits of the above foods.

Rob Heffernan: Walking.

"Normally in the morning, I will have porridge, toast and a cup of coffee. I also take a Kinetica recovery drink after morning training. Lunch is a salad, a pasta or rice with fish, with meat and with vegetables.

I have two dinners a day. I will get up after a rest at 5 o' clock, have a sandwich and a cup of coffee and go training again. Then I would have another dinner in the evening. You also need anti-oxidants because your body is toxic when you are training. You need supplements as well: a good fish oil, multi-vitamins and anti-oxidants. I have to replenish my glycogen stores all the time because my glycogen runs low and that's like a car running out of petrol.

You need good meat and good fish to help your muscles recover. I use protein shakes from Kinetica just for recovery".

Gavin Noble: Triathlon.

"I'm a big coffee man. I'll always have one before I go swimming. I'll come back then and have a big breakfast because I like to eat quite a lot early in the day. I'll start with porridge and bananas and sometimes a scrambled egg with that.

When I'm out on the bike I will drink lots of water and I will eat energy bars as I'm cycling. After that it's more small meals. I would probably have soup and sandwiches for lunch. I never eat meat for lunch as it's too heavy and I like to run after lunch. I will have a rest and then I will have a coffee and some bananas. I like to eat biscuits then also.

Dinner is vegetables with a little bit of carbohydrate like pasta or rice. If I'm adventurous, I'll try to do something special like chicken. I've got to watch my iron levels a lot so I may have to eat more red meat on occasion.

I've got a sweet tooth so I like to eat ice cream and jelly after my run. But I don't go out for random pints or anything like that. No chips at night."

Make out the grid for Gavin Noble with the information he provided.

	A TRIATHLETE'S DAILY DIET: GAVIN NOBLE

Did you know? The brain takes up about 2% of our body but uses 20% of the oxygen going into our bloodstream. The brain generates the same amount of power as a 10-watt light bulb.

Which of the 3 athletes is the most disciplined, in your opinion?

Are there any foods that are common to all 3 athletes? Do you think this means they are 'super foods'? Research their nutritional value by looking them up on Google.

If you had to live on a desert island for a year, what five foods would you pick to survive?

Make out a nutrition plan for tomorrow using only the best available foods in your house. Are you happy that your nutritional needs are being met?

The Irish Rugby Football Union (IRFU) has a great website where it explains the five main food groups. It can be accessed at **irishrugby.ie nutrition.** The five main groups are:

1. Cereal and cereal products (e.g. bread (wholegrain), breakfast cereals (oatmeal etc.), rice and pasta.

2. Fruit and vegetables.

3. Milk and milk products (e.g. whole milk, skim milk, yoghurt, cheese).

4. Meat and alternatives (e.g. meat (lean), fish, poultry, nuts, legumes (beans etc.) and eggs.

5. Fats and oils (e.g. butter, margarine, olive oil, cream and salad dressings).

The website has many great tips for eating habits and gaining or losing weight. Why not access it and do a project on healthy eating habits?

New scientific studies have shown that eating 'inner glow' foods give a better skin tone than sunbathing! The 'super foods' and liquids below have powerful properties that help the hair, skin, teeth and eyes to glow with health. Look up each on the internet to write in one magical benefit they give to your body, skin or hair.

SUPER FOOD	BENEFITS	SUPER FOOD	BENEFITS
coconut oil	slows Alzheimer's	coffee	slows heart disease
wild salmon		sweet potatoes	
almonds		walnuts	
tomatoes		red peppers	
sea vegetables		blueberries	
papaya		apple cider vinegar	
kiwis		kale	
yoghurt		acia berries	
radishes		water	
spirulina		mangos	
organic vegetables		avocadoes	
flax and hemp seeds		spinach	
cacao beans (chocolate)		olive oil	

'THE HUFFINGTON POST'S' LIST OF SUPERFOODS

The Huffington Post is an online news publication and blog which was set up in 2005. It encourages freelance (i.e. independent) writers to send in articles on nature, politics, news, healthy living, education and technology. It recently did a survey on the healthiest foods on the planet and the top 50 is below. It has a great website where photographs of the foods below may be accessed. It also lists the special qualities of the foods. Write into the grid the magical benefit each food has to help your body. Try to give each food a points system or just access the '*Huff*'. Do any of them match the 'inner glow' grid? Make a list of those that do.

ITEM	POINTS/BENEFITS	ITEM	POINTS/BENEFITS
almonds		kefir	
apples		lentils	
artichoke hearts		oatmeal	
avocado		olive oil	
beetroot		oranges	
beans		pistachios	
bell peppers		pomegranate	
black/rasp/berries		potatoes	
black tea		quinoa	
blueberries		red wine	
broccoli		salmon	
brown rice		sardines	
Brussels sprouts		seaweed	
cherries		shiitake mushrooms	
chia seeds		skim milk	
coffee		spinach	
cranberries		strawberries	
dark chocolate		sunflower sprouts	
Edamame		sweet potatoes	
eggs		tomatoes	
flax seeds		turmeric	
ginger		**tuna**	
Greek yoghurt		walnuts	
green tea		water	
kale		white tea	

Did you know? Some scientists are expressing reservations about recommending fish like **tuna** to the public. An Atlantic blue fin tuna can grow to quite a large size. The biggest recorded was 1,496 lbs. (108 stone! YouTube it) from Nova Scotia in Canada in 1979 and was almost 12 feet long. Fish this size can have a high degree of mercury in them. This build-up of mercury comes from eating smaller fish. Mercury in the sea can be naturally occurring but it is also caused by coal-fired industries, waste incineration and power plants. Sadly, high levels of mercury may be lethal to humans and it is one of the few substances the human body can never get rid of. It may be wiser to eat sardines and herring. These are plankton eating and do not have levels of mercury high enough to pose a health risk.

LEARNING BY ASSOCIATION

Fill in the blanks by finding the links between the words.

1. Wa_es are to the sea as st_rs are to the s_y.	Link word-in.
2. Vol_a_o is to me_d_w as as mo_nta_n is to fo_n_a_n.	Link word-rhyme.
3. L_ll_ng is to r_ll_ng as tu_b_ing is to s_m_rsa_lting.	Link word-motion.
4. Sun sp_a_s are to sun la_c_s as moon ar_o_s are to moon da_g_rs.	Link word-weapons.
5. La_oo_ is to l_ke as st_e_m is to riv_r.	Link word-water.
6. S_c_le is to sc_t_e as h_ok is to h_rse_h_e.	Link word-shape.
7. Gl_nt is to g_e_m as gl_t_er is to gli_m_r.	Link word-reflect.
8. R_u_h is to so_t as ba_k is to c_t_on.	Link word-texture.
9. Night's c_o_k is to night's r_b_ as night's v_il is to night's sh_o_d.	Link word-metaphor.
10. A s_up of smells is to br_th as a st_w of smells is to go_l_sh.	Link word-metaphor.
11. O_ly is to f_s_y as s_l_y is to b_i_y.	Link word-smell.
12. I_f_r_a_ is to fo_mal as b_a_k is to w_i_e.	Link word-opposites.
13. S_o_e is to f_i_t as ei_e_d_wn is to f_a_h_r.	Link word-texture.
14. K_ng is to br_a_f_st as pa_p_r is to d_n_er.	Link word-eating.
15. M_l_en is to o_e as E_en is to J_r_s_ic.	Link word-colours.
16. A_m_nd is to w_l_ut as sa_m_n is to s_r_i_e.	Find the link.
17. Va_p_re is to z_m_ie as w_r_o_k is to w_t_h.	Find the link.
18. Cr_st_l is to i_e as fl_me is to f_re.	Find the link.
19. O_b is to e_e as g_o_e is to ci_c_e.	Find the link
20. Pa_c_ed is to de_y_r_t_d as ti_g_i_g is to b_rn_ng.	Find the link.

Riddle # 6: John was killed one Saturday morning. The police know who they are going to arrest from this bit of information:

Alyssa was doing the laundry.

April was getting the mail.

Reggie was cooking. Mark was tending to the garden.
How do the police know who to arrest?

ADVICE FOR 11-16-YEAR-OLDS FROM THOSE WHO HAVE GONE BEFORE U

The following statements are a selection of advice from ordinary people who have been in the situation you find yourself in now. They were once 11 to 16 and going in a new, school environment just like you are. Read them and write down a list of the best advice given. Then write out why that particular piece of advice appeals to you and discuss it further. Ask your teacher to have a class conversation on the problems of being a young man/lady. See if there is anything obvious that has been missed and discuss those issues. The first two points and the last one are written out in full. You should do the same for the points you agree with.

1. Appreciate what you have and show gratitude. It is easy to be negative about the world around us. The real truth is that humans have never had it so good. Our choice of food in the supermarket, our clothes, our houses and quality of life is so much better than it was only 30 years ago. It is also a world of great opportunity. Our educational systems give everyone a chance to succeed in life. All you need to do is develop your motivation, your vision and your work rate. A simple 'thank you' to a teacher after class or to a parent will make you, and them, feel better. It might seem difficult sometimes, but having gratitude for what you have is a gift.

2. Walk faster, think better, talk proper. We are living in a world that is getting so much faster. People can take this to mean that we should run around in a headless rush and that will bring success. Wrong. If you are dragging your feet coming to school, change the habit. Make simple plans that enable you to do the work assigned, get more sleep and eat better foods. People who walk faster live longer, according to scientists. It's not a surprise, as they are probably building up their energy stores with exercise, with positive behaviours, and planning for times ahead. The future job market will need people who can think ahead, work on their own initiative, and be creative with solving problems. Think like a person of action. Act like a person of thought. Think about what you want to be and act towards being it. Dreamers are nice, doers are great, but a dreamer who does is a very happy person.

3. Being perfect is over rated. Be comfortable with who you are. A little bit of self-improvement every day goes a long way. Then you are becoming a very rare person indeed.

4. Having good friends is essential. Choose them wisely. If they are destructive, too negative, or leading you into bad situations, think carefully about the future life you want to lead.

5. Don't hold grudges. Life is too short for that. Forgiveness gives the power back to you. No one is saying you have to like them. Confucius said: "If you seek revenge, dig two graves."

6. Endure! Being a pre-teen is difficult. We are all a bunch of chemicals and emotions and, sometimes, the going gets tough. If you can enjoy school with humour and grace, you win.

7. Be a good friend to others. That means being loyal, considerate and dependable. Loyalty does not mean blind loyalty, however. If they are doing something wrong, tell them they are.

8. Try out many activities and enjoy them. Not because you want to feed your ego or look cool, but because you want to improve yourself. Music, drama and book clubs will help you.

9. Worry can eat you up from the inside out. So you don't have your homework done? So your 'friends' don't like you anymore? So what? Talk to a teacher or parent and feel better.

10. Always learn from people who are successful. They may be all around you but you haven't noticed. Don't take them for granted. Watch how they behave and copy their habits.

11. There's a massive difference between courtesy and respect. Respect has to be commanded, not demanded. Courtesy should be shown to everyone, student and staff alike.

12. Take a deep breath before reacting to something or creating more fuss. Those who show dignity when provoked are admired. That's because they think and breathe before they act.

13. Plan, plan, plan and plan! Life can drift past you before you know it and your options are limited. Find a pal who likes to plan ahead also and you have a great platform for success.

14. 'Bullies' is the wrong word for people whose insecurities result in anger, violence and nasty words. Perhaps they should be called victims too, perhaps not. You can talk to someone or you can get stronger, mentally and physically. Or you can forgive. Either way, you win.

15. Always follow your own path (but put in the research and practice first). Success only comes easily to those who have put in the time. If you are to be your own leader, start now!

16. If you hurt someone, have the good grace to say you are sorry. The world is full of people regretting that they didn't have the strength to say it. In Latin it is: "Mea culpa." Try it.

17. If someone offers you alcohol, cigarettes or drugs, say: "I tried them before. They don't suit me." Then walk away. You will be giving yourself the best favour you can ever give.

18. Just because the human body can take incredible punishment doesn't mean it should be taken for granted. Cut down on fizzy drinks, drinks with concentrate, and junk food. Be well.

19. You and your friends should have a code word. Something like 'toothache' will work. When a situation becomes uncomfortable or unpleasant, use it and get out of there.

20. **"Bitterness is like cancer. It eats upon the host. But anger is like fire. It burns it all clean."** **Maya Angelou**

She is a wise woman. Anger is a natural reaction. It is the body and mind telling you that it is not happy. It should also to be expressed in the right way. Expressing anger should be done with physical exercise, by sharing your feelings with others, or by telling yourself that you are aware of the problem and that you are going to take steps to solve it yourself. Lashing out at teachers, family members, fellow students or members of the community, is not anger. It is stupidity. Identify the cause of your anger and do one of three things: calm down with deep breaths or exercise, share it with others, or laugh at it and let it go. If you feel like self-harming, tell your closest friend and the two of you should discuss it with one of your parents, the school counsellor/principal, or the teacher you respect the most. Having feelings of anger is the most natural thing in the world. It is supposed to be turned **outwards**, however, never inwards. Help is always just a chat away in a school environment. Use it.

CLASS IDEAS REVISION GRIDS

The grid below can be filled in as the class is doing a creative page of fill in the blanks. It may also be used at the end of the module for revision purposes. The teacher might also decide to put different headings in the grid. Some classes may decide to put in words; others may decide to put in phrases or sentences. The template for the first two pages is done for you. The rest needs to be filled in by the student.

IMAGES FOR A BEACH
SKY COLOUR
CALM SEA SOUNDS
COLOUR OF THE SAND
SHAPE OF THE BEACH
PHYSICAL SENSATIONS

RIDDLE # 7: SOLVE THE MYSTERY

A crime has been committed at Freemont Street. The main suspect is a man named Sean Baker. It was said that a man had been walking along the pathway when he was suddenly shot in the stomach. The suspect had brown hair, blue eyes and wore a baggy Armani suit just like Sean Baker's.

Sean was asked to tell the story right from the beginning. "Well," said Sean, I was just hanging around the park when I saw this man walking along the pathway. Suddenly, a guy came up from behind him and shot him! I ran home as fast as I could." The policemen asked him to give a description of the murderer. "He had a red moustache, red hair and an Armani suit on," he said. Sean was immediately arrested. How the policemen know he did it?

THE PAINTER IN THE FOREST

The Latin phrases provide a great store of knowledge with the least amount of words. There is a great story from Pliny the Elder, a Roman writer and philosopher. It tells of a shoemaker (i.e. cobbler) who approached a master painter pointing out a mistake he had made when drawing a sandal in his masterpiece. The painter had the wisdom and grace to agree with him and changed it. Encouraged by his success, the cobbler began to criticise other aspects of the painting. At this point, the painter, Apelles of Kos, said:

"Sutor, ne ultra crepidam."   (Cobbler, not above the sandal.)

If you can understand what this quote means in later life, you are on the path to wisdom. For students, however, they should always question *why* something is presented as best practise.

For that reason, picture yourself walking in a forest. You see a painter working in a clearing.

He has filled in a beautiful scene. Titan's fiery wheel hangs in the sky. Fingers of light poke through the trees and touch the shadows, making the earth steam. The leaves are hanging silently, dressed in their small, green slippers. A waterfall falls down into a bliss-pool and an otter is eating a fish on the bank. The colours he uses are deep in places, a light pastel in others.

"Stick to the painting," you tell him. "You wouldn't be able to get a job as a writer."

Why would you say such a thing? Maybe it is because you can do things as a writer that he can never do. You have to visualise a scene also, just like he does. More than that, though, your job is to make it come alive for the reader with words. In your wisdom, you know that describing a wide, open scene like a beach is based mainly on the visual sense. For an enclosed space like a forest, that won't be enough. You need to use other techniques in order to catapult the reader into your world. You write down a list and give it to him. This is it:

COLOUR: The sun is a glowing ball of nectar-gold.

METAPHOR: The mist is soundless, voiceless and soulless.

COLOUR: The leaves are mint-green and the waterfall is neon-blue.

TEXTURE: The leaves feel like satin and the water feels like warm, rippling velvet.

ONOMATOPEIA: The waterfall is tumbling and the otter is crunching the bones.

ACTION: The otter plunges into the pool when he sees you and slaps his tail in warning.

SENSATION: The scene is soul nourishing.

SMELL: The earthy cologne of the forest drifts all around you.

TASTE: You eat some wild berries and they taste tutti-fruity, like little pearls of heaven.

"Painter, not above the grass," you say, and you walk away, leaving him staring at the list.....

Date: __/__/__	Title: **DESCRIBING A FOREST: 1ˢᵗ GRID**	Lesson number:

Latin phrase: Medicus curat, natura sanat.

Definition: D_c_ors/c_r_, nat_r_/s_ves.

Meaning: _____

_____

Spelling revision	New words	Dictionary definitions, corrections, and synonyms.
m_cr_sc_p_c	gl_de	
n_rr_t_r	sur_eal	drea_l_ke
par_c_u_e	fr_gm_n	
h_ng g_id_r	gin_erbr_ad	
b_o_h_re	E_en	
b_rbe_u_s	Ju_as_ic	
m_lt_n	E_er_la_es	

You are walking in a forest on a sunny day. What's in the forest?

1 POINT	2 POINTS	3 POINTS	4 POINTS

tr_es	spe_ific a_im_ls	gl_des/gr_v_s	mo_nli_ht
a_im_ls	nothing-you are b_ind	su_li_ht	st_rli_ht

5 POINTS	6 POINTS	7 POINTS	8 POINTS

a fi_e	a u_ic_rn	a m_g_c/ca_t_e	an e_il/m_gi_ian
a r_v_r	spe_ific/f_re_t/b_r_s	a l_st/w_r_d	an e_il/w_t_h

9 POINTS	9 POINTS	10 POINTS	10 POINTS

a/s_r_al killer	va_pi_es/zo_bi_s	a gin_erbr_ad/h_u_e	a d_ad/fr_gm_n
a/t_o_l	an_th_ng/sur_eal	a wa_er_all/r_ck po_l	

super student ideas

Magical forest words

a sile_t/Ed_n	wo_dsor_el	ber_l-gre_n	all_ring
si_k/so_t/lea_es	clo_dbe_rri_s	jas_er-gre_n	a potpo_r_i of scen_s

POINTS SCORE

0-50 good first try	51-100 well done	101-130 very good	131-148 excellent

"I've learned that people will forget what you said, people will forget what you did, but people will never forget how you made them feel." **Maya Angelou**

Do you agree with the above quote? Why? Why not?

Can we learn anything from what she says and would it make you think about how you treat other people? If we are polite and courteous to everyone, do you think they will respect that?

Maya Angelou is an African-American poet. She was born in 1928. She worked with Martin Luther King and Malcolm X. Do you think her quote has extra meaning because of her experiences of fighting for justice? Look up Martin Luther King or Malcolm X on Wikipedia and do a short project on their lives.

Trying to figure out which of these: there/their/they're, is the correct term to use, can be a challenge. The best way to remember it is the following:

1. 'There' refers to **location** (i.e. the forest is **there**. Think of **'every there is everywhere'**).

2. 'Their' refers to **possession** (i.e. **their heir** is possessive).

3. 'They're' always replaces **'they are'** (i.e. **they're** a nice family).

Rewrite the following by choosing the correct terms:

1. The forest over _____ is tropical-green. **COLOUR**

2. The twigs were crunching under _____ feet. **SOUND**

3. _____ called the swaying towers of the forest. What are they? **SHAPE/MOTION**

4. I heard a badger snuffling over _____. **ANIMAL SOUNDS**

5. _____ looking up and the stars are shining like silver petals. **STARS**

6. _____ the green skyscrapers of the forest. What are they? **METAPHORS**

7. The ferns over _____ are Jurassic tall. **IMAGERY**

8. _____ experience of the forest was heart haunting. **SENSATION**

9. The forest over _____ smells pulpy and loamy. **SMELL**

10. _____ going to the forest to taste the sherry sweet cloudberries. **TASTE**

Did you know? The eldest and strongest crows roost at the top of the tree at night. The youngest and weakest crows perch on the bottom boughs. This is because nobody can drop a love bomb on you during the night if you are on the top of the tree! Is love bomb a metaphor?

Date: __/__/__	Title: **DESCRIBING A FOREST: 2ⁿᵈ GRID**	Lesson number:

Latin phrase: Crede quod habes, et habes.

Definition: B_li_ve/th_t/y_u/ha_e/it/a_d/y_u/d_.

Meaning: _____

_____

Spelling revision	New words	Dictionary definitions, corrections, and synonyms.
gl_de	on_mat_p_eia	
sur_eal	ech_ism	
fr_gm_n	cr_nk_y	
gin_erbr_ad	ru_tli_g	
E_en	clac_ing	
Ju_as_ic	gu_rdia_s	
E_ergla_es	pu_si_g	

the colour green

1 POINT	2 POINTS	3 POINTS	4 POINTS
j_de-green	po_tc_rd-green	ca_ni_al-green	Am_z_n-green
E_ergla_es	v_lv_t-green	E_en-green	J_ra_sic--green

onomatopoeic sounds

cre_king/tr_es	cr_nk_y/leaves	clac_ing/bo_ghs	ru_tli_g foliage
cru_ching/t_igs	cr_s_y grass	cr_ckly/fer_s	phut-ph_tt_ng/n_ts

metaphors for the trees

c_stl_s	h_gh/ri_es	c_ret_kers	sl_e_ing/soul
t_w_rs	sk_scr_pers	gu_rdia_s	pu_si_g/h_a_t

POINTS SCORE

0-10 good first try	11-29 well done	30-50 very good	51-60 excellent

Commas are used to indicate a pause in a list of words or a sentence. With the rise of digital technology, people don't seem to use them as much. Do you think the comma should be banished from English classes forever? This, of course, would mean that a lot of sentences would be read out in a breathless rush. Give two reasons why the comma should be saved!

What's the difference between a cat and a comma?

Mnemonic: One has **CLAWS** at the end of its **PAWS** and the other has a **PAUSE** at the end of its **CLAUSE**!

5 quick rules for commas

1. Place a comma to **separate a list of 3 or more words**.

Ex: The forest is spellbinding, magical, and alluring. The last comma here is called the 'Oxford comma', and not all writers use it. Look it up on **www.oxforddictionaries.com**.

2. Place a comma **to separate two adjectives before a noun**.

Ex: The forest is a green, woody paradise.

3. Place a comma to **separate two independent sentences** (or clauses) using a conjunction. A conjunction is a link word such as: **and, but, so, or, yet** and **for**.

Ex: He wanted to go to the lush forest. I did not.

He wanted to go to the lush forest, but I did not.

4. Place a comma **after introductory words**. An introductory word starts a sentence in an unusual manner. Make some sentences on the forest using these introductions:

1. No,

2. Yes,

3. Well,

4. However,

5. Meanwhile,

6. Therefore,

7. Curiously,

8. Obviously,

9. Still,

10. For example,

5. Place a comma when **switching from direct** (reporting) **to indirect** (reported) **speech**.

Ex. "Yes," he said, "the forest is enchanting."

Did you know? Cats are estimated to kill 55 million birds a year in England and 4 million birds a year in Ireland. There are approx. 700,000 'tame' and 200,000 feral cats in Ireland.

USING ONOMATOPOEIA

animal	onomatopoeia	sound	motion
bear	gr_w_s	rooargh	sha_bles
bee	b_z_es	biiiiiiiiz	sur_s
bull	be_lo_s	brooou	char_es
cat	mew_s	meeeow	p_ds
cow	lo_s	arrruuum	wan_ers
dog (big)	bar_s	rufffruff	clum_s
donkey	br_ys	heeeaaaaw	tro_s
duck	q_ac_s	grackgrack	wad_les
elephant	tr_mp_ts	buurrrrrrrrr	lumb_rs
frog	c_oa_s	ribbitribbit	lea_s
magpie	cha_te_s	kakkakkak	swo_ps
monkey	sc_ea_s	ooohahahah	clim_s
mouse	sq_e_ks	weakweak	scur_ies
owl	h_o_s	toohootoohoo	ghos_s
peregrine falcon	whi_es	waaaaaaaaaa	di_e/bom_s
pig	g_u_ts	hokkkhokkk	amb_es
robin	caro_s	feekeekeefee	fli_s
raven	c_o_ks	graawkgraawk	soa_s
serpent	hi_s_s	sssssssssssssss	slithe_s
wolf	ho_ls	owuuuuuuuuu	lop_s

Using onomatopoeia in a descriptive passage is the best way to bring the reader into your story. By recreating the sounds of animals, wind or a forest, you catapult them into your world. They don't even have a choice! Try to find an onomatopoeic word for the following forest sounds and then put as many of them as possible in a story. Add in colours if you wish:

ACTION	SOUND	ACTION	SOUND
a twig breaking	cr_c_ing	lightning in the sky	si_s_ng
a badger moving	sh_f_l_n	a rodent running	sk_t_e_i_g
a stream	g_r_l_n_	a flood river	r_a_i_g
a soft wind	s_g_i_g	a loud wind	ke_n_ng
a squirrel running	sc_mp_ri_g	deer hooves	cl_p_i_g
a jay on alert	sc_e_c_i_g	a dragonfly's wings	wh_r_i_g
conkers falling	th_n_i_g	thunder in the sky	r_m_l_ng
a bees' nest	dr_n_n	a lake rippling	e_b_ng
a small waterfall	ca_c_d_n_	a large waterfall	pl_m_e_i_g
a wildcat	sl_n_i_g	a troll yelling in pain	yo_l_ng

Did you know? The combination 'ough' can be pronounced in 9 different ways. Read this out loud: "A rough-coated, dough-faced, thoughtful ploughman strode through the streets of Scarborough; after falling into a slough, he coughed and hiccoughed!"

Date: __/__/__	Title: **DESCRIBING A FOREST: 3ʳᵈ GRID**	Lesson number:

Latin phrase: Cave ab homine unius libri.

Definition: Fea_/t_e/m_n/of/on_/bo_k.

Meaning: _____

_____

Spelling revision	New words	Dictionary definitions, corrections, and synonyms.
on_mat_p_eia	gnar_ed	
ech_ism	can_py	
cr_nk_y	tann_n	
ru_tli_g	al_o_d	
clac_ing	gro_e	
gu_rdia_s	hoa_y	
pu_si_g	mys_iq_e	

the colour brown

1 POINT	2 POINTS	3 POINTS	4 POINTS
ba_k-brown	con_er-brown	te_k-brown	umb_r-brown
b_m_oo-brown	n_t-brown	tann_n-brown	al_o_d-brown

nice images

a d_me of trees	a mo_s/vei_ed/tra_l	gnar_ed trunks	a can_py of le_v_s
a le_f/carp_ted path	se_ret/gro_es	hoa_y boughs	a le_fy/c_rt_in

metaphors for the moon

a glowing or_	a glinting h_lo	a blo_d/mo_n	a Ha_v_st moon
a gleaming glo_e	a glittering ri_g	a p_g_n moon	a H_nt_r's moon

magical words grid

the o_l/lig_t of du_k	pl_cid/riv_rs	moon-spl_sh_d trees	mis_y/mys_iq_e of
chimi_g/so_gbirds	sle_k/riv_rs	gli_me_i_ng/light	the lav_sh/fo_es_

POINTS SCORE

0-10 good first try	11-29 well done	30-50 very good	51-60 excellent

"You've got to dance like there's nobody watching

Love like you'll never be hurt

Sing like there's nobody listening

And live like it's heaven on earth.

(And speak from the heart to be heard.")   **William W. Purkey** b. August 22, 1929.

Do you think that this is an unfair quote to put in this book? Do you see this advice as being for people near the end of their life rather than for twelve year old students? After all, do you fear being ridiculed if you lived like this or are you strong enough not to care what people think? Write down your thoughts on these questions in your copy book.

Write down a 'bucket list' of things you would like to do if you had one day to live. Write out 15 first. Then cross off 5. Think about it and then cross off another 5. Finally, cross off 2 and you will be left with your dreams for the future. Your focus should be on achieving these.

ACHIEVING SUCCESS

Many experts believe that there is a formula for success in life. They see great sports persons, artists, businessmen and pop stars as sharing many of the same qualities. Read them below and see if you agree.

1. All successful people **visualise** their success in some way from an early age. This does not mean they dreamed about it. They **lived it** and **acted out** their dreams physically every day. For example, if you want to be a Formula 1 driver, you should be actually driving the car in a Formula 1 race as often as possible in your mind. Then you should be recreating the skills needed to win the world championship by pretending to be in the car. Do it in your bedroom, a quiet area or in your parents' car, but practice constantly. Live it, act it out, and visualise it. It will come true. Always remember; the universe is big enough to contain all your dreams. Believe it and it will happen for you. Watch **'The Secret'** on Netflix to find out more on this.

2. All successful people tend to **work harder** than their competitors. Some of the greatest competitors ever did extraordinary, possibly superhuman, feats in order to get to the top. Jack Nicklaus, the golfer, practised until his hands bled.

3. "Fail to prepare, prepare to fail." You may have heard of this, but actually it's not quite accurate. The difference between many successful people compared to others is that they are **prepared to fail**. If they suffer a setback, they do not let it deter them. It spurs them on to succeed even more. One of Einstein's famous quotes is: "I am thankful to all those who said No to me. It's because of them I did it myself." If you want to put it another way, the true test of a person is not just how they treat triumph, but how they deal with despair.

4. All successful people become **comfortable with repetition**. They break down their goals into clearly defined processes and achieve things an inch, a minute, a day at a time. Whether it is karate, soccer or learning off parts in a play, sometimes you have to put up with repetition, even boredom. It is also known as 'living in the now'. Look up **'The secrets of successful people'** on Google and make a list of 5 more common traits of successful people.

5. Some business people and sports stars have got an obsessive personality. This gets them where they need to go, but it doesn't always make them good human beings, unfortunately. Many have forgotten that life isn't always about the 'me'. Others realise early on that to be mega-successful, you should mix a pleasant, friendly personality with a competitive streak. David Beckham is the classic example of this. Every time he lost the ball playing soccer, he tracked back to retrieve it like an avenging angel. This is his inner, ruthless streak at work. People also say about him that he is very complimentary and always says something nice to make them feel better. This is because he practices his charm, his courtesy, and his manners, like a professional off the pitch. In short, he **is** a nice guy because he **wants** to be a nice guy.

6. My father always said: "If you have the reputation of being an early riser, you can get up at 3 o' clock." The importance of this is clear; early risers are seen as successful. You may have heard of the expression:

"Early to bed, early to rise,

makes a man healthy, wealthy, and wise."

Research has proven that you are more likely to be successful and healthy if you get an early night's sleep and wake up early in the morning. You will find you have more energy, better memory retention and increased powers of concentration. It is certainly better for your digestive system if you have an early, hearty breakfast. That is why it is recommended to: **"Eat breakfast like a king, lunch like a prince, and dinner like a pauper**." Joe Schmidt, the Irish rugby coach, has asked his players to be in bed for 10.30 each night. Breakfast is at 7.30 a.m. as it helps the players to lose body fat. This separates him from most other coaches. His preparation in everything to do with his teams is legendary.

7. The last point is to do with attention to detail and recall. Most successful people have a training routine that is meticulous, well planned and designed to replicate success. It may be mission statements, mental maps, or practising moves in slow motion the night before. As well as that, a lot of great sports people have a phenomenal ability to recall every moment of their games weeks, years and decades later. They don't just **play** the game, they **memorise** it and learn from their errors. Practising is half the battle. Being able to analyse your efforts after a game or performance is the other half. Keeping a mental diary is crucial. Try it out.

Having read this, do you agree with every point or not? List the 3 you feel are the most important and discuss why. Which points, in particular, struck you as being interesting? Are there any you would take out? Why? How can these ideas help you as an English student?

A mission statement might be a note to yourself telling you how to achieve your aims. Remember no. 1 on your bucket list above? Write down five simple points on how you could 'map' your way to your dream job (ex. diet, sleep patterns, courses, saving money etc.).

"Success is the sum of small efforts repeated, day in, day out." R. Collier   Do you agree?

Date: __/__/__	Title: **DESCRIBING A FOREST: 4ᵗʰ GRID**	Lesson number:

Latin phrase: Custode et cura natura potentior omni.

Definition: A_d/k_o_l_dge/i_se_f, is/p_w_r.

Meaning: _____

_____

Spelling revision	New words	Dictionary definitions, corrections, and synonyms.
gnar_ed	me_l_w	
can_py	aste_s	
tann_n	bal_	
al_o_d	su_de	
gro_e	pen_agr_m	
hoa_y	ba_l_d	
mys_iq_e	bas_l	

interesting phrases

1 POINT	2 POINTS	3 POINTS	4 POINTS
m_th/flut_er of da_n	be_rds of mo_s	su_de/s_ft/fl_w_rs	a ba_l_d of bi_ds_ng
wit_h/li_ht of du_k	kn_tted/ar_s of trees	G_rd_n of E_en	a m_s_y/ma_tre_s

edibles of the forest

ri_e/nu_s	ju_cy/b_rri_s	wild bas_l	sti_gi_g/ne_t_e
del_c_ous mus_roo_s	me_l_w/fru_t	wild g_rl_c	hea_ing/bal_

similes for the stars

like flashing p_t_ls	like silver p_n/p_ic_s	like di_mo_d/du_t	like f_i_y/fi_e
like silver sn_wfla_es	like spark_ing aste_s	like fie_y/pen_agr_ms	like wi_a_d/du_t

POINTS SCORE

0-10 good first try	11-29 well done	30-50 very good	51-60 excellent

Direct speech is **reported** speech. This means it is quoted exactly as the person said it.

Indirect speech is **reporting** speech. This means you are not quoting directly. Indirect speech does not take quotation marks.

The basic rule for direct speech

The inverted commas (i.e. quotation marks/ 66's and 99's) **open** and **close** the sentence.

For example, if you have a comma, a full stop, a question mark, or an exclamation mark closing the sentence, the inverted commas come **last.** Just remember; if the inverted commas open a sentence, why wouldn't they close it?

1. "The stars burned like druid dust**,"** he said.

2. "The forest is womb quiet at night**."** That's what he said to me.

3. "A symphony of birdsong filled the forest**!"** he shouted.

4. "Can you smell the ripe berries**?"** he asked?

Punctuate the following using the above rule:

1. what is a hunter's moon she asked

2. i love the owl light of the forest at dusk he said

3. look at the stars glimmering he shouted

4. the misty mystique of an autumn forest is special he declared

5. can you hear the birds chiming she questioned

6. this dark forest gives me goose bumps he yelled

7. listen to the snapping branches she shrieked there must be trolls in here

8. rivers are the motorways of the forest he said

9. doesn't the mist look like a magician's smoke he asked

10. a blood moon hung over the forest last night she said it was eerie

RIDDLE # 8: There is a man on an island prison. He cannot swim. One day he escapes using nothing but himself. How did he do it?

Did you know? New research has shown that dogs communicate secretly to each other with their tails. A dog wagging his tail to the right is showing happiness. A dog wagging his tail to the left is showing fear. If a dog wags his tail to the left, showing fear, the other dog will also show fear. Scientists have also figured out why dogs hate postmen. It starts with one dog barking at him, usually outside human earshot. Other dogs hear it and decide the next person coming to the house is a threat. As it is early morning, the poor postman is next and gets it!

Date: __/__/__	Title: **DESCRIBING A FOREST: 5th GRID**	Lesson number:

Latin phrase: Custode et cura natura potentior omni.

Definition: Na_u_e/is/m_g_t_er/th_n/ed_c_t_o_.

Meaning: _____

_____

Spelling revision	New words	Dictionary definitions, corrections, and synonyms.
me_l_w	cl_y	
aste_s	lo_m	
bal_	mul_h	
su_de	org_n_c	
pen_agr_m	inc_n_e	
ba_l_d	dec_d_ous	
bas_l	col_g_e	

physical sensations of surprise

1 POINT	2 POINTS	3 POINTS	4 POINTS
ha_r/raising	eye/op_ni_g	go_se/bu_ps	he_rt/th_m_ing
j_w/drop_ing	eye/wi_en_ng	sk_n/ti_g_ing	he_rt/cl_nc_ing

deciduous forest smells

cl_y/ri_h smell	oak_n/aro_a	mul_hy/fra_r_nce	w_o_y/inc_n_e
eart_y/sce_t	org_n_c/waf_	pe_ty/p_rfu_e	loa_y/col_g_e

taste

fru_ty/strawb_rr_es	or_h_rd sweet berries	sh_rry sweet berries	fr_itca_e rich
sh_rp/tas_ing berries	me_d_w sweet	trif_e sweet berries	wi_df_ll sweet apples

POINTS SCORE

0-10 good first try	11-29 well done	30-50 very good	51-60 excellent

Changing direct speech to indirect speech is our next challenge. It helps that there is a formula to help us with it. Are you up for the mental challenge? Remember that success lies in the sum of small efforts done well. Wasn't that the quote or was it different?

FUN CROSSWORD FOR REVISION ON THE FOREST

(crossword grid with numbered cells 1–19; visible letters: 4 across shows S and R; 5 shows O; 6; 7; 11; 12 shows M; 13; 14 shows E; 16; 17; 18; 19)

ACROSS

1 Stars flickering with light

4 Type of flower or shape of star

5 Like clay

8 Walks casually like a pig

10 Grey-haired or ancient

12 Plant used for healing

14 Plant used by Romans for soup

17 Metaphor for forest perfume

18 The limb of a tree

19 A robin might make this motion

DOWN

1 A magician's star

2 Type of soft fabric

3 Crooked fingers or trees

6 Wet leaves decomposing

7 Not unreal, not real, but bizarre

9 Onomatopoeia

11 Metaphor for forest aftershave

13 A small wood without undergrowth

15 A type of silver metal. Not expensive.

16 As round as a globe

Did you know? The longest word ever used in a published crossword is the Welsh town of:

Llanfairpwllgwyngyllgogerychwyrndrobwillllantysiliogogogoch. Its clue was an anagram!

Changing from direct speech to indirect speech

Direct speech example: "The clay rich smell of the forest **is** wonderful," he said.

Changing to indirect speech: He said the clay rich smell of the forest **was** wonderful.

Write down 3 changes that you notice in the above sentences:

a) **'He said'** changes from the start of_____.

b) **'Is'** changes to_____.

c) The **inverted commas** for direct speech_____.

The following words change tense when you are changing from direct speech to indirect speech.

IS--------------------WAS or AM   ARE----------------WERE

MAY----------------MIGHT   CAN----------------COULD

DO/DID-------------DID/HAD DONE   WILL---------------WOULD

WAS----------------WAS/WERE   SHALL-------------WOULD

Now try to change these sentences from direct to indirect sentences in your copybook:

1. "We **may** listen to the dawn chorus," she said.   She said they..........

2. "**Can** you smell the rich perfume of the forest?" he asked.   He asked if she........

3. "I **will** go while the witchery of the morning is there," he said.   He said he..............

4. "There **is** an alien beauty to a lavish forest," she said.   She said................

5. "We **shall** visit the willowy waterfall," he said.   He said.................

6. "They **are** going to see the lush forest," she said.   She said...............

7. "We **did** a tour of the enchanting forest," they said.   They said.............

8. "There **was** an old yew tree in the forest," he said.   She said..............

Did you know? The world's 2nd hardest tongue twister is: "The sixth sick sheikh's sixth sheep's sick."

RIDDLE # 9: Can you guess what the only word in English to end in 'mt' is? Hint: you may have done it yesterday in school but you shouldn't have! You should have done it last night.

RECAP ON LESSONS

Two parts of the course have been completed, the beach and the forest. Underneath are a selection of words and phrases from the two parts. The words only go down and across. Can you get them all before you know how many are there? If so, you're an impressive student!

b	a	l	l	u	r	i	n	g	o
o	s	o	r	g	a	n	i	c	b
p	t	s	a	h	l	o	a	m	i
n	e	y	g	n	a	r	l	e	d
e	r	o	m	e	r	a	t	l	s
n	s	w	c	l	a	y	s	l	c
c	o	l	o	g	n	e	l	o	e
h	p	l	z	i	k	b	d	w	l
a	s	i	d	o	p	e	a	t	f
n	c	g	h	o	a	r	y	m	m
t	y	h	e	x	r	y	s	o	i
i	t	t	d	m	c	l	t	l	s
n	h	g	e	r	h	i	a	t	t
g	e	k	n	a	g	m	r	e	z
i	l	d	a	d	i	v	i	n	e

If you were to include a waterfall in your forest essay, would you be able to describe its colour, sound, action and the images that might go with a waterfall? The sounds below are of a small waterfall and a large waterfall. Do you think those sounds would be very different? Try the grid below and see if you can complete it. You may need a friend to help you.

MAKING A WATERFALL GRID

	-silver	-blue	-white
COLOUR			
SOFT SOUNDS			
LOUD SOUNDS			
ACTION			
IMAGES			
IMAGES			
SOUND OF RAIN			
THE POOL	a bliss pool	an eternity pool	an infinity pool

Did you know? The average person will eat 8 spiders while asleep in their lifetime. Don't snore!

Riddle # 10: You walk across a bridge and you see a boat full of people, yet there isn't a single person on board. How is that possible?

"What the mind of man can conceive and believe, it can achieve."   **Napoleon Hill**

If you want to write a good descriptive essay, there are some factors to consider first. Should your essay have a structure? Do readers like to see new and creative phrases? Should you include direct speech in order to vary your writing style? If you think the answer is yes to these, try to change the underlined words and phrases below. It is only a sample, a template (i.e. an outline) to guide you. Punctuate the essay and correct the spellings where necessary.

INTRODUCTION: SETTING THE SCENE

The clouds began to cover the <u>ore-gold</u> sun and it gave off a strange, zombie glow. The last of the leeves dangeld from the trees <u>like tattered sails</u>. Night's <u>dark cloak</u> was closing in around us and we were getting nervus. We could hear <u>eerie</u> noises coming from the undergrowth. Both of us had that <u>skin crawling</u> sensation that we were being watched.

PARAGRAPH 1: DEVELOP THE PLOT

The local rumour was that a wicked witch lived in the forest. She had a house made of candy and karamel and her eyes <u>glowed like hot coals</u>. I knew we should not be here on Halloween night, but we were hopelessly lost in this maze of trees. A low, sad moan came from the bushes in front of us and the hairs on the back of my neck <u>rose</u>. What could cause such a noise? Then we laughed as <u>rays</u> from the <u>Harvest moon</u> spilled through the trees to reveal a glass bottel. The wind was making the bottel wail like a child!

PARAGRAPH 2: ADD A CRISIS TO THE PLOT (AND DIRECT SPEECH)

Then we had a branch <u>snap</u> and a <u>shuffling</u> sound and we both feared the witch was coming to get us.

Let's run Laura hissed.

It was too late. I had already beaten her to it.

My heart tumped in my chest as we ran for our lives. It was dark and <u>murky</u> in the forest. The <u>twisted</u> branches of the trees looked like human <u>limbs</u> trying to reach out for us. The stars looked <u>like diamund dust</u> through the bear trees. They were <u>enchanting</u> and it made our situation seem <u>surreal</u>. Then, up ahead, we saw a large figure blocking the path. He raised his large arms.

It's a troll Laura screamed We're finished

Then she fainted and collapsed in a heap leaving me to kill the troll on my own. I picked up a large stone and through it at him but he ducked. now were for it I thought to myself the troll seemed to loom over even larger over us and I thought to myself: this is it it's the end of life as you know it I decided to throw a rock at him if i was going to die I was to go out in style

PARAGRAPH 3: THE PLOT DEVELOPS

The <u>ghostly</u> light of the moon shone on the troll's face. It was <u>bat-black</u> and his nose was large and misshapen. He smiled and his teeth were as jagged as <u>a line of tombstones</u>.

He spoke and his voice was like the rumbel of <u>thunder</u>.

What are you doing in *my* forest he roared

Then he smiled and took out a mouth gard. His skin was covered in the black paint a hunter might put on.

Just joking kiddo he said It *is* halloween after all isn't it

It turned out that he was badger watching and his name was Jim He was a cheerfull fellow and explained that he had cracked a couple of teeth and broken his nose while walking in the dark the week previosly. That was why his nose was bandaged up and he had put his old rugby mouth gard over his teeth.

CONCLUSION: LINK TO INTRODUCTION

Until that night, I had seen forests as places of Eden-green <u>sorcery</u> and <u>mystery</u>. Now I know that they can be places of danger also. And what happened to Laura? after Jim carried her to the edge of the forest and into the ambulance, I never saw her again. Her father said I should have looked after her better!

Do you think this was a good story? Why? Why not? Could you write a better story?

Did you notice that there were very few colours, tastes, smells and sounds used? Would you put in more in your own story? Is there anything else you would put in to improve it?

Do you agree that putting the direct speech on separate lines makes your story look longer? Is this a good idea when you are doing your homework?!

3 FAMOUS QUOTES

1. Today I will do what others won't, so tomorrow I can accomplish what others can't.

2. You miss 100% of the shots you don't take.

3. I've missed more than 9,000 shots in my career. I've lost almost 300 games. 26 times I've been trusted to take the game winning shot and missed. I've failed over and over again in my life. And that is why I succeed.

The three quotes above are from Michael Jordan, the greatest basketball player ever, Wayne Gretsky, ice hockey's greatest ever player, and Jerry Rice, considered the greatest NFL player of all time. What do you think is the best quote?

Who said what and what do the quotes have in common, in your opinion?

Do you think they're talking about sport or life lessons they've learned? If so, what lessons?

RIDDLE # 11: What do you call a frog with no legs?

WRITING A DIARY ENTRY

The diary is your dog.

You can tell your dog your innermost secrets, your darkest fears, and your most precious hopes for the future. He will never speak of it to anyone. He will never betray you. That is why you should tell your diary everything. Use the K.I.S.S motto also-Keep It Simple, Student! There are two golden rules for a diary (i.e. as well as keeping it locked away).

RULE 1: Always picture yourself writing at your desk at night. You are writing about events of the past day and your **emotional reaction** to those events. The emotions you felt are as important as what happened that day.

RULE 2: You are writing to yourself. Never forget that. The language register should be simple, honest and direct.

Underneath are a list of 'do's' and 'don'ts' for a diary entry.

DO	DON'T
use the **past** tense. It's a diary of the past day.	use the present tense unless you need to.
use **short sentences**.	complicate the syntax (i.e. sentences).
explore many of your emotions.	just list emotions. Explain why you felt them.
write it as you **felt it** that day.	ramble or use stuffy language.
use it to **get things off your mind**.	ever think you are being over dramatic.
use descriptions but use them sparingly.	take up too much time describing
use **humour** as a writing technique.	put in words you wouldn't use with friends.
rhetorical questions.	put in direct speech or quote anyone.
look forward with hope for tomorrow.	use the past continuous tense.
sign in with '**Dear diary**'	forget to sign off! '**Till tomorrow!**

JUMBLE BOX OF EMOTIONS TO USE IN A DIARY

HAPPINESS	ANGER	SADNESS	A.N OTHER
gl_d/del_g_ted		cr_s_ed/dow_h_ar_ed	
over_o_ed/ecs_at_c		broken hearted/wre_ch_d	

LONELINESS	SHAME	FEAR	A.N OTHER
lo_ely/lon_so_e		ne_vo_s/fri_hten_d	
aba_do_ed/_is_lat_d		an_io_s/te_rif_ed	

Did you know? A dog should not be fed: alcohol, onions/garlic, coffee/tea, grapes/raisins, milk/ice cream, sweets/nuts/chocolate, raw eggs, raw meat **or bones** and salty or sugary foods. Surprised? Watch the slideshow on **pets.webmd.com** to see what he/she should eat.

THE GREAT FAMINE

Patrick Flannely was a historian who recorded famine stories from Attymass in Co. Meath in 1946. This was 100 years after the great famine in Ireland when 1 million people died. His sources were the sons and nephews of people who had lived through these times. Here are some of his reports. He starts with a description of Attymass just before the famine in 1844:

"The people were not too badly off. They tilled about ¾'s of the land which of course was not a lot in a very congested area, but they managed to live and had the reputation of being big, strong men. As many as could possibly manage it also, kept a couple of sheep in addition to the cow and calf.....The land supported the household for they lived on potatoes and now and again had oatmeal cakes and butter and milk.....rabbits and hares were caught, wild fowl trapped and the rivers and lakes supplied some fish. Poaching was rife. Flax was sown, a few quarts by each farmer, out of which they made their linens, and wool provided the heavier clothing which was provided locally."

On 19th November, 1846, Attymass was the first parish in Ireland to report a death:

"Tradition says it came from France in a thick fog and fell for three nights-some say one night. The year was extremely wet, so much so that there was little turf. In spite of this there was a fine crop of stalks and the year was good. Following the fog black spots appeared on the leaves of the stalks which gave out an unwholesome peculiar smell and in a short time the stems were also affected and the fields had a blackened appearance."

In actual fact the blight was brought in from trade ships coming and going to the Americas from Ireland. The first place where it struck in Ireland was the Botanical Gardens in Dublin in 1845. It had been reported in South America in 1844 and was in the Isle of Wight and France in early 1845. The people of Attymass would have been aware of the significance of crop failure. There had been 24 crop failures from 1728-1844. The crops had failed in 1821 also. This led to famine from 1822-1826. This is a **diary entry** from July 26, 1830, when there was yet another crop failure. The writer is Amlaoibh O Suilleabhain.

"The paupers are picking potatoes out of the edges of the ridges. The 'black famine' is in their mouths.....This month is now called 'Hungry July'.........'Yellow mouth' is its proper name in Irish. It is a suitable name, for the fields are yellow, and also the faces of the paupers are greenish yellow from the black famine, as they live on green cabbage and poor scraps of that most."

Potatoes that were grown in April/May would be ready in October/November. The spare potatoes were buried underground in pits and would stay edible until July. The months after July were known as the 'meal months' as there were no potatoes. The 'Lumper' was the most popular potato as it grew the most potatoes per holding. It required little manure but it had a bland and watery taste. It was only 16% dry matter. The rest was water. The potatoes we eat today are 20-24% dry matter. When people went to bed a few hours before blight struck, their fields were as green as jewels. When they went outside, they were black or dark brown from decay. Quite a few of the peasants blamed the 'static electricity' from trains as the cause!

"Conditions were terrible as few had any money. In one case a man drowned himself rather than suffer the hunger pains any longer. It is related of one family that someone called on them to find the children dead and the parents lying on the floor, nibbling grain from a sheaf of oats which lay between them and both unable to rise when the visitor entered………

……a man was reputed to have fallen dead at the door of his cabin with a parcel of meat in his hand for which he had travelled five miles. A woman and child were found on the roadside. The woman was dead and had the trace of grass or green food about her mouth. The child was alive."

The situation for most was getting desperate. There were quirky stories as well as tragic ones in this dark time. One man in particular was

"…. a local who had the only horse and cart in the immediate neighbourhood. He was paid at so much per head to convey the sick to the workhouse. The patient was put in a sack, feet first, and the sack was tied closely around the neck and labelled. Up to seven or eight patients were laid out in the body of the cart which then set out on its cogglesome journey to the workhouse. Few ever returned."

The contractor received the name of 'sack-'em-up' from the fact of putting the patients in the sacks.

Another remarkable story is that of Fr. Egan who fought for justice for the poor. The chairman of The Relief Committee (a landlord) referred to him as 'Bully Egan from the Gap' (i.e. the main road between Mayo and Sligo).

Fr. Egan replied: "Aren't you 'soap-the-rope'?

This was in reference to the landlord's habit of hanging people in his farmyard for minor offences. The same landlord, a few years before he died, became very violent and was locked up in his own cellar. Food was thrown in through the bars but he still managed to eat his own shoulders before he died!

This extract shows how wild and lawless Ireland had become for those whose crops survived.

"Man traps were set in potato fields etc. A hole about 8 feet deep and 2 foot wide was dug, filled with water and concealed with brambles and grass etc. People lay in wait and when the robber fell into the trap, he was pounced upon and beaten to death with sticks. In some cases, the trap held water and the robber drowned."

These are known as **graphic** stories. They bring home the despair, misery and extremes of human nature the famine brought to ordinary people. A lot of these extracts came from second-hand sources and may or may not be exaggerated. Your diary should have impactful stories in it too, stories that are rich, creative and interesting to a reader.

Did you know? The population of Ireland before the famine was probably closer to 10 million than 8 million which would suggest that over 1 million died and 2 million emigrated. The main diseases were: cholera, typhus, relapsing fever, dysentery, beriberi and influenza.

SAMPLE DIARY ENTRY

Dear diary,   26th November, 1847

I am so afraid. My hands are trembling as I write this. I don't know if I can go on any longer. Mary passed away yesterday and we had to leave her there and go on. We are trying to get to the workhouse in Clonmel but there are rumours it is closed down. If it is, we are surely doomed. I am terrified that we will be next to fall and that we won't get up again.

My teeth are beginning to fall out and my stomach is bloated from hunger. It seems that every nettle and weed has been plucked from the ditches and the trees are bare of leaves too. We got by on watery soup until now and Sean caught the last, wild rabbit left in Tipperary two weeks ago. We were overjoyed with that and it gave us both nourishment and hope. Every time we try to catch a fish from the river armed men drive us off and claim that we don't have the right to come onto their land. They are foul men and I hate them. Can they not see we are starving? They are worse than the packs of feral dogs that dig up the bones of the dead.

It is the brigands who are the worst, though. They gather in large groups and attack people like us who have been driven off the land. They take everything you have: pots, snares, rings and even your clothes. These are dark times. Through God's mercy we have avoided them and I am grateful for that. The potato fields are black with decay and a foul smell hangs over the country. I am broken hearted at what Ireland has become.

As I write, a sour mist is forming, driven towards us by a thin wind. Up to now, the weather has been mild but I have heard stories from the West of men and women being killed by the cruel winds up there. They just don't have the energy to fight off both man and nature. I have seen people who would make your soul bleed with pity. They are like scarecrows and their yellow faces are pinched, with sunken eyes. They stumble like they are drunk and cling to little children who look like a bundle of rags. I hope I don't look like them. Do you think God is punishing us for something we did to him? If that is true, I will say a few extra prayers tonight and he may save us.

I have to go now, diary. I just don't have the strength to write about this horror any more. If God is merciful, I will write again tomorrow. If not, you will know what has happened to me.

'Till then

Sarah

A diary should contain a lot of emotions. Write down the different emotions present in this one. Do you think this is a sad diary entry? Why? Why not? Do you think it is historically accurate or would it have been a lot worse back then than this diary entry?

Write the diary entry of a 12-year-old boy living through the famine using different emotions.

The grid below needs to be filled in. It is a grid for 'Describing a Lake'. Are you good enough to give the sounds, metaphors etc. needed for the grid? Try your best to complete it.

LAKE COLOURS		mirror-silver	
LAKE SOUNDS	lapping		
LAKE IMAGES		wisps of fog	
LAKE SILENCE			haunting silence
METAPHORS			
SENSATIONS		iceberg cold	glacial
LAKE SMELLS		pine trees	
WATER TASTES	fresh	crisp	nectar of the Gods

FILL IN THE COLOUR CHART

BLUE	SILVER	GREEN	BLACK
al_i_e-blue	al_m_ni_m-silver	Am_z_n-green	ab_ss-black
aq_ar_um-blue	arg_nt-silver	c_rni_al-green	bas_lt-black
astr_l-blue	ber_l_ium-silver	cel_ry-green	b_t-black
bi_be_ry-blue	b_bb_e-silver	Ed_n-green	c_t-black
br_ch_re-blue	cha_nma_l-silver	fe_n-green	ca_e-black
bu_ter_ly-blue	chr_sal_s-silver	f_r_st-green	c_ll_r-black
c_emi_al-blue	dew gl_nt-silver	gar_ish-green	coba_t-black
co_kt_il-blue	di_m_nd fl_me-silver	gra_e-green	co_ra-black
co_mic-blue	dr_g_n sc_le-silver	gl_de-green	cor_l-black
cr_st_l-blue	fraz_l-silver	ja_e-green	corb_e-black
dr_g_nfly-blue	gl_t_er-silver	ju_cy-green	cr_w-black
d_ck-e_g blue	hoa_fr_st-silver	la_e-green	de_il's clo_k-black
el_ctr_c-blue	i_e-silver	ma_ble-green	de_il's he_rt-black
g_sfl_me-blue	mer_-silver	me_d_w-green	de_il's so_l-black
g_mst_ne-blue	mo_n gl_w-silver	mil_y-green	do_m-black

HAVING FUN WITH COLOURS

Write a brief story on a lake adventure using your 2 favourite colours from each column. There should be 8 colours in total and you will see the difference it makes to a story. Add in 8 onomatopoeic sounds as well if you wish and you have the platform needed for a great story. Make the plot a murder mystery and you will find you can't stop writing.

RIDDLE # 12: A tennis ball has rolled its way into a hole. This particular hole is extremely deep and has a sharp bend in the middle, making the ball impossible to retrieve by hand. The ground around the hole is made of concrete, so digging the ball out isn't an option. If you had to choose one item to get the ball out (not explosives) what would it be?

Did you know? The best way to drive mice out of your house without killing them is to dip cotton wool in peppermint essence and put them around the house. The smell evicts them.

MAKING A PERSONAL STATEMENT

A personal statement is a phrase or sentence that sums you up. It could be what you are, what you hope to be, or the person you are determined not to be. Everyone should have their own personal statement locked away in their mind for when life gets rough. Underneath is a list of possible statements to use in your life. You may decide to write one in your diary, your English portfolio, or your journal. If none suits you, then make one up and keep it locked away in your brain gym for future use.

1. Better, smarter, nicer: Pick any two.

2. Walk a mile in my shoes before you judge me.

3. Those that doubt me don't know me.

4. God don't make no junk, baby.

5. No one defines me except me.

6. If I'm not learning, I'm not earning.

7. Courage is never loud. It's a soft voice saying: "I will try again tomorrow."

8. Let others doubt. I know the universe is big enough to contain all my dreams.

9. I must be the change I wish to see in the world.

10. If I treat others well, God will give me an alibi.

11. Real people fail. I'm going to fail better than anyone else.

12. Stupidity is repeating the same mistakes and expecting a different result.

13. I was sick, but I'm better now, and there's work to be done.

14. You can't get to me. There's ice in my hands, my friend.

15. Effort comes from the muscles, not from nerves.

16. I am the master of my fate. I am the captain of my soul.

17. Yesterday I did, today I do, and tomorrow I will.

18. I belong where I choose to go.

19. Pain is weakness leaving the body.

20. If I can't make them understand, I will make them marvel.

Pick your favourite 10 statements and write a detailed explanation of what you think they mean. You should also see what other schools/cultures/individuals adopt as their personal statement (or mission statement) and see if you have something in common.

MAKING A MISSION STATEMENT

You are going for a job interview. In the lobby of the company you are visiting, your eye drifts up to the poster on the wall. In big, bold lettering, it reads:

"WHAT WOULD YOU DO IF YOU WEREN'T AFRAID?"

Perhaps you should get up and leave now. You know the quote is by Spencer Johnson. You and your class have adopted this as your mission statement since day 52 in first year English. You have lived by its motto and you turn to your friend. You say: "Should we go?" Instead, he says: "We'll buy the company first." Congratulations. You are a multimillionaire and you are conducting an interview to see if the company is suitable to add to your portfolio.

Many companies have recently added mission statements and vision statements to their company mottos. A mission statement is a statement of your goals and ambitions. It is based in the present. It is who you are today and what your class represents. **It is also the statement that sums you up best and that you want the world to see.** Here are some famous companies and their mission statements:

1. **Dell**: Dell's mission is to be the most successful computer company in the world at **delivering the best customer experience** in markets we serve.

2. **Facebook**: Facebook's mission is to **give people the power to share** and make the world more open and connected.

3. **Google**: Google's mission is to **organize the world's information** and make it universally accessible and useful.

4. **Skype**: Skype's mission is to be the **fabric of real-time communication** on the web.

5. **Yahoo**!: Yahoo!'s mission is to be the most **essential global Internet service** for consumers and businesses.

As you can see, the statements are short and to the point. You (and your class) should make out a list of 'power' words that you feel represent your mission as English students. Compile them in a grid and then choose the most important two or three to go into a statement. The grid below should help with this.

COMPANY 'POWER WORDS'	ENGLISH CLASS 'POWER WORDS'
delivering the best customer experience	…nurture and
give people the power to share	…enrich and
organize the world's information	…harness and
fabric of real-time communication	…empower and
essential global Internet service	…educate and

The mission statement can now be printed off and put on the front of everyone's English portfolio and journals. It should also be made into a banner to put on the wall of the classroom.

YOUR DAILY NUTRITION GRID

The grids below contain a list of excellent breakfasts on the left and a grid of low-nutrition breakfasts on the right. Your job is to rate each from 1-15. 1 is the lowest score and 15 the highest. Read them carefully and maybe you should look up what Michael Phelps and other sports stars have for breakfast before trying it. His breakfast is in the grid! Can you guess it?

BEST BREAKFASTS	PTS.	LO-NUTRITION BREAKFASTS	PTS.
grilled sardines with tomatoes		any concentrated juices	
porridge with honey/berries/nuts		processed cereals laden with sugar	
cold muesli and milk		chocolate nut spread on bread	
scrambled egg/wholegrain (wh.)toast		instant oatmeal from microwave	
peanut butter/banana on (wh.) toast		breakfast drinks for kids full of sugar	
melons/kiwis/oranges on (wh.) toast		pizza reheated from night before	
grilled herring with eggs and beans		non wholegrain toast and sugary jam	
yoghurt and (wh.) cereal with apple		instant microwavable sandwiches	
fruit/cream cheese and oatmeal		pancake mixes made from powder	
(wh.) waffles, berries and milk		fried sausages/puddings/bacon	
veggie omelette/bran muffin/yoghurt		any type of 'fast' foods	
grilled cheese/peanut butter wrap		toasted pastries in a packet	
a fruit and yoghurt smoothie/water		non-homemade muffins	
(wh.) pancakes with grilled kippers		any fry cooked with vegetable oil	
porridge/eggs/honey with lime juice		any of last night's takeaway leftovers	

Now do the same for the dinner grid. You may decide to make out a lunch grid yourself.

BEST DINNERS	PTS.	LO-NUTRITION/RISKY HABITS	PTS.
turkey/potatoes/cabbage /carrots		frozen pizzas from packet	
mackerel grilled with olive oil		processed burgers covered in sauces	
venison/croquettes/taco sauce		takeaways as part of a daily routine	
grilled chicken/cheese/mayo		non-organic chicken nuggets	
Greek yoghurt/strawberries/nuts		supersized burgers from a take away	
steak/Brussels sprouts/kale		processed meat with fries/curry/mayo	
wild salmon/ mushrooms/spinach		hot dogs	
beef stew/turnips/parsnips/broccoli		any meal dripping in mayonnaise	
turkey/brown rice/peppers/lentils		processed meats in general	
potatoes/coleslaw/beetroot/peas/meat		Happy Meals with a big, fizzy drink	
grilled tuna/tomatoes/walnuts/lettuce		kebabs bulging with meat and sauces	
beef//onion/spinach/beans		potato wedges and hash browns	
salad with 7 'super foods'		frankfurters	
pasta meal/Bolognese sauce		any meat from a deep-fat fryer	
veg/tomato soup and chicken wrap		oversized takeaway pizzas	

Everyone loves a takeaway. None of the above is in any way harmful to your long term health if they are seen as a treat. A treat is something you decide to give yourself once a week or once a month as a reward. If the low nutrition foods are part of your regular diet, change them!

PLANNING A SUCCESS MAP

Fill in the grids by ticking the boxes that you agree with strongly. You must fill in the point values by giving each row a value of: 10, 8, 5, 2 or zero. Zero is to be used if you disagree strongly with a statement. Each sentence starts with: **I am aware that..........**

NUTRITION   POINTS

I am what I eat and if I eat well, I will be well.	
'fast' foods are a tasty treat but should not be seen as part of my every day diet.	
processed foods such as hot dogs and chicken nuggets are very low in nutrition.	
small changes to my quality of diet can have a very positive impact on my life.	
making a written or mental checklist of my weekly intake of food will benefit me.	

SLEEP   POINTS

the body and mind start to shut down after 3 days without sleep. Sleep is precious.	
as an 11/12-year-old, I should be getting a minimum of 10 hours sleep per night.	
the pressures of time and school work don't allow me to get the sleep I require.	
I must manage my nightly food intake and social media time so I can sleep better.	
if my sleeping patterns are healthy, I will have more energy and it will help me.	

EXERCISE AND PLAY   POINTS

the health of my mind is linked to having a minimum of 30 minutes exercise daily.	
having fun, playful activities are of as much benefit as a very active sporting life.	
looking up YouTube for the best stretching exercises is more important than sport.	
exercise is what I do, not what I am. Sport does not define me, my mentality does.	
activities like yoga, karate, meditation and Pilates complement my mind and body.	

STUDY PATTERNS   POINTS

learning is a lifelong ambition of mine and school is one step on the road of life.	
if I get into the habit of studying on weekend mornings, I will be very successful.	
researching how to use mental maps will help me to study more effectively.	
a little bit of extra study because it's my choice is more valuable than homework.	
trying to study when I'm tired is silly and I will try to build up my energy levels.	

TEACHERS/FRIENDS/PARENTS/OTHER INFLUENCES   POINTS

talking to them about my daily or weekly successes in school is positive for me.	
being proud of small gains in my progress is more important than overall results.	
my strategy is to succeed in the long term and they are there to encourage me.	
I will come across negative people and I will choose not to listen to their opinion.	
I will thrive not only because they want me to but because it is part of my strategy.	

AVOIDING NEGATIVE PATTERNS

Fill in the grids by ticking the boxes that you agree with strongly. You must fill in the point values by giving each row a value of: 10, 8, 5, 2 or zero. Zero is to be used if you disagree strongly with a statement. Each sentence starts with: **I am aware that..........**

SOCIAL MEDIA   POINTS

technology is my friend but only if it helps my ambitions to succeed in life.	
most students spend between 8-13 hours a week networking and that is too much.	
everything I communicate can be used against me later in life as it is stored.	
I have a responsibility to communicate with others in a fair and proper manner.	
SM can sometimes be destructive and I'll never let it define my value as a person.	

MOBILE PHONE   POINTS

we are privileged to live in a world where communication with others is so easy.	
my mobile phone is a perk and not an entitlement and I must use it wisely.	
spending endless hours talking to others may not advance my strategy for success.	
uploading and sharing data on others without their consent may lead to problems.	
I have a responsibility to others not to cause them distress because of my actions.	

TECHNOLOGY   POINTS

YouTube is one of the greatest educational tools ever invented.	
Facebook and Twitter may give me pleasure but talking to my friends is better.	
I am living in a world where the opportunities to succeed have never been greater.	
an appreciation of the power of technology with hard work can help my ambitions.	
very few of my SM friends will be there to help me if I have a genuine problem.	

PEER PRESSURE   POINTS

the modern world can be a cruel place for a teen but I have the tools to cope.	
most of my friends wish me success but 'virtual' friends may not want the same.	
my peers on social networking sites at times will ask me to do things I shouldn't.	
there is no issue so serious that I can't discuss it with a counsellor or teacher.	
communicating my problems to an adult is now seen as a strength, not a weakness.	
a rumour is half way around the world while the truth is putting its boots on.	

THE VALUE OF READING OVER TECHNOLOGY   POINTS

reading will broaden my knowledge base in a way that PlayStation cannot.	
PlayStation is better for kinaesthetic intelligence. Reading covers the other seven.	
knowledge lies in reading information. Wisdom is in applying it to better my life.	
there will be thousands of occasions in life when I am bored and I'd love a book!	
one day I will wish my children to become great readers because it will help them.	

MY SUCCESS MAP

Write down the list of statements you gave 10 points to underneath.

I am aware that:

Nutrition:

Sleep:

Exercise and Play:

Study Patterns:

Influences:

Social Media:

Mobile Phone:

Technology:

Peer Pressure:

Reading:

Write out the list of statements you gave zero points to.

I am aware that:

Nutrition:

Sleep:

Exercise and Play:

Study Patterns:

Influences:

Social Media:

Mobile Phone:

Technology:

Peer Pressure:

Reading:

You have now made a list of points that you feel may benefit you or have a negative influence on your daily life as a student. If you can work on turning one bad habit into a good habit every day or week, you are achieving something that is beyond most people. Congrats!

ASSOCIATIVE LEARNING

Fill in the blanks by finding the links between the words.   **LINK WORDS**

1. Ed_n is to J_r_ss_c as E_e_gl_d_s is to Am_z_n.   colour

2. G_a_e is to g_o_e as m_ad_w is to v_ll_y.   open/closed spaces

3. C_i_k_y is to c_is_y as is to c_a_k_y is to r_s_l_s.   sounds

4. C_s_l_s is to t_w_r as hi_h/r_s_s is to s_y_c_ap_r.   tree metaphors

5. G_o_l is to b_l_o_ as g_u_t is to ba_k.   warning sounds

6. Sq_e_k is to s_re_m as bu_z is to h_s_.   opposite sounds

7. A_bl_s is to s_a_bl_s as l_p_s is to lu_be_s.   same motions

8. S_a_s is to s_oo_s as s_r_s is to d_ve/b_m_s.   air motions

9. Sc_a_b_ing is to s_u_r_ing as s_a_pe_ing is to s_it_e_ing.   rodents

10. D_o_ing is to b_z_ing as h_m_ing is to b_m_li_g.   bees

11. Ba_k is to ba_b_o as te_k is to ta_n_n.   colour

12. Do_e is to a_c_ as c_i_i_g is to c_no_y.   leaf cover

13. Lu_h is to p_u_h as ri_h is to la_i_h.   a deluxe forest

14. Ca_m is to pl_c_d as s_e_k is to l_t_e.   rivers

15. D_li_h_ed is to e_st_t_c as cr_sh_d is to w_etc_ed.   emotions

16. P_t_l is to s_ow_la_e as a_t_r is to pe_t_gr_m.   Find the link.

17. Wa_t is to f_ag_an_e as i_ce_se is to c_lo_ne.   Find the link.

18. S_er_y is to t_if_e as fr_i_y is to fr_itc_ke.   Find the link.

19. E_rt_y is to l_a_y as w_o_y is to m_lc_y.   Find the link.

20. A_pi_e is to a_tr_l as cr_st_l is to c_s_ic.   Find the link.

Riddle # 13:   I stare at you, you stare at me.

I have three eyes, yet can't see.

Every time I blink, I give you commands.

You do as you're told; you move your feet and hands.   What am I?

MY NUTRITION PATTERNS

The grid on this page is designed for you to keep a log of your daily food intake. No one is asking or telling you to change anything to do with your diet. No one is going to judge you. All that you have to do is write in your average meals and snacks/treats/fizzy drinks for one week. If, after the week is out, you believe you need to change your diet, well then do so. If you feel you don't, then don't. The key point is that you are aware of what you are eating weekly and that you are happy with it. You might decide yourself to make out a list of the 'super foods' that you eat each week also. If so, you deserve extra points for your initiative.

	BREAKFAST	LUNCH	DINNER	SNACKS
MONDAY	eggs			
MONDAY	porridge			
MONDAY	natural juice			
TUESDAY				
TUESDAY				
TUESDAY				
WEDNESDAY				
WEDNESDAY				
WEDNESDAY				
THURSDAY				
THURSDAY				
THURSDAY				
FRIDAY				
FRIDAY				
FRIDAY				
SATURDAY				
SATURDAY				
SATURDAY				
SUNDAY				
SUNDAY				
SUNDAY				

The average recommended exercise for everyone is 30 minutes a day. In a lot of cases, walking to and from school might give you all the exercise you require. If you are the sporty type, don't burn yourself out by over training and playing too many sports. Try every sport and enjoy them, but pick your favourite after 14/15 years of age and stick to it. You will find that your health may suffer in old age if you overexpose yourself constantly to Irish weather.

	Less than 30 minutes	More than 30 minutes	More than 1 hour
MONDAY			
TUESDAY			
WEDNESDAY			
THURSDAY			
FRIDAY			
SATURDAY			
SUNDAY			

THE PROBLEM WITH INFORMATION

With the rise in awareness about our nutrition requirements, it appears that some things we were told about our diet and wellbeing have turned out to be not quite accurate. Recent research on food seems to contradict what we have been told before.

Let us look at vitamin pills, for example. The new evidence, based on research involving 50,000 people, is that they are no substitute for a healthy, well-balanced diet. The following quote is taken from an editorial that academics from Warwick University and John Hopkins University in Baltimore, USA, published recently.

"Most supplements do not prevent chronic disease or death, their use is not justified and they should be avoided. This message is especially true for the general population with no evidence of [vitamin and mineral] deficiencies."

The Health Food Manufacturers' Association agrees with them:

"For most, the best solution is to eat as healthy a diet as possible, combined with other health-related lifestyles."

However, they go on to say that vitamin pills are recommended for children aged 6 months to 4 years (vitamins A, D and C), for over 65's (vitamin D) and for women trying to conceive (folic acid).

Another change in advice comes from scientists regarding saturated fats. These include red meat, butter and cream. Up to now, it was thought that they increased the chances of heart disease. New evidence has shown that saturated fats are good for you. The grid shows how attitudes have changed toward other products over the years.

PRODUCT	YEAR AND ADVICE GIVEN:	YEAR AND NEW RESEARCH SAYS:
eggs	1970-high cholesterol content is bad for you.	2013-they are a great source of proteins and vitamins.
chocolate	1988-can cause migraines and indigestion.	2012- may help to lower blood pressure.
coffee	1988-increases a risk of heart disease.	2008-a little coffee may lead to slightly lower mortality.
saturated fat	1970-linked to coronary heart disease.	2013-now no longer linked to heart disease.
bottled or tap water?	1997-chlorine in tap water linked to risk of cancer.	2013-bottled water is not tested to the same standard and is more likely to be contaminated.

Did you know? Gout is known at the 'disease of kings' and with good reason. In Roman times, the rich used to have their houses plumbed with lead pipes ('plumbum' means lead in Latin). They also used lead casks to store the wine and added lead to food and drinks as a sweetener. Many Roman Emperors died of lead poisoning-after suffering from severe gout!

You have just read the chart on how information about our food products can change. Now let us take a look at what drinks we are consuming every day. Many people enjoy a 'smoothie' and think they are healthy. The grid below is based on an article published by 'The Irish Independent' on Tuesday, December 3rd, 2013.

FIZZY DRINKS	sugar per 200ml	amount in sugar cubes	SMOOTHIES	sugar per 200ml	amount in sugar cubes
Lucozade	34.4g	xxxxxx	Juice Press raspberry	30.4g	xxxxxx
Club Orange	26g	xxxxx	Naked orange juice	23.8g	xxxxx
Fanta Orange	24g	xxxxx	Innocent orange and passion fruit	21.8g	xxxx
7up	22.4g	xxxx	Tesco strawberry and banana	19.2g	xxxx
Coca Cola	21.2g	xxxx			
Pepsi	21.2g	xxxx			
Sprite	13.2g	xxx			
HIGH FRUIT SQUASH CORDIAL			FRUIT JUICE		
Royal Orchard (Lidl)	27.4g	xxxxx	Del Monte	23.6g	xxxxx
Royal Orchard		xxx	Cranberry classic	22g	xxxx
Tesco High Juice		xxx			
REGULAR SQUASH CORDIAL			UNSWEETENED FRUIT JUICE		
Ribena	21g	xxxx	Jaffa Gold orange juice	22.4g	xxxx
Vimto Original Squash	8.5g	xx	Copella	20g	xxxx
Mi Wadi Orange	4.5g	x	Tropicana	20g	xxxx
Robinsons	3.7g	x	Sqeez	18.2g	xxxx
Dunnes Stores orange squash	1.6g	o	Innocent	16.4g	xxx

Write down what you have learned from the information given in the last two pages.

What surprised you the most? Do you agree that researching something for yourself is the best way of finding out the truth about what is good and bad for you?
Do a research project on one aspect of your health or lifestyle and include a facts grid.

CLASS IDEAS REVISION GRIDS

The grid below can be filled in as the class is doing a creative page of fill in the blanks. It may also be used at the end of the module for revision purposes. The teacher might also decide to put different headings in the grid. Some classes may decide to put in words; others may decide to put in phrases or sentences. The template for the first two pages is done for you. The rest needs to be filled in by the student.

THE COLOUR GREEN
ONOMATOPOEIC SOUNDS
METAPHORS FOR THE TREES

THE STUDENT BY THE LAKE WITH WRITER'S BLOCK

You are walking in the forest when you suddenly break free from its leafy umbrella. Ahead of you is a wide expanse of water. It is a very calm lake and it is large. In the distance there is a mountain range and its reflection is painted on the surface. Then you notice a young man sitting on a rock. He has a thick mop of hobbit-curls over an artist's face and eyes of the clearest, nomad-blue. He is staring at the lake with longing and he looks sad. He has a notebook and pen in his hand, but the pages are empty. You decide to approach him.

"Good morning," you say. "You look sad. Is something the matter?"

"Yes," he says. "I am trying to describe the lake but I fear I have writer's block. I can't do it."

"Fiddlesticks," you say to him.

"Excuse me?" he splutters. "Writer's block can happen to any student. It comes and goes."

"Bah! Humbug! Balderdash and claptrap too! If you took care to look at the patterns of nature and writing, you would be able to finish your observations in a jiffy."

"What patterns are you talking about?"

"Every aspect of describing nature requires a different set of skills. If you feel that the lake does not give enough detail for inspiration, make it up yourself. *Visualise it*. However, all lakes have patterns that anyone can write about. They all share some basic characteristics. I will help you to get started by writing down the pattern and one word or phrase to go with it."

COLOUR: mirror-silver

SILENCE: church-quiet

SOUNDS OF FISH: plopping

THE MIST: gauzy

THE CLEARNESS OF THE WATER: glass-clear

THE REFLECTION OF THE MOUNTAIN: stamped onto the lake

THE IMAGES: geese honking and flying in a 'V' formation like a Celtic fairy tale

THE RAIN: clinking off the lake

THE SENSATION OF THE BREEZE: refreshing

THE SMELL OF THE FLOWERS: a bouquet of sweet scents

THE TASTE OF WATER: it was like drinking sunshine.

"Thank you," he says, and you whistle as you make your way towards the mountains.......

Date: __/__/__	Title: **DESCRIBING A LAKE: 1ˢᵗ GRID**	Lesson number:

Latin phrase: Orta recens, quam pura nites.

Definition: Ne_ly/r_s_n, h_w/b_i_ht y/y_u/s_i_e.

Meaning: _____

_____

Spelling revision	New words	Dictionary definitions, corrections, and synonyms.
cl_y	frin_ed	
lo_m	feng sh_i	
mul_h	cur_a_h	
org_n_c	ti_k_r/ta_e	
inc_n_e	ald_r	
dec_d_ous	col_n	

You are walking by a lake on a sunny day. What do you see?

1 POINT	2 POINTS	3 POINTS	4 POINTS
w_t_r	an_m_ls	g_e_e/s_a_s/d_c_s	a c_o_d of f_i_s
a b_at	b_r_s	ot_e_s/be_v_rs etc.	fi_h_r_en

5 POINTS	6 POINTS	7 POINTS	8 POINTS
h_z_l/ald_r trees	an is_a_d	a cur_a_h/c_n_e	a s_il/b_at
re_d/frin_ed	a m_s_y/is_a_d	a k_y_k	a c_ui_e/l_n_r

9 POINTS	9 POINTS	10 POINTS	10 POINTS
a wh_rl_o_l	a lake m_n_ter	police s_u_a/d_ve_s	lo_g/lo_t/co_s_n
a w_te_spo_t	pack of w_l_es/be_r	police ti_k_r/ta_e	

super student ideas

magical words grid

a/gl_s_y/la_e	moo_shi_e clear	God-go_de_ed light	feng sh_i silent
p_n/cu_hi_n/re_ds	moo_light/p_le/li_i_s	he_v_n-spil_ing light	rain-pe_rl_d grass

POINTS SCORE

0-50 good first try	51-100 well done	101-130 very good	131-148 excellent

RULES FOR COLONS

1. The key word for a colon is that it **introduces** something. It can be: a word, a phrase, a sentence, a list or a quote.

Let's take a look at what that means with examples.

a) There is only one word for the glory of the morning: rapture. **A WORD**

b) The morning had only one thing on its mind: being blissful. **A PHRASE**

c) The morning light was layered in gold: it looked precious. **A SENTENCE**

d) The lake's light blazed with colours: zinc-silver, sunrise-gold and astral-blue. **A LIST**

e) The morning wind seemed to whisper to me: "We are alive." **A QUOTE**

Note that the quote after the sentence in e) takes a capital. This is a general rule.

2. A colon should be used when putting someone's name before direct speech. Example:

John: "Are you serious? I thought that ball was in."

Umpire: "Are *you* serious? The computer is never wrong."

John: &!

3. A great tip is that you should be able to substitute the word '**NAMELY**' for a colon. Rewrite sentences a) to e) above by replacing the colons with '**NAMELY**'. Does it make sense now?

The **only** piece of advice I will give in this book is not to use colons unless it's a **list** or a **quote**. Reorganise your syntax (sentence construction) in order to avoid them altogether if you can. It works for me!

PUT IN THE COLONS AND PUNCTUATE

1. The sky was a riot of colours bruised-blue grate-grey and warlock-black.

2. the teacher said to me you are a certified genius young sir.

3. I bought three items in the shop potatos milk and peas.

Riddle # 14: Mosquitoes have killed more people than any other animal in history. Can you guess which animal causes the most deaths in the U.S yearly? Take 3 guesses for 10 points.

Date: __/__/__	Title: **DESCRIBING A LAKE: 2nd GRID**	Lesson number:

Latin phrase: Tolle, lege; tolle, lege.

Definition: T_ke/up/a_d/r_a_! T_k_/u_/a_d/r_a_!

Meaning: _____

_____

Spelling revision	New words	Dictionary definitions, corrections, and synonyms.
fri_g_d	se_ic_l_n	used for
feng sh_i	hoarf_o_t	
cu_ra_h	chry_al_s	
ti_k_r/t_pe	apost_op_e	used for
al_er	span_le	
c_l_n	thu_king	
d_cid_o_s	plu_king	

the colour silver

	1 POINT	2 POINTS	3 POINTS	4 POINTS

d_w-silver	st_rfla_e-silver	s_yl_ne-silver	hoarf_o_t-silver
dra_g_n scale-silver	m_on_eam-silver	span_le-silver	chry_al_s-silver

the silent lake/valley

ca_e quiet	nu_ne_y quiet	wo_b quiet	cataco_b quiet
ch_r_h quiet	mo_a_te_y quiet	to_b quiet	confe_si_nal quiet

fish sounds

flo_pi_g	flip-flo_pi_g	plo_p_ng	plu_king
sl_p_ing	thu_king	plip-plo_p_ng	ker-plun_ing

the mist on the lake

gh_st-grey	spo_k-grey	voi_e_ess	sou_less
gho_l-grey	spe_tre-grey	so_n_less	bl_o_less

POINTS SCORE

0-20 good first try	21-49 well done	50-69 very good	70-80 excellent

RULES FOR APOSTROPHES

N.B every correct sentence in the grids is worth one point.

1. An apostrophe can take the place of **one** letter. These are called **contractions**.

contraction	put into a sentence	**contraction**	put into a sentence
all's	**All is** not well.	isn't	
can't	**I cannot** stand up.	they're	
couldn't		wasn't	
didn't		we're	
doesn't		wouldn't	
I'm		you're	

2. An apostrophe can take the place of **more than one letter**. These are called **contractions**.

contraction	put into a sentence	**contraction**	put into a sentence
he'd	**He would** be a great scholar.	she'll	
he'll	**He will** be a super parent.	they'd	
I'd		they'll	
I'll		we'll	
I've		who've	
shan't		you'll	

3. An apostrophe is used to show possession **of one thing**. This is called **singular possession**.

singular possession	explaining the sentence (**one** forest etc.)
The forest's lake was mirror-silver.	The lake in the **forest** was mirror-silver.
The mountain's peak was heaven swept.	The peak of the **mountain** was heaven swept.
The moon's rays were like lasers.	
The star's light was brilliant.	
The sun's glow was radiant.	
The valley's colour was mint-green.	

Did you know? Chewing gum while peeling onions will stop you from crying.

Riddle # 15: What five letter word becomes shorter when you add two letters to it?

"They say in China that if an old man dies, a library burns down." Chinese proverb

4. An apostrophe is used to show possession **of many things**. This is called **plural possession**. When this happens, it comes at the end of the word.

singular possession	plural	plural possession (more than one forest)
(apos. **before** last letter)	(**no** apos.)	(apos. **after** last letter)

The forest's lake	many forests	The forests' lakes were salmon-silver.
The mountain's peak	many mountains	The mountains' peaks were heaven touched.
The cat's eyes	many	were luminous.
The lion's fur	many	was tawny-yellow.
The waterfall's edge	many	were laced with white.
The meadow's grass	many	
The river's bank	many	
The cloud's colour	many	
The stream's rocks	many	
The tree's leaves	many	

5. There are many exceptions to the rule. If in doubt, just **put an apostrophe after 's' for plurals**. An example is below. You will be right over 90% of the time!

MNEMONIC HINT

Think of an apos-trophe as **the apostle's trophy**.

If trophies ends with an 's', it is **the apostles' trophies**.

EXCEPTIONS

	SINGULAR	PLURAL	PLURAL POSSESSION
words ending in S	Christmas	2 Christmases	Christmases' past
words ending in ES	spectacles	2 pairs of spectacles	the spectacles' cracks
words ending in CH	church	2 churches	the churches' doors
words ending in O	volcano	2 volcanoes	the volcanoes' fires
words ending in X	box	2 boxes	the boxes' holes
words ending in F	loaf	2 loaves	the loaves' price
compound nouns	mother-in-law	2 mother's-in-law	mother-in-law's sons

Did you know? It is true that a cockroach can survive without his head. 9 days is the most recorded and then they starve to death. Ants are the only creatures known to survive a microwave. They dance between the beams as they can sense them. Dinosaurs were wiped out by an asteroid, but not a single species of toad or salamander was affected. No one knows how crocodiles and tortoises managed to survive either. Why not do a project on it?

Date: __/__/__	Title: **DESCRIBING A LAKE: 3rd GRID**	Lesson number:

Latin phrase: Verba volant, scripta manent.

Definition: W_r_s/f_y, w_i_t_n/s_ays.

Meaning: _____

_____

Spelling revision	New words	Dictionary definitions, corrections, and synonyms.
se_ic_l_n	min_ed	
hoarf_o_t	d_w/po_d	
chry_al_s	lic_en	
apost_op_e	tat_o_ed	
span_le	fer_l	
thu_king	qu_ll	
plu_king	deca_ter	

nice images of a lake

1 POINT	2 POINTS	3 POINTS	4 POINTS
du_k/p_nd round	gl_s_y lake	reflections min_ed on	hi_d_n/hea_t of lake
d_w/p_nd round	cr_st_l lake	reflections tat_o_ed	fat_oml_ss depth of

the clear lake

p_ne clear	g_n clear	va_ni_h clear	mo_nsh_ne clear
wi_d_w clear	v_d_a clear	di_mo_d clear	deca_ter clear

nice images around lake

cru_b_ing/cas_le	re_d/frin_ed island	a g_l_xy of flies	fer_l/goa_s
we_th_r/b_at_n boat	qu_ll/sha_ed reeds	a pl_to_n of flies	lic_en/enc_us_ed rock

magic words grid

wis_y/mi_t	ced_r/swe_t smells	mo_k/h_m of bees	the nec_oman_y of
nect_r of the Gods	pol_ergei_t-white mist	bumb_i_g bees	bur_li_g streams

POINTS SCORE

0-20 good first try	21-49 well done	50-69 very good	70-80 excellent

RULES FOR SEMICOLONS (a.k.a. the super comma)

There is only one rule to a semicolon; **don't use it until you're 18**! The other rule is underneath.

1. The reason a **semicolon** is used, in general, **is to link two related sentences** (or clauses). If they are not related to each other, they don't take a semicolon. Think of a **semi-detached** house as a mnemonic to remember it. A semi-detached house is related (i.e. joined) to another one but they are still separate houses. Which of these sentences should take a semicolon?

a) The thunderclouds started to appear it rained like a winter's day.

b) Dogs can jump mountains have snow.

As you can see, both of these sentences would be more effective with a full stop. Therefore, **don't use a semicolon**! Why do writers use them? It is an effective technique (and a stylish one) if you are using long-winded sentences. As a young student, however, you should keep your sentences short. Use the K.I.S.S philosophy- **Keep It Simple, Student**!

Below are three sentences that could use either a semicolon or a full stop. Put in a full stop.

a) The lake was womb quiet plopping trout broke the silence

b) The surface of the lake was pane clear it was like something out of a fairytale.

c) The cedar sweet smell of the trees was refreshing the air was nirvana pure

The 14 punctuation marks in English. Copy this into your grid into your notebook.

PUNCTUATION MARK	EXAMPLE	PUNCTUATION MARK	EXAMPLE
apostrophe	'	braces	{}
comma	,	brackets	[]
colon	:	dash	—
exclamation mark	!	ellipses	.....
full stop/period	.	hyphen	-
question mark	?	parentheses	()
semicolon	;	quotation marks	" "

Did you know? Punctuation as we know it wasn't invented until the 15th century. The invention of mass printing in the 1450's led to the need for better punctuation. A man from Venice called Aldius Manutius and his grandson are credited with: inventing the semicolon, creating the modern comma, and using parentheses. Why not do a project on the invention of punctuation? Start with Aristotle; he was the original master of speech and punctuation.

Riddle # 16: How can you take nine matches and make ten without breaking the matches?

Date: / /	Title: **DESCRIBING A LAKE: 4th GRID**	Lesson number:

Latin phrase: Quam bene vivas refert, non quam diu.

Definition: H_w/w_l_ /y_u/l_v_/is/th_/s_c_et, n_t/h_w/l_n_.

Meaning: _____

_____

Spelling revision	New words	Dictionary definitions, corrections, and synonyms.
min_ed	alle_u_a	
d_w/po_d	Tolki_n	
lic_en	idy_lic	
tat_o_ed	yo_i	
fer_l	wink_ed	
qu_ll	amp_ith_at_e	
deca_ter	Budd_a	

interesting phrases

1 POINT	2 POINTS	3 POINTS	4 POINTS
rain wink_ed grass	ave_ue of pi_e trees	he_v_n/lea_ing light	nature's/am_hith_at_e
drag_nfli_s/whi_ri_g	Tolki_n-esque ferns	idy_lic scene	alle_u_a moment

the still lake

st_t_e still	yo_i still	vau_t still	f_ng/sh_i still
shri_e still	Budd_a still	cry_t still	Z_n still

metaphors for rain

bea_s of rain	d_wdro_s of rain	pr_gna_t drops of	di_mon_s of stinging
pear_s of rain	dr_ple_s of rain	te_rdro_s of rain	j_w_ls of sha_p rain

words for light rain

ai_y	dri_z_ing	tin_ling	miz_ling
mi_t like	sp_ayi_g	sprin_ling	like a Scottish smi_r

POINTS SCORE

0-20 good first try	21-49 well done	50-69 very good	70-80 excellent

ADJECTIVES, NOUNS AND VERBS

You may have noticed that the three terms above are listed in alphabetical order. That is because most sentences containing all three tend to have them in that sequence. Read the rules below and see if you agree. A good mnemonic for adjec**tive** is that it is descrip**tive**.

ADJECTIVES

An adjective is a word that describes a noun. Fill in the grid with describing words.

oxblood-red			
	glinting stars		
		singing rills	
			megawatt smiles

NOUNS

A noun is a **p**erson, **i**dea, **p**lace or **t**hing. A good mnemonic is the word **PIPIT**.

Let's try to figure out the person, place, thing or idea first. Fill in the rest of the grid. Do not put in any words that take a capital. Each word in the grids for the next two pages is a point.

person	place	thing	idea
man		snow	
			love
	forest	bone	
godfather			friendship

A proper noun gives us the **actual name** of this person, place, thing or **title**. A proper noun **always takes a capital letter** so it is easy to spot. Make up a mnemonic for: P, P, T and T.

Name of person	Name of place	Name of thing	Name of **title**
			'Hips Don't Lie'
		English	
	Miami		'Blue-Sky Thinking'
Shakira		Hallowe'en	
			'Jaws'
		Friday	
			'The Field'

A good way to remember it is to shout out to a friend: "You're a **Proper Noun**, you are!"

Did you know? Scientists have discovered that raindrops are shaped like hamburgers.

VERBS

A verb is an **action** word. It adds energy to a sentence so the mnemonic is **vibrant verbs**.

Fill in the grid below.

VIBRANT VERBS

LIGHT REFLECTING	MIST MOVING	RIVERS OVER ROCKS	BEE MUSIC
gl_a_ing	c_e_t	d_n_ed	hu_mi_g
gli_me_i_g	cr_wl_d	le_p_d	dr_ni_g
gli_ti_g	gl_d_d	sk_p_ed	mu_bli_g
glis_e_i_g	sa_l_d	h_rd_ed	b_m_li_g
gli_te_i_g	fl_at_d	va_l_ed	m_rm_ri_g

VERBS FOR DIRECT SPEECH

a_d_d	ba_bl_d	c_uc_led	gru_bl_d
an_o_nc_d	ba_k_d	co_plai_ed	hi_s_d
ans_er_d	b_wl_d	cr_w_d	ma_vel_ed
a_g_ed	bo_st_d	de_la_ed	pr_te_t_d
a_k_d	b_o_ed	dra_led	si_h_d

The story below has 20 underlined words. Write in **A**, **N** or **V** after each one. If you think it could be an adjective **and** a verb, for example, write in **B** (i.e. for **both** adjective and verb).

Punctuate the story after you read it once. Then rewrite it and change the adjective, noun or verb for a similar word or phrase.

INTRODUCTION: SETTING THE SCENE

"Never argue with a <u>fool</u>; he has the benefit of experience." That's what my grandfather, God rest his <u>eternal</u> soul, told me many years ago. It's a pity that I didn't heed his advice. I wouldn't have ended up in hospital listening to the <u>beep-beep</u> of a heart monitor.

PARAGRAPH ONE: DEVELOP THE PLOT

The day started like all horror stories do. Titan's <u>fiery</u> wheel was rising in the sky and I let the <u>ballad</u> of birdsong wash over me. My nostrils inhaled the fresh, crisp scent of pine and I admired the sky punching mountains in the distance. They <u>loomed</u> over us, us being my English class. We were here to describe "God's garden", or so my teacher called it. In reality, it was a sprawling forest of leaf and limb. We were supposed to find the lake in the centre of this forest by using a map and compass. He called the lake "God's teardrop", even though I discovered it was sausage shaped later.

PARAGRAPH TWO: ADD A CRISIS (AND DIRECT SPEECH)

We split up into groups of three and off we went on our <u>ramble</u>. It was going great until I decided we should try to find the old, Roman fort rumoured to be in the forest.

"That would be a history class then, wouldn't it?" barked John. "This is English."

I had never liked John. He had a squint in one eye and was always punching me.

"Yes, but there's a trove of treasure buried underneath it," I complained.

"Then that would be a science class, wouldn't it? Kate babbled.

I remembered my grandfather's quote and stopped arguing. I just grabbed my bag and stormed off. Thirty minutes later, I opened the bag. It had mascara, a hair brush and lipstick in it. There was no food, no water, no map and no compass. I felt like a right prat. I backtracked the way I had come but I lost my bearings. I shouted out time and again but no one answered. I wasn't too <u>concerned</u> because I watch Bear Grylls on The Discovery Channel.

PARAGRAPH THREE: THE PLOT DEVELOPS

Then I remembered that we were on a school tour to Norway and I thought of the bears and wolves. The shadows started to grow longer and I decided to <u>climb</u> up a tree. I reached the top and looked around as the <u>gloaming</u> of the evening arrived. I could see the lake twinkling with the last of the light. It was a <u>bright</u>, star flame-silver and looked like it was miles away. I heard a noise beneath me, and to my horror, a brown bear was <u>shambling</u> his way along the path. He didn't see me but I <u>swore</u> I wasn't climbing down until the morning. In a <u>strange</u> way, the stars kept me company that night. They looked like the <u>lost</u> souls of the world, <u>winking</u> at me as if we shared the same <u>destiny</u>. I must have fallen asleep at some stage because a <u>loud</u> crack woke me up.

CONCLUSION: LINK TO INTRODUCTION

It was the park ranger. He didn't look happy. He explained that a helicopter was waiting in a nearby clearing with medical supplies in case I had hypothermia. We had to take it as part of procedure.

"It's hot dog shaped," I <u>shouted</u> as we passed over the lake.

"Are all Irish people as idiotic as you?" he asked. "The only reason we found you is that you're wearing a white jacket...."

"Only the adults," I declared.

….."in the summer. In Norway. Clinging to the top of a <u>swaying</u> pine tree."

I thought of my grandfather's quote and promised that I would never argue with myself again. The only fool in this story is me.

QUESTIONS ON STORY

The narrator is the person telling a story. In this story, it was a young student. Do you think it was a male or a female? Why?

Did you like the narrator in this story? Give three reasons why/why not.

Do you think he/she was a foolish person or a clever person? State the reasons for your answer.

Do you think there were too much or too little descriptive passages in the story? Say why.

Rewrite the last paragraph and give a different conclusion (i.e. humorous, sad, surprising etc.).

MAGICAL WORDS/PHRASES GRID

stars like pixie dust			
	glistering		
		lambent	
			postcard perfect
		gloaming	
	diamond clear lakes		
cascaded			
	fluting song birds		
		juicy berries	
			mystical
		picture perfect	
	magenta		
fulgent			
	argent-silver		
		lithe rivers	
			opaline moons
		cerise	
	lemongrass		
a-flash			
	a waterscape of		freeze-frame perfect

Fill in the grid with magical words from the last three chapters or other words not in this book. Each word will be worth one point if the teacher agrees it would be nice to put in a story. Look up the meanings of the words provided in the grid and write them into your copybook. Pick 10 words going **down** the grid or 2 rows of 5 words going **across** the grid.

Did you know? The English language draws from 3 main sources for its words: **Latin** 30%, **French** (including Norman French and Anglo-French) 30% and **Germanic** (Anglo-Saxon, Old Norse and German) 30%. **Greek** is at 6% and others are at 4%.

Blue-Sky Thinking

Date: / /	Title: **DESCRIBING A LAKE: 5ᵗʰ GRID**	Lesson number:

Latin phrase: Quidquid discis, tibi discis.

Definition: W_a_e_er/y_u/l_a_n, y_u/l_a_n/it/f_r/y_u_s_lf.

Meaning: _____

_____

Spelling revision	New words	Dictionary definitions, corrections, and synonyms.
alle_u_a	al_e/V_ra	
Tolki_n	crysta_li_e	
idy_lic	ruf_ling	
yo_i	spr_te	
wink_ed	salv_	
amp_ith_at_e	myr_h	
Bu_d_a	calami_e	

physical sensations of the wind

1 POINT	2 POINTS	3 POINTS	4 POINTS
a co_l sensation	a so_t_ing sensation	the re_re_hi_g wind	the ruf_ling wind
a ple_s_nt sensation	a salvi_g sensation	hair tou_ling wind	the care_si_g wind

flowery smells

air was pet_l sweet	bl_ss_m sweet	calami_e sweet	myr_h sweet
air was pol_en rich	al_e/V_ra sweet	hone_suc_le sweet	jasmi_e sweet

the taste of water

cri_p	glas_y	crysta_l_ne	mo_n_a_n pure
spri_g fresh	tasted of sp_ite	sprigh_ly	tun_ra pure

metaphors for heavy rain

silver na_ls of	hi_sing/wi_ch-sp_t	A_a_o_ian rain	No_h's-A_k-hea_y
silver cr_st_ls of	the bi_li_n-fold pi_g	fo_nt_in from heaven	Ar_age_d_n rain

POINTS SCORE

0-20 good first try	21-49 well done	50-69 very good	70-80 excellent

FUN REVISION CROSSWORD

ACROSS

1 Bottomless, as in sea (10)

2 Wizardry of the black sort (10)

4 Not quite a wraith, but alike (7)

5 Trees that live near water (6)

6 A type of metal (4)

8 Not quite moss, but alike (6)

11 A biblical scent (4)

14 First part of a healing plant (4)

16 Slim and supple (5)

18 Acronym for a missing soldier

DOWN

1 A type of Oriental meditation (4,4)

3 A pink colour (6)

4 A glitter of bracelet (7)

7 Praise the Lord (8)

9 The taste of water (11)

10 The head of the wizards in T. L. of the Rings.

12 A healing plant to finish 14 across (4)

13 Wild and free (5)

15 A spring animal (4)

17 A type of blue colour and a type of duck (4)

Did you know? An estimated 14.7 million people in the U.K. play the crossword every week. The largest crossword ever compiled had 12,842 clues down and 13,128 clues across and appeared in Russiky crossword.

RECAP ON THREE MODULES: QUIZZES AND QUESTIONS

1. What word beginning with '**l**' was given for a yacht moving lazily on the waves?

2. What was the compound noun used to describe a horizon?

3. What metaphor beginning with '**e**' was used to describe the colour gold.

4. Name two physical sensations of being burned by the sun.

5. Write down two metaphors for the sun.

6. Name as many of the 8 types of intelligence as you can.

7. What was a butterfly previously called?

8. Butterflies are cannibals. True or False?

9. Name two metaphors for water.

10. What word beginning with '**p**' is listed as a sea smell?

11. What word that sounds like lolling is an emotional sensation of the soul?

12. What is kelp?

13. Name three green adjectives that start with a '**j**'.

14. What did Maya Angelou say that people will always remember?

15. Give two adjectives which mean 'twisted' for trees.

16. Name two types of moon which start with an '**h**' (or '**H**').

17. What is a placid river?

18. Nettles contain more vitamin c than oranges. True or False?

19. Define the word 'aster'.

20. Give four other words that can replace the word smell.

21. Vending machines kill four times as many people every year as sharks. True or False?

22. What is a catacomb?

23. Give 4 sounds a trout would make slapping the water. (not aaaaarghhhh)

24. What two words beginning with '**g**', and two words with '**s**', were given as mist colours?

25. What is feng shui?

Bonus Question: Take one letter away from the word **starling** each time to make 7 new ones.

MNEMONICS REVISION

1. Give the structure of an army command using a mnemonic of your choice.

2. What is the mnemonic for and definition of a metaphor?

3. What is the mnemonic for and definition of a simile?

4. Give the mnemonic for the word 'there' and put it into a sentence.

5. Give the mnemonic for the word 'their' and put it into a sentence.

6. What word can be used to replace a colon and what was the mnemonic for a semicolon?

7. What is the mnemonic for using both adjectives and apostrophes?

8. What is the mnemonic for both a noun and a proper noun?

Can you see how the phrases below are mnemonic and help with your spellings? Learn 5 today and 5 for the next 2 days. Try to change the wording to form your own mnemonics.

1. Argu lost an e in his argument.

2. Never believe a lie.

3. Dara checked the calendar every day.

4. Eileen found her e's in cemetery.

5. Emma faced a dilemma.

6. I'm really red and embarrassed. So sorr (drop the 'e' for embarrassment).

7. A new environment will iron me out.

8. Goofy Greg loved to exaggerate.

9. Generally, a general is your best ally.

10. Mom ate immediately.

11. An island is land surrounded by water.

12. Miss Pell never misspells.

13. It is better to give than to receive.

14. Rhythm helps your two hips move.

15. Sep was the farmer's wife. She saw a rat. "Sep. A rat. E!" she squeaked.

PLANNING A STORY WITH ONOMATOPOEIA

We know by now that onomatopoeia is when the meaning of a word is obvious from its sound. But what exactly does it do for a passage of writing? Quite a lot, as it turns out.

When a writer uses onomatopoeia, the reader is catapulted into the world of the writer's creation (i.e. without having a choice). The sounds used **imprint** heavily on the reader's mind. Onomatopoeia is the whizzing, 'silver bullet' of writing techniques and is used to create **atmosphere** and **action**.

With the flick of a pen from the writer, a murmuring wind can become a howling storm. A peaceful scene with humming bees can be turned into a disaster by swarming, buzzing wasps. The soothing sea song of the waves can be turned into a sea that lashes and claps your tiny boat. Screeching banshees can spill out of windy bottles and lazy trout can become the fizzing torpedoes of the river. Whatever onomatopoeic words you choose, ensure you are using them to fit in with the tone you are trying to create.

In the next two sample stories, onomatopoeia is needed to give a mood of calm, followed by men banging their swords and spears off their shields. Look at the grid below to see which words **you** would choose.

SOFT WINDS	LOUD WINDS	HARSH 'ng' SOUNDS	DEEP 'nk' SOUNDS
bre_th_ng	me_l_ng	cla_g_ng	cl_nk_ng
ex_a_ing	shri_k_ng	clango_rous	clon_ing
si_h_ng	scre_m_ng	go_ging	clu_ki_g
so_gh_ng	scre_c_ing	jan_l_ng	pl_nking
wh_s_er_ng	wa_l_ng	tw_ng	thu_king
mu_m_ri_g	sn_r_ing	**SOFT 'ng' SOUNDS**	**MUSICAL 'nk' SOUNDS**
sus_ir_ng	ho_l_ng	di_ging	chi_king
w_im_er_ng	y_wli_ng	ji_g_ing	cl_nking
ga_pi_g	ke_ni_g	p_ng_ng	p_inking
pu_f_ng	cat_rwa_ling	r_ng_ng	ti_k_ing

Next the story needs the sound of a stone or an arrow going through the air. Luckily for us, we now know that the 'zz' sound is the fastest in the English language. The next fastest are words with a double letter in them. Which of those below would you choose for a projectile?

ARROWS THROUGH THE AIR	FAST WORDS WITH DOUBLE LETTERS	
b_z_ing	h_m_ing	his_i_g
f_z_ing	st_u_ming	s_s_i_g
fi_z_ing (for fire arrows)	t_r_m_ing	p_rri_g
si_z_ing	w_ir_ing	wh_o_hi_g
w_iz_ing	zo_m_ng	z_p_ing/z_n_ing

Did you know? The tallest man documented was Robert Wadlow. He was 8'11'' and died in 1940 at the age of 22. He was 5'4'' tall by the time he was 4! Wikipedia has his photograph.

DAVID AND GOLIATH IN THE VALLEY OF ELAH

David, the little shepherd boy, faced the mighty Goliath of Gath, but he was not afraid.

The whispering wind twirled a few grains of sand as he bent down to pick up a stone from the brook. The water felt like warm silk on his hand and he looked up to the heavens as he rose. The sky was cosmic-blue, but he could not see anyone up there who could help him. A few ragged clouds of oyster-white were all that he had for inspiration. The breathing of the wind was warm and the stillness was eerie.

Across from the stream, he could see Goliath sizing him up. Behind Goliath, a great army of men stood in silence looking at him. Their armour flashed with sardine-silver and bronze colours and only the plumes on their helmets moved limply in the breeze. Then Goliath laughed, a deep, booming sound like the rumbling of bottled thunder, and the silence was shattered.

The Philistine army laughed also and clashed their weapons off their shields. The sound of the clanking and clanging caused a few vultures to rise up in surprise and David watched them soar into the sky. Goliath stood in front of the men like a myth from an old book. He was 6 cubits and a span, 9'9'' from toe to tip. He was an oak amongst a forest of holly trees and David's mouth became dry and his palms sweated.

"Do not look for the sky to help you, boy. My Gods don't like it!" Goliath bellowed. He slashed his huge sword twice through the air and David could hear it whistling from where he stood.

David summoned up the courage to defy him and it was as if someone else was answering.

"This day Jehovah will deliver you into my hand, and I will strike you down; and I will give the dead bodies of the host of the Philistines this day to the birds of the air and to the wild beasts of the earth; that all the earth may know that there is a God in Israel."

Then David bent down to pick up four more stones, one for each of Goliath's brothers. Goliath the Brute roared and charged at him. David could feel the vibrations of the giant through his sandals. Slowly and deliberately, he chose the most perfectly smoothed stone. He placed it carefully into his sling and the sling hummed as it swished around and around his head. His 5'3'' frame needed all the energy he could muster.

He let fly as Goliath neared the brook. The stone hissed through the air and caught Goliath right in the centre of his forehead. Goliath stopped, stumbled, swayed on his feet, tottered, and crashed to the ground with a howl of outrage. He twitched twice and died.

Silence returned to the Valley of Elah. The murmur of the brook was the only sound that reached the ears of the stunned armies. Then a great cry rose up from the Israelites behind David and he had never felt so alive. He strode across the brook and chopped off the head of Goliath.

"David! David! David!" the Israelites roared as he held the bloody head up to the sky.

Did you like this story? Give your reasons why or why not.

Who do you think is the hero and who is the villain in this story? Is it very obvious?

Do you feel glad that David killed the giant Goliath? Do you have any sympathy for Goliath? Why? Why not?

Make a list of all the onomatopoeic words used in this passage. Do you think they helped the story? Write down some ways they helped the mood of the story.

What is the best image in this story, in your opinion? Did you notice any metaphors or similes? Make a list of those also.

Rewrite the story using the words and phrases in the grid below. Why not let Goliath win?

galaxy-blue sky	voice rumbling like a volcano
sighing wind	a sissing stone
like soft velvet	swayed and collapsed
hushed silence	jerked once
host of men	a pregnant silence
salmon-silver	lopped off his head
thunderclap	raised it aloft
clattered	"Victory!" he screamed.

POINT OF VIEW

Point of view in literature is the way the narrator allows you to hear and see the world described. Every narrator has a camera in descriptive writing. The narrator decides at what angle, what type of images and what scene is shown. The screen is what the reader sees, much like a cinema. **You are the camera: think about what is going up on the screen.**

In the 'David and Goliath' story, sympathy was suggested by the "little" shepherd boy versus the "mighty" figure of Goliath. David appears to be all alone at the start of the story. No one can help him and there is no mention of an army behind him. Goliath has the support of his army and they laugh at David's size. This is one point of view, a hero against a cruel enemy.

A good story will always have a blend of colour, sound, dialogue and action. Point of view helps you to decide which person you want to write the story in: first, second or third. The 'David and Goliath' story was written in the third person. The key pronouns are: **he, they** and **it** in this story. A diary is normally written in the first person.

Did you know? A cubit is the length from elbow to middle finger tip and a span is the length from the tip of the thumb to the tip of the pinky!

Riddle # 17: Two people are in a barn. Ten cats follow them in. How many feet are in the barn now?

"Ever tried. Ever failed. No matter. Try again. Fail again. Fail better." Samuel Beckett

HEROES AND VILLAINS

David, the king's weapons' bearer, looked at the hulking figure of Goliath the Philistine and laughed. He wasn't the little boy that Goliath thought he was. He was a veteran of many battles and all his enemies had fallen like skittles at his feet. True, he was only 5'3'', but that was quite tall for 1,015 B.C. Goliath was only a head taller at four cubits and a span.

"This guy isn't even worth a sword stroke," he thought, as he bent down to pick up five stones from the brook. The cool water felt like satin on his hand and the puffing wind swirled a few dust grains as he picked the best stones. Goliath, his cousin from his mother's side, had four brothers. If they felt like a blood feud after he butchered Goliath, he would cut off their heads too.

He looked up to the sky. Not because he was looking for help, but because he could see Goliath was favouring his right hand and was slow and clumsy. The sky was brochure-blue with a few wispy clouds and David thought he would take a holiday after today. The Lord above knew he needed it. His life up to now had been a never ending series of blood and battles. His mouth was dry but that was because they were in the middle of a heat wave.

"And to think none of the Israelites will fight this oaf," David thought, as Goliath the Village Idiot boomed out some words in that alien accent of his. David couldn't understand a word he said, but it must have been funny because the Philistine army laughed like braying donkeys. Then they smote their weapons against their armour and all the clunking and clonking nearly caused him a headache.

"Let's get it over with!" he screamed because his patience was running out. Goliath pounded the ground with his feet and David could swear he could feel the vibrations through his sandals. He took a round, oval stone and placed it in his sling. He twirled the sling in neat circles around his head, waiting for the right moment. Goliath was nearly inside the kill zone and he didn't want to have to fight him. The day was just too hot. The sling whirred and strummed with the violence of his hand. Then he released it and the stone fizzed through the air like a hummingbird's wings.

A hit! It had struck him in the centre of his forehead. David couldn't believe it. What happened next stunned him even more. Goliath groaned and staggered backwards. His huge legs buckled underneath him and he collapsed onto his knees. He tried to rise, but there were blood bubbles coming from his mouth. He fell forward. His face hit the sand. He twitched once and was still.

A pregnant silence descended on the battlefield. The only sound was the burbling of the brook and the scream of a happy vulture. Then a roar arose from the vast, Israelite army behind him and David felt proud of himself. He had never seen anyone dying from a slingshot before.

"Right. Let's go get that head, I suppose," he said out loud. "And if those brothers of his want it back, there's another four stones where that one came from."

Has your opinion of David changed from the first story? What do you think is the reason for that? Discuss your answer and refer to the term point of view in your answer (see page 59).

Which of these stories is closer to what happened in 1015 B.C. in your opinion? **"What is history but a fable agreed upon?"** Do you think Napoleon's quote rings true?

Do you feel any sympathy for Goliath in the second story? Make a list of the words and phrases used to describe him in the first and second stories. Is there a big difference?

FILL IN THE COLOUR CHART

GREY	RED	OTHER GREYS	OTHER REDS
a_h-grey	b_r_y-red		
cind_r-grey	b_o_d-red		
cl_y-grey	bo_fi_e-red		
fli_t-grey	cl_ret-red		
g_o_e-grey	cri_s_n-red		
gr_te-grey	d_v_l-red		
gra_i_e-grey	d_v_l blo_d-red		
gr_v_l-grey	d_a_on blo_d-red		
gr_v_s_one-grey	d_a_on fla_e-red		
griz_led-grey	em_er-red		
h_ll mi_t-grey	fi_eb_ll-red		
ir_n-grey	fire f_a_e-red		
to_bs_one-grey	he_lh_u_d-red		
u_d_ad-grey	h_l_y-red		
wo_f-grey	p_p_y-red		

The grid below needs to be filled in. It is a grid for 'Describing a Mountain'. Are you good enough to give the sounds, metaphors etc. needed for the grid? Try your best to complete it.

MOUNTAIN COLOURS		ermine-white	
MOUNTAIN SOUNDS			rumbling
MOUNTAIN IMAGES		an eagle circling	
MOUNTAIN SIMILES	like rose thorns		
MOUNTAIN METAPHORS		steeples of the sky	
MOUNTAIN SENSATIONS			numb
MOUNTAIN SMELLS	sweat and oil		
MOUNTAIN TASTES	heavenly chocolate	divine	Arcadian

Did you know? Do you want to calculate the age of your dog in human years? Up to recently, most scientists seemed happy with the formula of multiplying a dog's age by 7. Hence, a dog aged 3 would be 21. Wrong. A dog matures much faster than a human at the early stage of his life. So would you if you had a gene in you that said: "Hunt deer or die." A dog's rate of growth slows down after 2 years of age, however. They then age about 4 years for every human year. If you want to calculate his/her age, subtract two from his/her age. Then multiply by four and add 21. You heard it here first.

THE HISTORY OF THE ENGLISH LANGUAGE

It is September 25th and the Battle of Stamford Bridge is underway. It is not Chelsea versus Arsenal. The screams and war cries of men fill the length of the meadow. The smoke is thick from fire arrows and they fizz and frizzle as they whine through the air. Steel rings, swords bite and men die.

The flowers are still fresh on the grave of Edward the Confessor, but the battle to be the next king of England has started. On one side of the river is the Anglo-Saxon army led by Harold Godwinson, the new English king. He has 7,000 men, but they are exhausted. They have just marched an incredible 185 miles in 4 days to get here. They were carrying heavy armour on this miracle march and it has taken its toll. The year is 1066.

On the other side of the river is the Viking army of Harald Hardrada, King of Norway. He has 10,000 men. Unfortunately, the other half of his army is a day's march away, so only 5,000 are with him. They are resting up on their 300 ships as no one expected Godwinson to get here so soon. The bad news for Harald is that most of the armour is back with the ships as well. This September has been unnaturally hot and the men were happy to discard their armour. The sun beats down on their bare flesh as they lounge around, laughing and donkey calling each other.

Godwinson's army streams up from the south and the Vikings are stunned. How did he manage to arrive so quickly? Although his men are bone tired, Godwinson launches into battle. The Vikings on the west side of the bridge are quickly overcome by the front of Godwinson's army. The rest flee over the bridge and gather more forces. They stop to get weapons and what armour they can. Then they face Godwinson's army again. This time they will fight on the bridge. The bridge has only enough room for 4 men across and that suits the big, bloodthirsty men of the North.

An hour later, Godwinson shouts out: "In the name of all that's holy, what is happening up there?"

He knows the Vikings have sent word to the ships and that more men are on the way. It is vital that they get over the bridge and defeat this half of the Viking army before the reinforcements come. It is a lot easier to defeat 5,000 men in two separate battles than 10,000 in one. His horse is jittery but he reaches up on his stirrups and strains his neck to see. There must be a hundred of his men pressed together on the bridge. They are fighting in deadly hand-to-hand-combat and the sounds drifting back to him are sickening: bones cracking, shields splitting and flesh slicing. Then he sees what the holdup is.

There is one man on the bridge who is a head taller than the next tallest man. He is a titan of a man, a true giant, and he is causing havoc. This man would not have put on his armour even if he had it. He is a Viking berserker, a special breed of warrior who doesn't care whether he lives or dies. His berserker name comes from two Norse words, 'berr' (bare) and 'serkr' (shirt). He is the lunatic on the bridge and, besides the battle axe he wields, he also has the fate of the English language gripped in those huge, clumpy paws of his....

THE BERSERKER ON THE BRIDGE

His axe smoked with steam and blood. He was weary beyond measure but they kept coming. The Vikings around him had withdrawn from the bridge because he was swinging his weapon in such huge arcs. He was also blood-drunk and they knew better than to be around him.

The world had narrowed down to two slits in the helmet he wore. It was an old bear skull fitted with metal plates and his father's father had worn it before him. He was proud of his ancestors. He wanted to meet them with pride in his heart when he walked to the gates of Valhalla. That would be today, he knew, but he did not mind. He was born for this life of fighting and he would die well today no matter what happened.

His great chest heaved like a bellows as he drew in horse-breaths of air. The English dogs were moving back from the bridge! Then he saw the size of the men who were replacing them. His heart sank as he realised they were sending all their champions at once to face him. He knew his time was short so he took one last look around.

The trees were a-fire in a patchwork of colour and the light-haze of the sun on the corn was spectacular. Then the sun dimmed behind the hills and the Technicolor faded.   **COLOUR**

The noise of battle turned down like a switch as the two armies waited to see what would happen. A Viking titan fighting against the best of the Saxon army. A pin drop silence descended. There was no insect-hum, no leaf-rustle, no wind-music.   **SOUND**

He touched the cold, smooth steel of his axe head as he sharpened the edge of the blade with his whetstone. It felt like pond ice. He laughed at the memory of his father falling into the frozen pond when the snow dragon had come in May all those years ago.   **TEXTURE**

The memory released his tension and he inhaled the sweet, September air for the last time. Above the stench of horse bowels and blood, pollen drifted in the air. Air gold, the Viking women called it, but gold didn't smell of red poppies and white lilies.   **SMELL**

The Saxon champions were ready. The last one was clomping up in his battle boots and they were forming in line to face him. He looked down and saw a sleek trout lazing in the river. Its spots were blue and red and white and he knew he would look like that tonight.   **IMAGE**

He only knew one Latin phrase. His son in Norway had it now. It was hundreds of years old and it was engraved on a Roman coin. It was a metaphor for how his family had lived its life. "Melium est nomen bonum quam divitae multae," he whispered and charged up the bridge. "Will I be remembered?" he wondered, as he swung his axe in frenzy. Voices rang, swords sang and men died.   **METAPHOR**

Find out what happened next by typing it into Google. Then write the ending once you get all the facts. What is for certain is that the Battle of Stamford Bridge had the potential to change the direction of the English language. Less than 3 weeks later, the winner of this battle fought the king of France in the Battle of Hastings to see who would rule England for once and for all. You should consider doing a project on these battles and relating them to English class.

A QUICK HISTORY OF ENGLISH: A CLASS ACTIVITY

Fill in the blanks by researching the times, customs, words and legacy the following tribes left behind them. If a tribe or race back then has been remembered by history, it means they were ruthless, cunning and brave. Put an extra column in your copybook for the second grid.

	CELTS	ROMANS	ANGLES
Dates of arrival	500-100 B.C.	A.D. 43	
Famous for	Queen Bouddica	Julius Caesar	
Famous for	druids	Coliseum	
Traditions	fighting naked	the legion's standard	
Battle traditions	woad tattoos	'the tortoise'	
Festivals/Names	Hallowe'en	January/March	
Technology introduced	swords/glass beads	indoor plumbing	
Technology introduced	bronze mirrors	53,000 miles of road	
Technology introduced	hair gel (limewater)	public libraries	
Technology introduced	harvesting machine	cement/bricks	
Food introduced	cheese	stinging nettle/peas	
Animals introduced	hens	cats/fallow deer	
other facts	heads on doorways	Rome population 1m	
other facts	swords in rivers	'decimate' a legion	
words	basket/bog		
words	bother/clan		
words	glen/ keening		
words	poteen/slob		
words	whiskey/uisce beatha		

SAXONS	JUTES	VIKINGS	NORMANS

WHAT THE GREEKS CAN TEACH US

The ancient cultures of Greece and Rome can teach us a lot. Greece, in particular, was the cradle of democracy. Recently, the 'Huff' ran an article entitled: 'What Greek wisdom can teach the rest of the world about living well.' Underneath are the 11 main points of the article. You may decide to look it up in more detail with your teacher's blessing and base a project around it.

1. **They eat a healthy, Mediterranean diet**: The Greek diet was (and is) based around vegetables, olive oil, healthy fats, fish and whole grains. Recent research concluded that those who followed a Mediterranean diet had a reduced risk of heart disease, obesity, cancer and Alzheimer's.

2. **They take naps**: Most Greeks take a siesta in mid-afternoon and re-open for work again at 5p.m. It can be argued that students do too! This is great for resting the body properly.

3. **They appreciate the value of a good walk**: During the warmer months, small villages and towns obey the tradition of *volta* (strolling). It is normally done when the sun goes down.

4. **They ask the big questions**: Greek people love to question the meaning of life and how others can be treated better. There is a strong sense of identity and community also. Socrates said: "**The unexamined life is not worth living.**"

5. **They take hospitality and generosity very seriously**: Greek people are famous for their hospitality. If you are their guest, they take your welfare very seriously.

6. **They've unlocked the secrets to longevity**: Ikaria is a tiny island off Greece. Ikarian men are nearly four times as likely to reach the age of 90 as American men. They say it is because they wake up late and always take naps, as well a healthy diet and strong family ties.

7. **They take a lot of leisure time**: Very few people in Greek islands wear watches. If they invite you to lunch, you can arrive at 10 a.m. or 6 p.m. They don't care! It's 'island time'.

8. **They tell stories**: Telling a story is a great way for our brains to give structure and meaning to our lives. The Greek tradition of Gods battling mortal men links heaven and earth for them in a way that makes sense.

9. **They spend a lot of time outdoors**: The heat of the Greek sun has obvious health benefits.

10. **They eat food together**: Food is the glue that binds social ties, whether friend or family.

11. **They know where to find happiness**: The Greeks believe unhappiness is a choice. They do not see stress as an external matter, but rather something that must be conquered from within. To this day, the Greek word '*stoic*' means to bear hardship and suffering very well.

Do you agree with every point in this article? Write a brief explanation for each one you agree with. If you disagree with any point, explain why.

Write out a list of points about living well that are not mentioned above and discuss them.

ASSOCIATIVE LEARNING

Fill in the blanks by finding the links between the words.

LINK WORDS

1. G_o_t is to gh_ul as s_o_k is to s_ec_re.   fog

2. Nu_ne_y is to m_na_te_y as ca_a_o_b is to c_y_t.   silence

3. Vo_c_l_ss is to _ou_d_e_s as b_o_d_ess is to s_ul_ess.   fog

4. M_z_li_g is to d_iz_li_g as s_r_yi_g is to sp_in_li_g.   rain

5. P_un_i_g is to t_un_i_g as f_o_pi_g is to p_op_i_g.   fish

6. M_n_ed is to ta_t_o_d as p_i_t_d is to e_g_a_ed.   reflections

7. A p_a_o_n is to a l_gi_n as a c_us_er is to a g_la_y.   flies

8. S_a_u_ is to s_ri_e as y_g_ is to Bu_d_a.   stillness

9. B_a_s are to p_ar_s as d_a_on_s are to j_w_ls.   rain

10. Co_l is to p_ea_a_t as r_f_li_g is to c_re_si_g.   wind

11. P_t_l is to p_l_en as m_r_h is to ja_m_ne.   flowers

12. C_i_p is to c_yst_l_i_e as m_u_ta_n is to t_nd_a.   water purity

13. B_z_i_g is to f_z_i_g as s_z_li_g is to f_iz_li_g.   arrows

14. C_nd_r is to g_a_e as g_a_el is to g_a_e_t_ne.   colour

15. Gi_ is to g_a_s as v_d_a is to d_c_n_er.   water clarity

16. H_m_i_g is to t_r_m_ing as w_ir_i_g is to w_iz_i_g.   Find the link.

17. C_a_e_ is to c_ims_n as f_r_b_l_ is to he_l_o_nd.   Find the link.

18. _la_sy is to c_y_t_l as p_n_ is to w_n_o_.   Find the link.

19. S_ip_ed is to l_a_e_ as h_r_l_d is to v_u_t_d.   Find the link.

20. C_ep_ is to cr_wl_d as s_i_ed is to f_oa_e_.   Find the link.

Riddle # 18: You stand at a fork in the road. Next to each of the two forks, there stands a guard. You know the following things: Firstly, you know that one path leads to paradise, the other leads to death. You cannot see any differences between the two paths. Secondly, you know that one of the two guards always tells the truth and that the other one always lies. You have permission to ask each guard one question to discover which path leads to paradise. Which one question would you ask to guarantee your path to paradise?

THE BERSERKER ON THE BRIDGE

The t_t_n was dying. The c_pp_ry taste of blood was in his mouth and his arms were covered in w_u_ds.

A H_r_e_t moon h_ng in the sky, c_st_ng spl_n_ers of Sol_m_n-gold down onto the bridge. The men were ba_hed in its cold gl_w and their be_l_ws rang into the bla_k_t of darkness that c_ver_d the sky. Try as they might, they couldn't dislod_e this insane No_t_man from the bridge. A pi_e of co_p_es blocked them from getting to him. Every time someone tried to move them out of the way, he c_t them down like wh_at under a sc_t_e.

His vo_ce was ha_sh and cra_ked through the air like a w_ip, scr_a_ing at them and da_ing them to be next to fight him. He looked like a t_o_l from an old fairytale, wa_ing his axe like a m_dm_n and g_i_ting his tee_h at them if they tried to a_van_e. That great axe he wie_ded gl_t_er_d as co_d as mo_ni_g fr_st and his hair was clo_ted with blo_d.

Godwinson called out an order and a bl_z_a_d of ar_o_s bu_z_d and hu_med into the do_m-bl_ck sky. The berserker grabbed a shield from the dead hand of one of the sl_in men and laughed as they th_m_ed into its metal surface.

"Fight me like men," he screamed and stood up again when the vol_ey was over.

He ba_hed his axe against the shield and let it drop to the ground with a cl_ng. He had held his ground for nearly an hour and he was mor_a_ly tired. His heart pou_d_d against his r_b ca_e and his ne_k hai_s felt like pins with the adr_nal_ne pumping through him. Gas_es covered his f_ce, his ar_s and his ba_e body. Two of the fi_g_rs on his right ha_d were lace_ated beyond use and that entire side of his body was nu_b from a spe_r thr_st.

He stood up for the last time.

"Just let me hold it for five more mi_u_es," he whispered. Then he leaned his head back and let out an an_m_l scream that ter_if_ed the Anglo-Sa_on army op_osi_e him. Three more men came towards him, sc_am_ling to climb over the heap of corpses. He rus_ed towards them and the axe came down. The first man let out a h_wl as the weapon sm_s_ed into his helm. It bu_kled the metal and the man fell. He sw_ng it around again using his weaker left hand but his op_on_nt blocked it easily. Titan jumped onto the man with the full force of his we_g_t. The man wasn't expecting it and wh_mp_red when the berserker grabbed a dagger from the ground and pl_n_ed it into him.

The last man was lo_m_ng over him. Quick as a flash, Titan rai_ed the dead man above his head and fl_ng him into the last war_i_r left. Both of them cr_s_ed to the ground and Titan sp_ang like a tiger to finish him off. He was the last man s_a_d_ng. He felt inv_n_ib_e.

Just then he felt a sh_rp, pai_f_l jab on the inside of his thigh. It was as if Gr_ek fi_e had been poured all over it. He looked down and saw the wi_k_d tip of a spear sticking through.

He collapsed onto the bridge and lay his head down. Through the planks of wood, he saw a man on a barrel floating away. "Di_bo_ical," he thought, as he waited for Valhalla to appear.

POPULAR GREEK AND LATIN SUFFIXES

The amount of words made up from Greek and Latin suffixes in the English language is remarkable. Research it for yourself by looking up **www.msu.edu** and typing in 'Greek and Latin suffixes.' There is an excellent grid on that site to help you complete the ones below.

SUFFIX	MEANING	WORDS MADE UP FROM
able, -ible	able or capable	remarkable, visible
-ade	result of action	parade, cascade
-age		
-algia		
-ian		
-ance		
-ary,-ery,-ory		
-cian		
-cy		
-dom		

MORE SUFFIXES

-er	one who	baker, builder
-ence		
-escent		
-ess		
-ful		
-ice		
-ine		
-ion, -sion, -tion		
-ure		
-y		

FILL IN THE GREEK AND LATIN GODS/GODDESSES

NAME	**GREEK GOD OF**	*ROMAN GOD OF*
Aphrodite=*Venus*		
Apollo=*Apollo*		
Ares=*Mars*		
Eros=*Cupid*		
Hades=*Pluto*		
Hephaistos=*Vulcan*		
Hermes=*Mercury*		
Kronos=*Saturn*		
Poseidon=*Neptune*		

Did you know? All the gold that has ever been mined in history would barely fit into two Olympic sized swimming pools. Half of that has been mined in the last 50 years.

GREEK AND LATIN STEMS

The English language is interconnected by a strong series of patterns. Think of it as a tree. The roots never change, even in the winter, but the word-leaves are constantly falling off to be replaced by others the following spring. That is because languages are being mixed together at an increasing rate in this global world. Travel and multi-culturism has seen to that. To put it in perspective, the last century saw three technological advances. Can you guess what they are? This century will see **nine** or more.

Educators always mention the eight intelligence forms, but the ninth and tenth may be the most important in this new world: your awareness of your place in the world and a lifelong zest for learning. The ability to see patterns is part of this adaptability process. English borrows from Greek and Latin more than any other languages. The swirling, leaf-stripping winds of change that the airplane and the internet bring are blowing stronger and faster. The roots of grammar, tenses and word stems shall not change in our lifetimes, however. That is why you should fill in the grid below and **enjoy working with the patterns it reveals.**

prefix	Greek meaning	Latin meaning	etymology	find two words
athl-	prize		athlos	**athl**ete/pent**athl**on
aqu-		water	aqua	**aqu**arium/**aqu**amarine
audi-				
bibl-				
bi-				
bio-				
cogn-				
dul-				
dexter-				
galact-				
gen-				
gramm-				
inter-				
intra-				
kine-				
libr-				
ling-				
luc-				
lumin-				
mus-				
nat-				
neg-				
phot-				
plur-				
post-				
semi-				
spa-				
sub-				
tele-				
viv-				

TEXT MESSAGING AND NEW WORDS

As a student, you might argue that grammar and spellings do not matter if you are texting. You are right!

Grmr iz ded baby. Bttr git uzd to it.

The English language is like a river on an estuary; it is ever-changing, it is fluid and it will move where the tide decides. The problems begin, however, if a student loses the ability to change back into the correct form of spellings. It can affect application forms, job prospects and lead to embarrassment. Try to put the 5 sentences below back into their correct syntax (sentence construction), grammar form and spelling. If you find you are having some difficulty with them, try to text in formal English for a week. Then you can lol with relief!

1. Datz wots gonna hppn.

2. Gud dayz ahed.

3. Tnx and hppy bday bud.

4. R u gng to de koncrt.

5. Gng to be a long dy in Englsh.

The amount of new words creeping into the dictionary is speeding up as technology gets more advanced. Test your skills with the most recent additions and look up their meanings if you don't know them.

New word	Meaning	New word	Meaning
chillaxing		nail tat	
chick lit		newbie	
cloud computing		nevertiree	
daycation		podcast	
flame war		screenager	
frenemy		smirt	
funkinetics		snail mail	
Glamazonian		solopreneur	
mailbomb		trolling	
meh		webinar	

A new book has ranked the most famous figures in history according to their internet 'meme' strength and their historical reputations. A 'meme' is: *"an idea, behaviour, style or usage that spreads from person to person"*. It is a controversial list, but why not do a small project on one of these figures? Include their quotes and how their language affected people forever more. Can you guess the top 10 based on their impact on the human race?

Alex. the Great	Mohammed	G. Washington	Thom. Jefferson	Napoleon
Abe Lincoln	Adolf Hitler	Aristotle	Jesus	Shakespeare

CLASS IDEAS REVISION GRIDS

The grid below can be filled in as the class is doing a creative page of fill in the blanks. It may also be used at the end of the module for revision purposes. The teacher might also decide to put different headings in the grid. Some classes may decide to put in words; others may decide to put in phrases or sentences. The rest needs to be filled in by the student.

THE COLOUR SILVER
THE SILENT LAKE
FISH SOUNDS
THE MIST ON THE LAKE

Find the definition in the words below and try to put them into a sentence in your copybook. Which word was the most hated, in your opinion? Which of these, if any, would you use in a creative essay? Your class should try to invent 10 words that nobody has ever thought of!

LIST OF MOST HATED WORDS 2014 FROM LAKE SUPERIOR STATE UNIVERSITY	
selfie	-ageddon (snowmageddon)
hashtag	-pocalypse (icepocalypse)
twittersphere	intellectually bankrupt
Mister Mom	adversity
newbie	(anything) on steroids

Did you know? The caterpillar fungus, a rare plant, is worth more per ounce than gold.

WHAT'S ON THE GROUND?

You are walking towards the mountains. The snow is glinting like angel fire and the mountains are shaped like the crooked teeth of a hag. That's when you see the man in the mercury-red suit. He is on the ground holding his head and he is moaning. A short distance away, you see a broken sled and dead reindeer litter the ground.

"Goddamned geese!" he roars at the sky. "Came out of nowhere like fluffy bullets and smashed into us. What the hell is wrong with people these days?"

He is not a happy man. His neck is bulging and the vein on his forehead is throbbing. Flecks of spittle are foaming at his mouth and his fists are clenching and unclenching. His eyes are looking this way and that and then he sees a bundle of white feathers sticking up from the snow. He kicks them and a shower of blood stains the snow red. You fear he is going to get a banger so you try to calm him down.

"Ice in the hands," you tell him. "Just think of having ice in your hands."

"Am I getting this correct?" he asks. "I'm just after falling 16,000 feet to the ground, all my reindeer are dead, I'm in shock and suffering from hypothermia in the middle of a prison of freezing snow-and you want me to imagine myself having ice cream in my hands?" He put his hands to his head in distress. "I need a snow day," he said as he sat down. Then he began to cry. "It's the constant stress" he sobbed. "It's too much."

"There, there," you tell him.

"My arse is getting too fat," he continues. "If my farts weren't like thunderclaps, I'd never get back up all those chimneys. It's too much for one man to take. It's just too much." He buries his bushy beard in his chest and rubs his face in distress. His chest heaves up and down and tear-streaks line his cheeks.

"Your mascara is running," you tell him.

"Is it?" He suddenly becomes alert. "That won't do. I'm supposed to be on Jay Leno later tonight. Thanks for the heads up." He takes out a mobile and rings for a back-up sleigh. While he is on the phone, he is professional and business-like. "Yeah. Just under the mountains that look like an old crone's teeth. Where? How the hell do I know? The sat nav is broken. Just do it. Thanks. And bring some more deer. Later. 'Bye."

"Sorted," he says. Then his eyes narrow. "Do I know you?" he asks suspiciously.

"You're Santa. You know everyone," you tell him.

"Harrumph!" he coughs. "Of course I am. Took a bang on the old noggin, you know. Now I have you. You're the lad who visualised the geese in the last chapter. You caused this. You'd better do something to make up for it. Why not describe Xmas for me while we're waiting?"

You sigh. "Christmas in the house or outside the house?" you ask. "Both," he says.......

Date: __/__/__	Title: **DESCRIBING CHRISTMAS: 1ˢᵗ GRID**	Lesson number:

Latin phrase: Qui vult dare parua non debet magna rogare.

Definition: H_/w_o/w_s_es/t_/gi_e/l_t_le/sh_u_d_'t/a_k/f_r/mu_h.

Meaning: _____

_____

Spelling revision	New words	Dictionary definitions, corrections and synonyms.
al_e/V_ra	sw_g bag	
crysta_li_e	war_ling	
ruf_ling	fra_kince_se	
spr_te	Yul_ti_e	
salv_	whi_eo_t	
myr_h	win_ers_a_e	
calami_e	St. Nic_ol_s	

You are asked to name the images associated with Christmas. What do you pick?

1 POINT	2 POINTS	3 POINTS	4 POINTS
t_rk_y/siz_li_g	d_c_rati_ns on tree	pr_s_n_s under tree	cr_c_ers/ex_lo_ing
C_ris_mas tree	a_g_l on tree	ti_s_l and l_g_ts	r_bi_s/war_ling

5 POINTS	6 POINTS	7 POINTS	8 POINTS
the m_n_er	h_l_y/b_r_i_s	Christmas p_d_i_g	a bl_c_o_t
ba_y in a cr_b	the N_r_h/st_r	m_st_et_e	a whi_eo_t

9 POINTS	9 POINTS	10 POINTS	10 POINTS
myr_h	f_o_en/p_n_s	s_et_d/c_n_l_s	Yul_ti_e logs
fra_kince_se	win_ers_a_e of snow	Ja_k/F_o_t	

super student ideas

POINTS SCORE

0-50 good first try	51-100 well done	101-130 very good	131-148 excellent

Did you know? In 1931, Coca-Cola ran an ad campaign showing Santa as the swag-bellied, twinkle-eyed bearer of presents we know today. Before that, Santa Claus (from the Dutch 'Sinterklaas' or 'Sinter Niklaas', St. Nicholas) had been dressed in green and brown and was thin. Did Coca-Cola invent Santa? No, but they helped to give him the image we know today.

THE COLOURS WHITE, YELLOW, BROWN AND ORANGE

WHITE	YELLOW	BROWN	ORANGE
ar_h_n_el-white	b_t_er_up-yellow	a_m_nd-brown	am_er-orange
j_s_ine-white	citr_s-yellow	a_t_mn-brown	b_azi_g-orange
m_rb_e-white	go_d/se_m-yellow	ba_k-brown	b_il_ng-orange
o_b-white	h_n_yco_b-yellow	c_r_m_l-brown	b_r_ing-orange
o_c_id-white	l_m_n-yellow	ci_na_on-brown	e_ber-orange
o_st_r-white	l_g_t_i_g-yellow	c_c_n_t-brown	gl_w_ng-orange
p_is_ine-white	m_l_n-yellow	c_n_er-brown	fe_eri_h-orange
se_sh_ll-white	mo_n/be_m-yellow	co_p_r-brown	fi_ry-orange
s_u_l-white	sa_fr_n-yellow	m_h_g_ny-brown	h_t-orange
sno_d_op-white	s_n/fl_sh-yellow	m_nk-brown	och_e-orange
sw_n-white	s_n_i_e-yellow	r_s_et-brown	sc_rc_ing-orange
tall_w-white	s_r_p-yellow	tan_n-brown	smo_lde_i_g-orange
u_i_o_n-white	y_m-yellow	te_k-brown	s_n_et-orange
w_al_bo_e-white	yo_k-yellow	t_a_t-brown	swel_e_i_g-orange
wa_e_l_ly-white	ze_ty-yellow	w_ln_t-brown	vulpi_e-orange

TRY TO GET SIX MORE OF EACH AS A CLASS

WHITE	YELLOW	BROWN	ORANGE

A fox and a scorpion were looking at a river. It had just flooded and it was deep and cold. The fox was just about to jump in and swim across it when the scorpion spoke up.

"Mr Fox, would you mind terribly carrying me across on your back? I'm afraid that if I try to cross it, I will drown. After all, I am small and the river is fast."

"Why would I do that?" asked the fox. "If I carry you and you sting me, I will drown and die."

"Why would I sting you?" asked the scorpion. "If I sting you, we will both drown. It won't happen."

"Fine," said the fox. "Hop on."

Halfway across the river, the scorpion got nervous. His tail flicked up and whipped down, stinging the fox.

"Why did you do that?" asked the fox, as he sank into the river. "Now we're both dead."
"You can't change the nature of the beast," said the scorpion.

Date: / /	Title: **INTERNAL SCENE: 2ⁿᵈ GRID**	Lesson number:

Latin phrase: Dum vita est, spes est.

Definition: W_e_e/t_e_e/i_/l_f_/t_e_e/i_/h_p_.

Meaning: _____

_____

Spelling revision	New words	Dictionary definitions, corrections, and synonyms.
sw_g bag	sor_e_y	
war_ling	dre_ms_ape	
fra_kince_se	mag_e_i_m	
Yul_ti_e	haml_t	
whi_eo_t	glis_e_ing	
win_ers_a_e	cin_am_n	
St. Nic_ol_s	he_rth	

Christmas lights reflecting

1 POINT	2 POINTS	3 POINTS	4 POINTS
fla_hi_g	gl_a_ing	gli_ti_g	gli_me_ing
flic_e_ing	gl_wi_g	glit_e_ing	glis_e_ing

sounds in the house

spar_le_s/fi_z	cra_ke_s/e_p_o_e	gla_s_s/c_i_k	la_g_t_r/r_n_s
li_h_s/h_m	o_en/p_r_s	pr_s_n_s/r_s_le	ke_t_es/h_ss and boil

images in the house

Christmas s_c_s	si_v_r/gl_t_er	fi_e/l_c_ing/he_rth	mag_e_i_m bright
large pi_e/c_n_s	ca_d_es/twi_k_ing	jo_ly/j_g of the fire	st_r-br_g_t angel

magical words grid

the ji_g_e of the sled	chi_ing bells	snow like a_g_l/fi_e	sl_e_y/h_mle_s
sh_rb_t sweet t_ea_s	cin_am_n smells	the sor_e_y of Xmas	dre_ms_ape of snow

POINTS SCORE

0-20 good first try	21-49 well done	50-69 very good	70-80 excellent

USING PERSONIFICATION IN YOUR WRITING

Personification is giving non-human things human terms. The key to understanding it lies in its name: **person**ification. It is one of the most powerful weapons in your English armoury. Explain why the following sentences use personification. The first two are done for you.

1. The pellucid-blue river jumped over the rocks.

This river is personified because **jumping is a human term** and the river is not human.

2. The saffron-yellow stars smiled down at me.

The stars are personified because **smiling is a human term** and stars are not human.

3. The spring wind exhaled gently.

The wind is personified because

4. The mountains stared down at me.

The mountains are personified because

5. The flowers were nodding their heads at me.

The flowers are personified because

Put the following words into a sentence. Then find a synonym (similar word) for each word.

		synonyms	
The lake	n_k_d	bare	The lake lay naked under the wolf moon.
The sea	r_ar_d	b_llow_d	The churning sea roared out its rage.
The heavens	wept	c_i_d	
The sun	k_s_ed		
The moon	b_es_ed		
The trees	s_iv_r_d		
The beach	r_n/t_		
The desert	c_o_ed/us		
The rain	sp_t		
The lightning	f_u_g		
The mist	c_a_l_d		
The waterfall	sa_g		
Spring	g_e_f_l		
Summer	s_i_ing		
Autumn	g_o_t_y		
Winter's	i_y/g_ip		

The last exercise is to think of ten **micro** parts of nature. It could be grass, leaves, snow or hailstones. Then personify them without anyone's help. Use the human terms above if you are stuck. Ideally, you should try to do it with a classmate using different words.

Date: / /	Title: **INTERNAL SCENE: 3rd GRID**	Lesson number:

Latin phrase: Credula est spes improba.

Definition: H_/w_o/l_v_s/o_/h_p_/a_o_e/w_l_/d_e/o_/h_n_e_ .

Meaning: _____

_____

Spelling revision	New words	Dictionary definitions, corrections, and synonyms.
sor_e_y	cl_v_s	
dre_ms_ape	tan_i_s	
mag_e_i_m	j_g	
haml_t	sul_h_r	
glis_e_ing	ci_r_s	
cin_am_n	ex_t_c	
he_rth	g_my	

the Christmas fire

1 POINT	2 POINTS	3 POINTS	4 POINTS
the sun_i_e/gl_w of	the da_c_ng fire	to_g_es of flame	b_t_ed in warmth
wall sh_do_s/cha_e	a bl_z_ng/j_g of fire	fire l_c_s the h_ar_h	c_c_li_g and spi_ti_g

emotional sensations of Christmas

h_p_y	c_e_ry	j_y_ul	m_r_hful
j_l_y	m_r_y	pe_c_f_l	gl_e_ul

smell

s_i_y beef	pi_e/tr_e/ar_m_s	sul_h_r of crackers	o_k_n/o_en smells
p_p_e_y/sc_n_s	sh_rp smell of cl_v_s	ro_e/sc_n_ed/ca_d_es	ex_t_c/s_o_e smells

taste

bu_te_y/p_t_t_es	he_vy/fr_it_a_e	t_a/tan_i_s	he_b-stu_f_d du_k
pl_m_y/pu_di_g	g_my/g_o_e	ci_r_s/dr_n_s	t_y_e-filled tu_k_y

POINTS SCORE

0-20 good first try	21-49 well done	50-69 very good	70-80 excellent

THE CHRISTMAS TREE AND THE GENESIS GENE IN ALL OF US

Frost-spikes hang off the window sill like a phantom's glassy fingers. The pine sweet smell of the tree ghosts through the room, mixing with the oaken oven scents.

The star-flash of tinsel glitters brightly and ribbons of flame dance in the hearth of the fire. They chase away the burglar-black wall shadows and you sink deeper into the couch. A sunrise warmth heats up the room and you are content. Your eyes drift up to the angel at the top of the tree. It reflects like river-light and you wonder why it stirs up memories you never knew you had.

Outside the window, the world is a moonscape of white. Jack Frost's fangs have bitten deep into the flesh and blood of the earth, leaving it clay-cold and drained. The night before he was out, plunging his vampire-white teeth into what's left of nature's trembling, dying heart. There is no bird song, no grass whisper, no footfall. Jack hates every living thing. He seems to swoop down quietly from the iron sky and strangles the world into silence. His cold gleam and icy eye polish everything with glassy hatred. Then his undead fingers creep and crawl across the land, leaving it as pale and drawn as a zombie's face.

You hear a sound, however, and you go to the window. The noise of feet on the powdery snow is like muffled grenades. It is your dog and he is rolling around the snow. There is a rabbit lifeless on the ground and he rolls on him too. The faint crackling of turkey juices dripping onto tinfoil can be heard from the kitchen. Its unique smell of McDonald's paper mixed with a delicious, gamy scent swirls around the room. The exotic whisper of stuffing and parsley burning into the flesh makes your stomach rumble and your mouth water. The sweet, cedar fragrance of the Christmas tree wafts around the room and it conjures up a memory you never thought you had.......

There are between 30 and 40 of the Magdalenian tribe sitting around the fire and they are happy. It is Christmas Eve, 11,000 B.C. and they are at the foothills of the Pyrenees Mountains in Northern Spain. They are the first humans to look and think exactly as we do today: homo sapiens sapiens (man wise wise). Their long hair is not the Rapunzel-gold of fairy tales. It is caramel-brown, long and glossy from a diet of eggs, nuts, fish and fruit. They hunt wild boar, reindeer, wild goats, horses, bison and aurochs. Aurochs are the biggest bulls that have ever lived and the only herbivore which will stalk and kill the hunters if given the chance.

The women wear animal skins which look exactly like the expensive fur coats we wear. They love the white fur of the Arctic wolf, fox and hare, but the Ice Age has just ended in Europe and these animals are getting hard to find. They make seashell necklaces and bracelets and their shoes are made from tough leather lined with fur. The men wear carnivore teeth from lions, bear and lynx. They punch holes through them with ivory pins to wear them around their neck. The more you wear, the higher your status as a hunter.

A few wild turkeys are roasting on the fire. They have already killed 3 wild boars and eaten them and the turkeys are for the eldest and the youngest in the tribe. There's an assortment of other small animals ready to roast for dessert: hare, squirrels, snowy owl, hedgehog, badger, weasel, gopher and dormouse. In 11,000 years' time, Julius Caesar will find that the only Spanish tribe he cannot conquer are the descendants of the Magdalenians. However, the Magdalenians and the Romans have one thing in common; a love of stuffed dormice served with honey, herbs and pine cone seeds.

The Magdalenians are ferocious, as Julius Caesar will find out. They also love their children, are very caring towards the elderly and are Europe's first cave artists. The men wear beards for the winter and ignore the huge, dark shapes prowling around the campfire. These are the hunting wolves of the Magdalenians and they are strong and fierce also. The men can relax in this wooded glade while the wolves are patrolling. Watchful eyes, none of them friendly, lurk elsewhere in this forest. The human race in Europe numbers only 3 million souls, but most of the tribes are warlike and savage.

The dripping blood from the turkey makes the fire spit, hiss and cackle. It is a cold, starry night and it is as if dream dust has been sprinkled in the sky. The Bethlehem star shines above one cypress tree and the women point to it and call it a good omen. They do not believe in angels, but if they did, they would call it one. Tongues of flame dart up from the fires, banishing the bat-black shadows.

There is no light pollution here and the moons dazzling brilliance flings spears of light into the holly glade. Five juicy salmon, fished from the River Elbo, are skewered on sticks next to the boar. Their silver skin blisters and sizzles over the fire. A pot is on the boil next to them containing wild mushrooms, periwinkles, thyme and almonds. Dinner tonight is a surf 'n turf delight. The mint-fresh lungs of the Magdalenians inhale deeply and take in the fragrances of the forest. A phantom of smells lingers in the air: grilled meat, charred cedar boughs and the sap-sweet smell of burning wood. The river glitters like jewels in the cat-light of the night.

The wolves roll over the cast away carcasses of the boar and reindeer. It will help them to disguise their musty smell when they are hunting game tomorrow. The Magdalenian men know this and laugh at their behaviour. They are happy, contented and proud of their tribe. The forests they live in are a real danger and challenge, but they are beginning to conquer those challenges. Little do they know it, but their genes will soon be travelling over to refresh the newly-thawed lands of England and Ireland.

Back in the present, you open your eyes and let the ghost of Christmas smells waft up your nostrils. The scene you had of a tribe in a forest came and went so quickly, you have forgotten it already. The glossy-green holly stirs up a memory again, but you can't recall it: the smell of your new, leather shoes: the amber scent of the tree sap: the fresh, crisp smell of the pine needles. They all scream at you to remember your genesis gene. You don't know it, but the Christmas tree is a gateway to the past, an anchor of the present and a bookmark for the future that family comes above all else. That is why the Magdalenian gene still exists.

You look out the window and you see the dog rolling around. "Now what's gotten into him?" you mutter. Just then you hear the greatest sound in the world. The bell chimes for dinner. A boom of heat and a carnival of laughter greet you as you open the door to the kitchen..............

Date: __/__/__	Title: **EXTERNAL SCENE: 4th GRID**	Lesson number:

Latin phrase:　　　　　Non nobis solum nati sumus.

Definition:　　　　　W_/a_e/n_t/b_r_/f_r/o_rs_l_es/a_o_e.

Meaning: _____

_____

Spelling revision	New words	Dictionary definitions, corrections, and synonyms.
cl_v_s	fest_o_ed	
tan_i_s	dra_ed	
j_g	ra_p	
sul_h_r	enc_s_d	
ci_r_s	wrea_h_d	
ex_t_c	scre_k	
g_my	mant_ed	

snow colours

1 POINT	2 POINTS	3 POINTS	4 POINTS
d_ve-white	f_o_r-white	h_lo-white	p_t_y-white
do_gh-white	g_o_e-white	h_i_sto_e-white	p_w_er-white

sounds

crea_i_g trees	cra_k_ing snow	t_u_p of s_ows_o_s	the ra_p of gates
cra_ki_g ice	the h_ss of s_e_s	s_is_i_g/s_at_s	the scre_k of hinges

land covered in snow

snow ve_led	snow cl_a_ed	snow dra_ed	snow fest_o_ed
snow ca_pe_ed	snow c_r_ai_ed	snow mant_ed	snow wrea_h_d

terms for ice and snow

the p_li_h_d/i_e	Ja_k/F_o_t's/f_n_s	sta_b_d by ice sp_a_s	enc_s_d in ice
i_y/br_a_h of winter	gl_s_y/fi_ge_s of ice	s_rge_n's coat of	a sno_dri_t

POINTS SCORE

0-20 good first try	21-49 well done	50-69 very good	70-80 excellent

USING POINT OF VIEW FOR A CHRISTMAS STORY

Let's write a story together. We have mentioned how point of view can be seen as a film camera. Think of the opening scene of a film about Christmas. This is what the director wants:

OPENING SCENE: A helicopter flies slowly over a sleepy village on Christmas Eve. The village is in a valley in Finland and it is surrounded by mountains. Smoke drifts up from the chimney pots towards the stars. The air is cold and crisp and there is no wind. Write an introduction:

_____

_____

_____

_____

_____

_____ .

The helicopter flies over a lake. It is frozen over and there are pine trees around it. The director wants you to write about how it looks now under the light of a yellow moon. He also wants you to picture how the scene will look tomorrow. Shall there be children skating on the lake? Recreate the sights and sounds of the lake and what is around it:

_____

_____

_____

_____

_____ .

Tomorrow_____

_____

_____

_____ .

The helicopter lands outside one of the houses. It flies away and you are on your own. Everything is silent except for three sounds. One of them is a robin whose voice cuts through the air as sharp as glass. Write about him and two other sounds of your choice.

_____

_____

_____

_____

_____

_____ .

You have been given permission to enter the house. You go into the living room and sit on a comfortable chair. You need time to gather your thoughts for this scene. People are asleep upstairs so you sit there silently. The fire's warmth is welcome and it casts shadows onto the wall. There is a beautiful smell from the Christmas tree. There is tinsel draped around the tree and an angel on top of it. Presents lie at the foot of the tree and there is a candle on the window sill. Describe the sights, sounds and smells of this scene.

_____

_____

_____

_____

_____

_____.

The director wants you to visualise sitting on the same chair tomorrow. The children are running in to open their presents. The turkey and goose are being cooked in the oven. Describe the sounds and the smells. There is a nice scent from the Yuletide logs also. What is it? Write about the joy the children feel also.

_____

_____

_____

_____

_____

_____.

Finally, you are back to the present. All is quiet. A mouse appears in the corner. The fire makes his shadow seem huge. Give a good metaphor or simile for this. Mention two other small details about something in the room that other students may not think of. With luck, someday you may be paid for your writing skills.

_____

_____

_____

_____

_____.

Add in a small conclusion of your choice.

_____

_____

Did you know? There are four sources of light when you are walking in the countryside at night: the moon, the stars, airglow from our own atmosphere, and zodiacal light caused by meteors burning up.

Riddle # 19: The word CANDY can be spelt using just two letters. Can you figure out how?

Date: __/__/__	Title: **EXTERNAL SCENE: 5th GRID**	Lesson number:

Latin phrase: Citius venit malum quat revertitur.

Definition: Misf_r_u_e/c_m_s/o_/h_rs_b_c_/a_d/l_a_es/o_/f_ot.

Meaning: _____

_____

Spelling revision	New words	Dictionary definitions, corrections, and synonyms.
fest_o_ed	som_re	
dra_ed	coro_a	
ra_p	c_n_er	
enc_s_d	do_eful	
wrea_h_d	bli_g	
scre_k	sh_c_le	
mant_ed	quiv_ri_g	

winter skies

1 POINT	2 POINTS	3 POINTS	4 POINTS
em_ty sky	ble_k sky	ha_n_ing sky	c_n_er-grey
l_n_ly sky	b_t_er sky	w_n sky	sh_c_le-grey

images for winter

no_e-ic_c_es	pl_m-p_r_le sky	bli_g-silver s_a_s	pe_r_y moons
sta_v_ng/b_r_s	La_la_d-white p_is_n	tr_es like s_e_et_ns	the moon's coro_a

sad 'o' sounds for atmosphere

o_d	l_n_ly	s_rr_w	m_u_nful
co_d	w_e	s_m_re	do_eful

sensation

shi_e_ing bodies	sti_f limbs	cha_te_ing teeth	s_in-se_p_ng cold
quiv_ri_g bodies	s_re joints	tin_li_g fingertips	s_u_fling noses

POINTS SCORE

0-20 good first try	21-49 well done	50-69 very good	70-80 excellent

HOW TO PLAN A SHORT STORY

The short story can be a very rewarding genre (i.e. style) to write in. Every novel is cut down to between an hour and half to three hours when it is put on the big screen. Think of the short story as being five minutes of action on You Tube. You need to get your story across in a short time. How do you do that? It is very simple. **HAVE A PLAN!** The plan is underneath:

1. Introduce your setting and the weather.

Will your story start in a dark forest, a city or inside a house? Give the details required to paint a scene for the reader. Is it raining or misty? Is the sunny or gloomy? Are the stars out or are they peeping from behind the clouds? Give the sort of detail that this book encourages but don't waste time giving too much.

2. Introduce a character.

Will your central character be a hero, a villain or an anti-hero (i.e. a man who may do bad things but can is essentially a good person)? Is he young or old, strong or weak? Give some physical details if you think they are needed. You can also make yourself the hero or villain.

3. Start the action (i.e. rising action).

In a short story, something dramatic or life changing usually happens. Start the action flowing by introducing a problem. It could be a burglary you happen upon, an event like a tsunami or an accident you caused yourself.

4. Give the story a climax.

The high point of the story should be dramatic and unusual. This should be pre-planned and keep the reader guessing as to what will happen.

5. Falling action.

The action is still taking place but the crisis is over. If it was a burglary, the police could have arrested the burglar but are still taking statements, for example. For a tsunami, the land is flooded and you are describing the devastation it caused.

6. The resolution.

The effect of this unusual climax should be outlined. How did it affect you? How did it affect others in the story? Is there a moral to your story and was your central character a winner or a loser in all this?

The art of the short story takes time and practise in order to get it right. Look out for unusual things that happen in your school day or your life outside school. If anything dramatic, impactful or unique happens, put it in your notebook. Jot down how people responded to the crisis. Write out the exact words they used. That is your dialogue taken care of. All the great writers keep a notebook close at hand for ideas. If you are serious about writing, you will too.

"It is the tale. Not he who tells it."   **Stephen King**

A CHRISTMAS SHORT STORY

INTRODUCTION:

Reading the newspaper today made me laugh out loud. It also brought back a memory that I thought had been buried forever. Let me paint the scene for you…

It was roughly fifteen years ago on Christmas Eve. The snow was falling in a cloud of Merlin-white and the air was beautifully cold. The sky was bleak and cinder-grey. It wasn't the skin-seeping pinch of a windy day, more like the powdery cold of a crisp, Alaskan whiteout. I was standing outside the front entrance of a shopping mall in New York, enjoying the high spirits of the shoppers as they swarmed around me. My mother was inside getting some Christmas presents. I suppose I was about twelve at the time.

INTRODUCE CHARACTER:

There was a homeless man in the middle of the street weaving his way through the traffic. I could only assume that he was homeless as his actions and clothes were bizarre. He held a brown paper bag in one hand and he would occasionally put it to his mouth to take a drink from the bottle within. The other hand was being used to make rude gestures and to thump the bonnets of the honking cars. All the while he let loose a string of swear words and vile curses. Not just your ordinary curses either. This guy was threatening the motorists that the milk would curdle in their fridges, their food would turn to sawdust and that he would make them infertile for eternity. He was like a one man comedy show with the outrageousness of his performance.

He had a strange appearance, almost as if it was made up. His hair was wizened and straw-like, nearly fossilized it was so dry. He had the sad eyes of a basset hound and a distinctive beard. It wasn't a thick, captain Ahab beard but rather something a lunatic might have: bushy and spittle flecked. His face was toil worn and tanned from exposure to the elements and he walked with a weary, sad air until he would suddenly explode in a burst of rage. His fingers were gnarled and knobbly and the clothes he wore were musty and smelly judging by the reaction of the people he passed. Their noses would crinkle in disgust and they would peel away from his presence. I don't want to sound pass remarkable, but he was a truly unpleasant character. What made it worse is that he made a beeline to where I was standing.

RISING ACTION:

I shuffled uncomfortably as he approached. His eyes seemed to laser in on me as if I was his target for the day. His voice was surprising, a gravel-and-gravy mix of whiskey roughness and educated accent.

"Hey kid. Gotta buck to spare?"

He seemed very gentle, a complete contrast to the South Park character I had witnessed earlier. I normally didn't entertain vagrants or weirdoes but I was so grateful he wasn't shouting at me that I gave him the first note out of my pocket. It was twenty bucks. I felt a pang of regret then as it was part of my money to get Christmas presents. He looked at the note and I remember that he said: "You're a nugget, kid. God bless all generous and good looking people."

With that he was off. He zigzagged his way across the street, screaming at anyone who honked. I saw him going across to another shop front and some old lady gave him money. That was the last I ever saw of him.

CLIMAX:

Now my eyes drifted to an article in the Obituary column of the New York Times. The caption was 'New York's Unlikeliest Billionaire.'

Died Monday, aged 65: Lloyd 'The Tramp' Carson, heir to the Carson Steel Empire, and notorious practical joker. Lloyd, who was a dedicated actor and keen observer of human life, liked nothing better than to dress up as a vagrant and shout insults at his fellow New Yorkers. Although knocked down twice as a result of these escapades, he played out the role until his last day on this earth. His last words were known to be: "You're a nugget, man. God bless all good looking people." Indeed, these are the exact words which shall be on his epitaph as per his wishes.

It is believed that Mr. Carson has left an estate worth north of $1.7 bn. As he does not have any immediate family, speculation is mounting as to who shall be named in his will. Rumours are rife that he had a team of private detectives following him. Apparently, they would discover the identities of people who were particularly generous to Mr. Carson's alter ego. It may be another urban myth, of which New Yorker's are particularly fond of, but sources at the New York Times are adamant that Mr. Carson intended to pay back those who had a generous spirit.

FALLING ACTION:

I laughed out loud again as I finished the article. He was most definitely a character, this guy. I had to hand it to him. He knew how to get a kick out of life.

RESOLUTION:

I thought nothing more of it until a letter arrived three months later. Then I didn't laugh at all. I cried with happiness.

Did you like this story? Do you think it is better to give to those less fortunate than you or to ignore them? Can you think of any practical way you could help people in your community? Are there people in your community who are alone and who your class could help?

ASSOCIATIVE LEARNING

Fill in the blanks by finding the links between the words.   **LINK WORDS**

1. W_nt_rs_a_e is to w_i_e_ut as s_o_sc_pe is to d_ea_s_a_e.   dreamy scene

2. M_r_h is to f_a_ki_c_n_e as c_n_am_n is to s_n_a_wo_d.   smells

3. J_s_i_e is to o_c_id as s_o_dr_p is to w_t_rli_y.   flowers

4. B_r_i_s are to r_b_n as t_r_ey is to h_m_ns.   eating

5. F_o_en is to f_ee_i_g as e_c_s_d is to i_e_ou_d.   icy

6. A_m_nd is to c_r_m_l as t_a_ is to m_h_ga_y.   colours

7. C_in_i_g is to ri_gi_g as h_m_ing is to p_r_i_g.   sounds

8. D_n_i_g is to j_g as to_g_es are to r_b_o_s.   fire

9. J_l_y is to m_r_y as m_r_hf_l is to g_e_f_l.   emotions

10. P_n_ is to p_p_e_y as _a_en is to e_o_ic.   scents

11. B_t_e_y is to p_um_y as g_m_ is to t_y_e.   tastes

12. C_e_ki_g is to c_a_k_i_g as r_s_ is to s_re_k.   sounds

13. C_o_k_d is to c_r_e_ed as w_e_t_ed is to f_st_o_ed.   snow

14. G_in_i_g is to g_i_te_ing as g_im_er_ng is to g_ist_ri_g.   light

15. S_n_a is to Kr_s_K_i_g_e as p_d_in_s are to Y_l_ti_e_l_gs.   symbols of Xmas

16. E_p_y is to l_ne_y as b_e_k is to b_t_er.   Find the link

17. S_r_ow is to so_b_e as m_u_n_ul is to d_l_f_l.   Find the link

18. S_i_e_ing is to q_i_e_ing as ch_t_eri_g is to sn_f_li_g.   Find the link

19. P_li_h_d is to i_y as gl_s_y is to fr_s_y.   Find the link

20. D_ve is to do_g_ as p_t_y is to p_w_er.   Find the link

Did you know? You are more likely to be killed by a champagne cork than by a poisonous spider.

CLASS IDEAS REVISION GRIDS

The grid below can be filled in as the class is doing a creative page of fill in the blanks. It may also be used at the end of the module for revision purposes. The teacher might also decide to put different headings in the grid. The template for the first two pages is done for you. The rest needs to be filled in by the student.

CHRISTMAS LIGHTS REFLECTING
SOUNDS IN THE HOUSE
IMAGES IN THE HOUSE
MAGICAL WORDS GRID
THE CHRISTMAS FIRE
EMOTIONAL SENSATIONS
SMELL
TASTE

RIDDLE # 20: In olden days, you are a clever thief charged with treason against the king and sentenced to death. The king wants to look merciful in front of the crowd and lets you choose how to die. 10 seconds later you walk free. How did you choose how to die?

"To be nobody but yourself in a world which is doing its best to make you like everybody else means to fight the hardest battle which any human being can fight and never stop fighting."

E.E. Cummings

MAKE A CHRISTMAS CROSSWORD

Ask your teacher for guidance if you need it. This exercise should be done with a partner.

Date: __/__/__	Title: **DESCRIBING MOUNTAINS: 1ˢᵗ GRID**	Lesson number:

Latin phrase: Praemonitus, praemunitus.

Definition: F_r_wa_n_d /is/f_r_ar_e_.

Meaning: _____

_____

Spelling revision	New words	Dictionary definitions, corrections, and synonyms.
som_re	cove_a_t	
coro_a	Sha_g_i-La	
c_n_er	abo_i_able	
do_eful	fer_l	
bli_g	myt_ic_l	
sh_c_le	y_ti	
quiv_ri_g	fu_g_s	

You are walking high up in a mountain. What do you see?

1 POINT	2 POINTS	3 POINTS	4 POINTS
sn_w	f_g	ea_le/named bi_d	de_r/fer_l goa_s
the wo_ld/be_ea_h	mi_t	be_r/named an_m_l	ra_e/sn_w le_p_rd

5 POINTS	6 POINTS	7 POINTS	8 POINTS
a_v_ll_ge	abo_i_able man	cra_h_d/aer_pla_e	c_ve of tre_s_re
v_ll_ge not on m_p	y_ti/g_a_t foo_pri_ts	hel_co_t_r/fal_i_g	named c_lo_rs

9 POINTS	9 POINTS	10 POINTS	10 POINTS
Sha_g_i-La	cate_pi_lar/fu_g_s	ab_nd_n_d/vi_la-e	Ar_ of the Cove_a_t
myt_ic_l snow w_rm	und_sc_ve_ed/ani_al	man with b_o_en leg	

super student ideas

POINTS SCORE

0-50 good first try	51-100 well done	101-130 very good	131-148 excellent

"Nobody trips over mountains. It is the small pebbles that cause you to stumble. Pass all the pebbles in your path and you'll find that you have crossed the mountain."

Unknown author

DIFFERENT NARRATIVE STYLES

First person narration occurs when a story is written from the point of view of the character in a story. The personal pronouns **I**, **my** and **me** are used for this.

Second person narration is rare and involves the personal pronoun **you** and **your** (singular).

Third person narration is also known as the 'fly-on-the-tree' technique. Imagine a fly on the top of a tree. He can see, hear, smell, taste and sense everything going on in the forest. His job as narrator is to communicate this to the reader. He will use the personal pronouns **he**, **she**, **it**, **they**, **them** and **your** (plural) to write his story. Put the fly's personal pronouns in the grid below.

1st PERSON					
2nd PERSON					
3rd PERSON	he/she				

PERSONAL PRONOUNS

A personal pronoun indicates the person: a) Speaking (I, me, we, us)

b) Spoken to (you, your)

c) Spoken about (he, she, it, they, him, her, them).

Personal pronouns are divided into singular (one person) and plural (more than one person). They are further divided into whether they are the **subject** or the **object** of a sentence.

The **subject** of a sentence is usually the person or thing being talked about in a sentence. It is also the person or thing **performing an action**. The subject is usually a noun. The verb (i.e. predicate) follows the subject. Underline the subject and verb below.

The mountain soared.

The eagle swooped.

The **object** is usually the person or thing **receiving** the action and follows the verb (i.e. predicate). An easy way to remember it is this; **a subject needs an object**. In this case:

Subject is the **subject**. Needs is the **verb**. Object is the **object**.

Try to identify the subject, verb and object for the sentences below.

The snowmelt ran down the mountain.

The mountain soared into the sky.

The eagle swooped towards me.

PRONOUNS AS SUBJECTS AND OBJECTS

The sentences in the last page have used nouns in their examples. A pronoun can also take the place of a noun and be the subject or the object. For example, you could say:

I am going to the mountain.

In this case, **'I'** is the **subject** and **'the mountain'** is **the object**.

You could also say:

He threw the snowball at me.

In this case, **'He'** is **the subject** and **'me'** is **the object** as you are receiving the ball.

Underneath is a grid where personal pronouns are explained in simple terms. Ask your teacher to go through the grid in detail.

singular	person	subject	object
	1st	I	me
	2nd	you	you
	3rd	he/she/it	him/her/it

plural	person	subject	object
	1st	we	us
	2nd	you	you
	3rd	they	them

The difference between 'I' and 'me'

'I' is the first person singular. It is also the **subject** pronoun. This means it refers to the **person performing the action**.

Examples: **I** want to leave. You and **I** are going now. John and **I** are going away.

'Me' is the **object** pronoun. It refers to the person the action of the verb is being **done to**.

Examples: He gave **me** a book. He should agree with John and **me**.

If you are ever in doubt, just split the two sentences in your mind. For example, if the sentence is: He told John and (I/ me?) to get a shovel.

He told I to get a shovel?   **NO**

He told me to get a shovel?   **YES**

Practice this with 10 sentences from a newspaper and write them out using the I/me formula.

Date: __/__/__	Title: **DESCRIBING A MOUNTAIN: 2nd GRID**	Lesson number:

Latin phrase: Qui rogat, non errat.

Definition: Th_/on_y/s_u_id/q_e_t_o_/is/th_/o_e/n_t/_s_ed.

Meaning: _____

_____

Spelling revision	New words	Dictionary definitions, corrections, and synonyms.
cove_a_t	enwrap_ed	
Sha_g_i-La	p_l_r	
abo_i_able	bell_w_ng	
fer_l	grumbling	
myt_ic_l	porc_l_in	
y_ti	Ar_t_c	
fu_g_s	pi_rc_ng	

snow colours

1 POINT	2 POINTS	3 POINTS	4 POINTS
a_g_l-white	b_ne-white	p_l_r-white	va_p_re-white
Ar_t_c-white	b_e_ch-white	ph_nt_m-white	porc_l_in-white

sounds of an avalanche

c_as_ing	ro_r_ng	gr_w_ing	b_o_ing
cl_p_ing	ru_bl_ng	gru_b_ing	bell_w_ng

mountain peaks

sky pu_c_ing	sky sta_b_ng	heaven t_u_hing	snow cr_w_ed
sky pi_rc_ng	sky spe_r_ng	heaven k_s_ing	snow enwrap_ed

POINTS SCORE

0-10 good first try	11-29 well done	30-50 very good	51-60 excellent

Did you know? If you stood on a lonely mountain without any light pollution, you would be able to see approximately 2,000-3,000 stars (i.e. depending on the brightness of the moon). Some astronomers now estimate there may be 300 sextillion stars in the universe. That is a 3 with 23 zeroes after it. Write out the number to see how big it is.

ADVERBS

An adverb is used to modify a verb. They tell us when, where, how, in what manner, or to what extent, an action is performed. Here are some examples:

When: He ran **yesterday**.

Where: He ran **here**.

How: He ran **quickly**

In what manner: He ran **barefoot**.

To what extent: He ran **fastest**.

Although most adverbs are easily spotted, some can sneak in unnoticed to a sentence. Examples are given in the grid below.

Adverbs of time	Adverbs of place	Adverbs of manner	Adverbs of degree
to_or_ow	t_e_e	a_g_ily	v_ry
so_n	e_e_yw_e_e	b_dly	le_st
n_w	a_o_nd	ca_m_y	m_re
n_v_r	he_e	co_re_tly	le_s
s_m_ti_es	f_r	e_si_y	m_st
a_w_ys	i_si_e	el_ga_tly	lo_s
f_r_v_r	t_w_r_s	jo_fu_ly	s_

It is indeed true that many adverbs end in 'ly'. Some do not, however. In order to spot an adverb, ask yourself 3 questions.

HOW?   How does he run?   He runs **perfectly**.

WHERE?   Where does he run?   He runs **here**.

WHEN?   When does he run?   He runs **sometimes**.

Make a list of adverbs in the grid that end in 'ly'. Put in the question they answer after them.

WHEN	HOW	adverbs to avoid	HOW	WHEN
		very	gently (how)	
nightly (when)		quite		
		really		regularly (when)
	joyfully (how)	severely		
		extremely		

Riddle # 21: What are the only two words in English that end in 'gry'?
Believe you can, believe you can't. Either way, you're right."   **Henry Ford**

THE COLOURS PINK, GOLD AND PURPLE

PINK	GOLD	PURPLE
blo_s_m-pink	A_c-of-Cov_n_nt gold	bi_d-of-par_di_e purple
a bl_shi_g, pilgr_m-pink	bee_w_x-gold	bi_h_p's mitre-purple
cal_m_ne-pink	chro_e-gold	he_th_r-purple
can_yfl_ss-pink	fla_en-gold	indi_o-purple
ceri_e-pink	har_st_ing-gold (for sunbeams)	juni_er-purple
da_n-pink	ho_eyco_b-gold	la_e_d_r-purple
di_m_nd-pink	ho_eyd_w-gold	l_l_c-purple
dus_y-pink	l_gh_ing-gold	mag_n_a-purple
fla_i_go-pink	molt_n-gold	mona_c_y-purple
fuch_ia-pink	mo_ngl_w-gold	m_lber_y-purple
peo_y-pink	nect_r-gold	orpi_e-purple
p_t_l-pink	Nord_c-gold	peaco_k-purple
sorb_t-pink	sta_be_m-gold	pl_m-purple
su_ri_e-pink	Teuto_ic-gold	r_y_l-purple
or_h_d-pink	Valkyr_e-gold	vi_l_t-purple

TRY TO GET FIVE MORE OF EACH AS A CLASS

CAN YOUR CLASS SOLVE THE MYSTERY OF THE 'BLOOD RAIN'?

On November 14th, 2012, red rain fell from the sky in Sri Lanka. On December 25th, yellow rain fell and on December 30th, green rain fell. Scientists say that it is more than likely caused by a type of bacteria from the soil. It may have been carried up on winds and fell as rain.

Much more curious, however, is the 'blood rain' which fell on Kerala, India, from July 25th to September 23rd, 2001. It fell after a loud thunderclap and a flash of light. After DNA analysis was carried out, scientists discovered that the rain contained red blood cells. These blood cells do not contain DNA, however, which means they cannot have come from Earth. The cells, therefore, seem alien and must come from outer space. Some scientists speculate that a comet exploded and deposited a ton of red space dust which came down with the rain. This does not explain how the dust could fall over such a period of time. The fact that blood rain fell in Kerala in 1896 may rule out any chemicals from factories causing it. Other scientist claimed it was from lichen spores. The same scientists admit that this theory is improbable. The lichen spores would have to be released from July to September and many days didn't have any wind to carry them. The story is made more bizarre by the fact it happened again from November 15th to December 27th, 2012. Look up **en.wikipedia.org** or **YouTube** for more.

Date: __/__/__	Title: **DESCRIBING A MOUNTAIN: 3rd GRID**	Lesson number:

Latin phrase: Qui scribit, bis legit.

Definition: W_o/wri_e_, r_a_s/t_ice.

Meaning: _____

_____

Spelling revision	New words	Dictionary definitions, corrections, and synonyms.
enwrap_ed	eas_l	
p_l_r	griz_led	
bell_w_ng	rugo_e	
grumbling	irides_ent	
porc_l_in	spec_r_m	
Ar_t_c	harpo_n	
pi_rc_ng	kaleid_sc_pe	

similes for a mountain range

1 POINT	2 POINTS	3 POINTS	4 POINTS
like a r_w tips	like a s_w's teeth	like a dr_g_n's back	like a h_g's teeth
like sh_r_s' fins	like harpo_n tips	like a r_w of thorns	like a t_o_l's teeth

appearance of a mountain

cr_n_led	crag_y	gnar_ed	ru_p_ed
wr_n_led	cru_pl_d	griz_led	rugo_e

other images

gh_st-grey mist	we_p_ng waterfall	scre_m_ng eagle	ne_k_ace of snow
bli_s-blue lake	l_n_ly sky	i_se_t-like figures	irides_ent rainbow

a splash of colour

a carn_v_l of colour	a ri_t of colour	a pri_m of	an eas_l of
a fest_v_l of colour	a rai_b_w of colour	a spec_r_m of	a kaleid_sc_pe

Riddle # 22: A cowboy rides into town on Friday, stays 5 days, and leaves on Friday. How?

"Opportunity is missed by most people because it is dressed in overalls and looks like work".

                                        Thomas Edison.

PAST SIMPLE

We have already seen how the past tense is very useful for a diary. Now the question is: how many tenses are there in the English language? The answer is **two**. They are the present tense and the past tense. The future tense is not, technically, a tense as it uses a verb form in order to complete it. There are, however, thirteen different ways to express an intent using time. Therefore, there are **thirteen tense forms** in English. We will start with the past tense simple. **It is used for something that happened sometime in the past.**

The **past simple** of regular verbs is formed by **adding an 'e' or 'ed'** onto the base form or stem (i.e. the infinitive) of a verb. An infinitive is very easy to work out. Put the word 'to' before a verb and you will get its infinitive. The grid below contains a list of verbs in different tenses. Change them into the infinitive in the second grid. Some examples are provided.

PAST PARTICIPLE	THE INFINITIVE	PAST TENSE SIMPLE
jumping	to jump	He jump**ed**
roaring	to roar	She roar**ed**
asking	to ask	He ask**ed**
shattering	to shatter	We
sleeping	to	I
studying	to	They
crashing	to	He
walloping	to	You
guessing	to guess	He guessed
sitting		We
carrying		They
joking		I
fishing		He
playing		She
chopping	to	They

Try to remember the infinitive with a mnemonic. You could try the catch-phrase of Buzz Lightyear in order to do this. Can you remember his phrase? The **infinitive** is **TO INFINITY** and beyond. Now you should remember that the infinitive takes a 'to' before it in order to work it out. A split infinitive is to put a word between the infinitives (i.e. to **boldly** go).

Write out the following sentences in the past tense simple form.

1. I (to walk) to the shop.

2. He (to visit) the cinema yesterday.

3. They (to shout) at the man to be careful of the ice.

4. We (to blink) in surprise when he told me that.

5. The water (to dribble) onto the floor while we were out.

PAST CONTINUOUS

The **past continuous** is used for actions happening at some time in the past. It is easy to recognise as it normally uses the words **was, were, wasn't** or **weren't** when it is being formed.

Try to fill in the rest of the grid with the help of a teacher. Choose the rest of the verbs yourself. If you can try some **irregular** verbs (e.g. to eat, to go) well done! An irregular verb changes in a different way from the infinitive to the past, present or future tense.

PAST SIMPLE	INFINITIVE	PAST CONTINUOUS
laughed	to laugh	I was laughing.
danced	to dance	We were dancing.
climbed	to climb	He wasn't climbing.
looked	to look	She wasn't looking.
ate	to eat	They
went	to go	You

Try to identify the past simple and the past continuous tense in the sentences below by rewriting them. Put in a PS (past simple) or PC (past continuous) after each tense.

1. You phoned while I was raking the leaves from the grass.

2. John laughed when I was painting the house.

3. When the river flooded the town, the noise was deafening.

4. You were joking when you said the rabbit hopped over the car.

5. What were you doing when the storm arrived?

6. Jane saw Robert and then she was trying to catch his attention.

7. We weren't working when you showed up.

8. Why weren't you driving the car when the police came?

9. I wasn't fooling when I said that you looked tired.

10. I ate the sandwich that you were keeping for me.

Date: __/__/__	Title: **DESCRIBING A MOUNTAIN: 4th GRID**	Lesson number:

Latin phrase:　　　　　Optimum medicamentum quies est.

Definition:　　　　　　R_st i_/th_/b_s_/m_d_c_n_.

Meaning: _____

_____

Spelling revision	New words	Dictionary definitions, corrections, and synonyms.
eas_l	ermi_e	
griz_led	somb_e	
rugo_e	quic_li_e	
irides_ent	kero_e_e	
spec_r_m	broo_ing	
harpo_n	zeph_r	
kaleid_sc_pe	Coss_ck	

nice phrases

1 POINT	2 POINTS	3 POINTS	4 POINTS
a wa_e of white	the somb_e mountain	therm_m_t_r plunged	Frank_nst_in cold
a t_unami of snow	broo_ing mountains	zeph_r haunted peaks	Coss_ck cold

mountain smells

your own st_le breath	w_ft of armpits	kero_e_e	p_ng of s_a_e clothes
oi_ed leather	w_iff of perspiration	mu_ty huskies	to_ic socks

movements of smell

bl_w towards us	dri_t_d towards us	fl_at_d towards us	gh_st_d towards us
ca_r_ed to us	draf_ed towards us	g_id_d towards us	st_a_ed towards us

other whites

ble_ch-white	ma_b_e-white	orc_id-white	zo_b_e-white
f_ng-white	se_s_ell-white	ermi_e-white	quic_li_e-white

Did you know? The world's most dangerous serial killer is out there and no one can catch him. His name is Gustave and he's killed over 300 people by most estimates. He lives in Burundi and he is a crocodile! The film 'Primeval' is based on him. Why not Google him?

PRESENT SIMPLE

The present simple is used for things that happen every day, all the time or as part a routine (i.e. regularly). For example, you could say: "I jump."

Does that mean you jump every day, all the time or is it just that you jump regularly?

The present simple is formed by getting the infinitive and using it for the pronouns: **I, you, we** and **they** (i.e. I jump, you jump, we jump and they jump).

An 's' must be added to the infinitive for the pronouns: **he, she** and **it** (i.e. He jumps, she jumps and it jumps). Can you guess why that is?

Fill in the grid below for the past simple rule. The first 8 verbs are regular and the next 6 are irregular.

VERB INFINITIVE (REG.)	I/You/We/They **PRE. SIMPLE**	He/She/It **PRE. SIMPLE**
to run	I **run**	He **runs**
to play	You **play**	She **plays**
to appear	We	It
to battle	They	He
to hope	I	She
to dance	You	It
to follow	We	He
to enjoy	They	She
VERB INFINITIVE (IRR.)	I/You/We/They **PRE. SIMPLE**	He/She/It **PRE. SIMPLE**
to go	I **go**	He
to do	You	She **does**
to have	We	It
to be	They	He
to catch	I	She
to flee	You	He

Make 5 of your own sentences in the present simple tense.

1.

2.

3.

4.

5.

Did you know? According to Tolkien, Edgar Allen Poe and many other authors, the most beautiful word in the English language is......on page 242. It has a beautiful sound that people find very appealing. This is known as a **euphonious** or a **phonoaesthetic** word. Before you look at page 242, take 5 guesses at the most beautiful word in English.

WHAT ELSE IS FALLING FROM THE SKY?

Leonardo da Vinci tried and failed to figure out why people sneeze. He might be glad to know that scientists are still not in full agreement about it. It is the same for yawning. Some things are better just left alone. Animals falling from the sky (usually fish and frogs) should have a rational explanation, however. Up to now, many people believed that tornadoes and waterspouts (i.e. tornadoes travelling over water) carried them from ponds, rivers or the sea. There are two scientific problems with that explanation.

The first is that waterspouts do not lift objects from anywhere. They are not capable of the suction required to do so as they are composed of condensed water vapour. Also, tornadoes cannot deposit objects such as frogs in one area alone. They would spit them out in random directions. Most people report the fish being alive. Scientists are not sure if they could survive being carried hundreds of miles inland by a tornado.

The second is that it always seems to rain with just one species. If they were coming from a pond, surely it should rain fish *and* frogs? If they were coming from a river, surely more than just one species would be swept up? How then can we explain animals falling from the sky? Try this case study:

On August 6th, 2000 a shower of 2-inch sprats fell on Greater Yarmouth in England. Fred Hodgkins, a retired ambulance driver, described it thus:

"There were a couple of claps of thunder and the sky went really dark even though it was only about 11am," he said.

"At first I thought I might have something wrong with my eyes because the whole of my back yard seemed to be covered in little slivers of silver. When I looked again, I saw scores of tiny, silver fish. I got my neighbours to have a look because I knew nobody would believe me. One of them had their garden shed covered in fish. It was quite extraordinary. I had never seen anything like it before in my life."

Andy Yeatman, from the Meteorological Office, said a small tornado building up under the thunderclouds out to sea was probably to blame.

"In this case, the tornado gathered over the sea and the fish got sucked up into the clouds. They were obviously carried along in the cloud for some distance before the cloud burst and the fish fell with the rain."

It seems probable in this instance that the sprats, a tiny fish, were swimming near the surface of the sea and carried up by a waterspout. The waterspout merged into the clouds. They were then carried half a mile inland and fell into a row of terraced houses in Greater Yarmouth. Or is it? What we have is one group of scientists saying it is probable and another group of scientists saying it is impossible. Did anyone see the tornado that carried them? Surely a waterspout or tornado would be noticed on the day? Write a newspaper article on it and interview all the neighbours again. Write your article on the basis that a tornado couldn't have caused it. Your name is Sherlock Holmes and you live by the quote on the next page.

Once you eliminate the impossible, whatever remains, no matter how improbable, must be the truth."   **Sir Arthur Conan Doyle, creator of Sherlock Holmes**

In 1997, the crew of a Japanese trawler were found clinging to the wreckage of their ship. When interviewed, they claimed that a cow had fallen from the sky and landed in the centre of their ship, smashing it apart. They were immediately arrested. They spent three weeks in prison.

This story was reported all around the world in the mainstream press. You are a journalist living close to the prison and are the first to interview the men. Write the story. Include a good caption (headline) and try to use a **pun**. A pun is a play on words. For example, you could use 'Miss-steak' or 'Fishy Tail' as your headline. Think of words that are related to cows or bulls for your caption and then apply it to the story. Underneath is a template you may decide to use or not.

CAPTION:	
Where is the story set? **When** did this happen?	**Introduction:**
Who is involved? **What** caused the cow to fall?	**Paragraph one:**
Describe the physical and mental state of the men. Are they lying? Give their story in their words.	**Main paragraph:**
Why is their story so difficult for the public to believe?	**Give public reaction with quotes** from different people (and/or the opinion of a scientist).
How is it part of a pattern of bizarre events of falling objects from the sky?	Give some **examples in history** of strange objects falling. If it is a tabloid article, link it to the end of the world.

Then a red-faced Russian Air Force general turned up. He explained that a flight crew taking off from Russia had seen a cow wandering near their air base. They had taken the cow on board as some sort of dare. When they were over the Sea of Japan, the cow started to smash up the cargo hold. At 30,000 feet, they had opened the cargo door in order to get rid of the cow. The cow duly obliged and plummeted from the aircraft, landing upon the ship of the terrified Japanese crewmen. The fishermen were immediately released with an apology.
Do you think this is a true story?
"Believe only half of what you see and nothing that you hear."   **Edgar Allen Poe**

Lex parsimoniae is the law of parsimony (or law of simplicity). It is also known as Occam's razor. It means that the simplest answer is the most likely.

A jug of milk has spilled from the kitchen table. A cat is lapping up the milk.

How did the milk fall?

Occam's razor says that the cat did it. It doesn't make it true, just the most likely to be true.

Bearing that in mind, take these examples and see if your class can solve the mystery of the falling frogs and fish and other objects.

1. 1st century B.C. Pliny the Elder writes about storms of frogs and fishes.

2. 1794 French soldiers stationed near Lille reported toads falling from the sky during heavy rain.

3. 1861 In Singapore, hundreds of catfish are reported to have fallen to the ground over a distance of fifty acres. An earthquake took place, followed by three days of heavy rain on February 20, 21 and 26. There is an eyewitness report at www.naturalhistorymag.com.

4. 1864 Quebec, Canada. A small frog is found inside a hailstone by a farmer.

5. 1873 Kansas City, Missouri. Frogs dropped from the sky during a hailstorm. There is no body of water nearby.

6. 1876 A woman in Kentucky reported chunks of meat falling from the sky. Two of her neighbours ate it. They guessed it was mutton or venison. They were right. Tests proved it was venison.

7. 1900 Providence, Rhode Island. Eyewitness Richard H. Tingley: "Streets and yards for several blocks were alive with squirming little perch and bullspouts".

8. 1901 Minneapolis, Minnesota. Frogs to a depth of several inches are reported, so much so that walking is impossible without killing them.

9. 1930 An 8-inch turtle fell during a Mississippi rainstorm.

10. June 16, 1940, Russia. A shower of 16th century coins falls on the village of Meschara. Archaeologists who analysed the currency believe soil erosion unearthed the treasure. Then a tornado picked it up and deposited it on the village.

11. October, 1947 Marksville, Louisiana. US marine biologist Alan Bajikov was having breakfast with his wife at a café. Suddenly, a shower of black bass, minnows and sunfish started to fall from the sky. They covered an area 1,000 yards long and 75 wide. This is what he said at the time: "There were spots on Main Street averaging one fish per square yard. Automobiles and trucks were running over them. Fish also fell on the roofs of houses….I personally collected from Main Street, and several yards on Monroe Street, a large jar of perfect specimens and preserved them in Formalin in order to distribute them among various

museums." The nearest sea was the Gulf of Mexico, 80 miles away. Some of the fish were frozen, some were rotten.

12. 1966 North Sydney, Australia. Father Leonard Bourne was dashing across a courtyard in a downpour when a large fish fell from the sky and landed on his shoulder. The priest nearly caught it as it slid down his chest, but it squirmed out of his grasp, fell to the flooded ground and swam away.

13. 1976 Blackbirds and pigeons rained down for two days in in san Luis Opisto, California.

14. 1981 Naphlion, Greece. Frogs showered down on top of their village. The frogs were native to North Africa, not Greece.

15. 1989 Ipswich, Australia. 800 sardines pelted the front lawn of a couple's house during a light rain shower.

16. 2005 Serbia. Thousands of tiny frogs bombarded the village of Odzaci. "I saw countless frogs fall from the sky," said resident Alexander Ciric. The frogs, a different species to those usually seen in the area, hopped around in search of water. Belgrade climatologist Slavisa Ignjatovic described the phenomenon as "not very unusual." She said: "A wind resembling a tornado can suck in anything light enough from the surface or shallow water. Usually, it's just dust, but sometimes also larger objects."

17. February, 2010. Lajamaun, Australia. Hundreds of spangled perch are still alive when they hit the ground, according to locals. Some were collected and put into buckets and the photographs may be seen on the internet.

18. December 31, 2010. Beebe, Arkansas, United States. 3,000-5,000 blackbirds were found dead after crashing to the ground. They all seemed to have suffered from blunt force trauma.

December 31, 2011. More than 1,000 blackbirds were found dead in the same manner in the same town the following year.

What disturbed people the most was that roughly 85,000 fish had died on a 20-mile stretch of river just a few days previously in the western part of the state. The fish were nearly all drum, and younger ones at that.

More than 500 starlings, blackbirds, brown-headed cowbirds and grackle were found dead around the same time in a different state, Louisiana. 50-100 jackdaws were found dead in a street in Sweden the same day. They seemed to have suffered blunt force trauma also. When 1,000 turtle doves fell from the sky onto the village of Faenza in Italy, the story went viral around the world. The turtle doves (and some pigeons) had a bluish tinge to their beaks, which may have indicated poison.

Did you know? There are between 10-20 billion birds in America and nearly half of these die every year. Mass bird kills are unusual, however. The biggest threat to birds is loud noises causing them to crash into buildings. Migratory birds also run the threat of freezing while flying through a storm. The most abundant **wild** bird in the world is the quealea (sparrow).

PRESENT CONTINUOUS

The present continuous tense is used for three main situations:

1. Things that are happening right now.

Ex: I **am talking** to you.

2. Things that seem to talk about right mow but are ongoing.

Ex: He **is studying** to be a doctor.

3. Future plans and arrangements.

Ex: I **am going** to enjoy Christmas.

The present continuous is formed by using: **am/is/are** and the **present participle** (i.e. **verb + 'ing'**).

In simpler terms, it is: **am/is/are + ing**.

The present participle is formed by using the infinitive (remember Buzz Lightyear?) and adding 'ing'.

Ex: Talking is the present participle of 'to talk'.

Ex: Laughing is the present participle of 'to laugh'.

Rule 1: For verbs ending in 'e', the 'e' must be dropped before adding 'ing'.

Rule 2: For verbs ending in 'ie', the 'ie' must be changed to a 'y' before adding 'ing'.

Rule 3: For verbs ending in consonant/vowel/consonant where the **last syllable is stressed**, double the last letter before adding 'ing'.

The verbs that **end in h, x, y and w never get a double letter**.

Rewrite the verbs below into their present participle form and put them in a sentence.

RULE 1		RULE 2		RULE 3 stressed		RULE 3	
type	typ-ing	tie	t-y-ing	be-**gin**	beginning	crash	crashing
joke		die		oc-**cur**		fix	fixing
bathe		lie		re-**fer**		play	playing
bounce		vie		hop		snow	snowing
create				run			
fire				stop			
pace				shop			
stare				hit			
capture				put			
slide				get			

There are fifteen vital clues to recognise the present continuous tense.

1. Now or 2. Currently,	9. Later today,
3. Right now,	10. Tonight,
4. At the moment,	11.Tomorrow,
5. Presently,	12. Next week,
6. I am constantly……..	13. Next month,
7. He is always……........	14. Next year,
8. They are forever……	15. At some time in the future

Put any 10 of the words and phrases in the grid above into a sentence. The first two are done.

1. Now I am going to visit my friend.

2. Currently, he is sleeping.

3.

4.

5.

6.

7.

8.

9.

10.

Did you know? The mnemonic for good weather has a scientific basis.

Red sky at night: shepherd's delight.

A red sky at night may show dust in the air. This means high pressure and good weather.

Red sky in the morning: shepherd's warning.

A red sky at dawn indicates a storm is coming from the west. This means rain is on the way.

Rainbow in the morning: travellers take warning.

If a rainbow is visible in the west, it means either rain or a storm is coming.

Rainbow at night: travellers delight.

If a rainbow is visible in the evening, the storm or rain has passed from east to west.

Date: __/__/__	Title: **DESCRIBING A MOUNTAIN: 5th GRID**	Lesson number:

Latin phrase: Qui non proficit, deficit.

Definition: He/w_o/d_e_/n_t/g_/f_r_ard, l_s_s/g_o_nd.

Meaning: _____

_____

Spelling revision	New words	Dictionary definitions, corrections, and synonyms.
ermi_e	astr_l	
somb_e	unea_t_ly	
quic_li_e	alg_d	
kero_e_e	astro_o_ic_l	
broo_ing	gel_d	
zeph_r	ha_d/ta_k	
Coss_ck	cos_ic	

sensation

1 POINT	2 POINTS	3 POINTS	4 POINTS
the fr_e_ing air	alg_d	Ar_t_c cold	numbing
the pin_h_ng cold	gel_d	Sib_ri_n cold	perishing

smell

p_t/r_a_t	bub_l_ng/bro_h	chargr_ll_d/la_b	p_t/no_d_es
ste_ed/mu_t_n	fl_sh-fri_d beef	me_ty/st_w	ha_d/t_ck

heavenly tastes

di_ine	gal_ct_c	astr_l	o_t of this w_r_d
cos_ic	st_llar	astro_o_ic_l	unea_t_ly

POINTS SCORE

0-10 good first try	11-29 well done	30-50 very good	51-60 excellent

Did you know? Children laugh, on average, 400 times a day. Adults laugh, on average, 15 times a day. Have some sympathy for your parents and teachers, you giddy bunch!

"Nothing is impossible. The word itself says: "I'm possible." Audrey Hepburn. Actress

FUTURE SIMPLE

The simple future tense is easy to recognise. The formula is: **will + base form of verb**.

Ex: I **will go**.

Ex: He **will dance**.

It is used for six different situations.

1. Making a promise: I **will** always **be** your friend.

2. Making a prediction: It **will rain** tomorrow.

3. Stating intentions: She **will be** a superstar.

4. A request for help: **Will** you **help** me, please?

5. Offers to help: **Will** I **paint** it with you?

6. Refusing things: He **will** not **go** to the match.

Numbers 1, 2 and 3 can overlap to a degree. Even so, try to put the sentences below into one of the six categories. The first sentence is done for you.

1. It will be a cold day.   **Making a prediction.**

2. The train will not be arriving soon.

3. Will you marry me?

4. Munster will win the Heineken Cup final.

5. Will we help him with his homework?

6. I will not do it.

7. Someday, I will be a success.

8. Will you stop talking out loud?

9. I will not rest until I have found it.

10. You will be a valuable member of our team.

Riddle # 23: You are in a bathroom built of stone and without windows. You start to run the bath when the handles come off and there is no way of turning the tap off. You can't open the door because it is locked. The room will flood and you will drown. How do you save yourself?

Blue-Sky Thinking

FUTURE SIMPLE

The future simple tense may be harder to recognise when it uses contractions. Fill in the rest of the contractions in the grid below.

SINGULAR CONTRACTIONS		PLURAL CONTRACTIONS	
I will changes to	I'll	You will changes to	
He will changes to		We will changes to	
She will changes to		They will changes to	
It will changes to		Who will changes to	

THE THREE SIMPLE TENSES (PAST, PRESENT, FUTURE)

Rewrite the sentences below and fill in the tense necessary to complete it. The base form of the verb is in brackets. Write in the tense in the parentheses.

1. She (scream) **screamed** when she saw the werewolf.   (PAST SIMPLE)

2. He (go) for a jog every day.   (   )

3. I (do) that tomorrow.   (   )

4. We (fight) a great battle but we lost.   (   )

5. He (visit) his friend in the hospital last week.   (   )

6. They (meet) up for the study session later.   (   )

7. I (build) a raft so I could go fishing on the lake.   (   )

8. We'll (organise) it immediately.   (   )

9. He (receive) a distinction for his project.   (   )

10. They (do not) pass their exam and they were unhappy.   (   )

Did you know? Many T.V programmes state that the rat or mouse is the most successful mammal in the world. This is not true. The answer is the fox. He lives wild in 83 countries and all seven continents. An urban fox only needs 80 gardens in his range in order to survive.

Riddle # 24: A boy is stuck on a deserted island. There is a bridge to connect the island to the mainland. Halfway across the bridge there is a guard. The guard will not let anyone from the mainland to the island or anyone from the island to the mainland. If the guard catches someone, he sends him or her back. The guard sleeps for 30 seconds and stays awake for 5 minutes. The island is surrounded by man-eating sharks and the boy does not have anything with him except for his shirt and his pants. It takes the boy one minute to get across. How does he get across the bridge without getting caught?

FUTURE CONTINUOUS

The future continuous is one of the easiest tenses to recognise. It is formed by using:
will + be + verb root + 'ing'.

Ex: I **will be go-ing**.

Fill in the grid below with sentences in the future continuous tense. The first one is done for you.

USING THE FUTURE CONTINUOUS

PERSONAL PRONOUN	WILL	BE	FINISH THE SENTENCE
I	will	be	driving us to the match tonight.
You			
He			
She			
They			
We			
I			
You			
He			
She			
They			
We			
I			
You			
He			
She			

FUTURE CONTINUOUS WITH SHALL

The future continuous tense may also be used with the word 'shall'. The original interpretation of 'shall' was 'to owe', but nowadays it is probably used more as 'to intend'.

The rule is the same as with 'will' (i.e. shall + be + verb + 'ing'). Using 'shall' instead of 'will' is a more formal way of saying the same thing. As the English language is constantly evolving, slang terms like 'gonna', 'hafta' and 'wanna' shall eventually replace 'shall'! What term would you use in the sentences below: will or shall? Does it make a difference, in your opinion? Rewrite the sentences using **both** words and see if you can decide.

1. I (will/shall) be (repay) you the money I owe you soon, sir.

2. I (will/shall) be (go) to the Doctors' Dance next month.

3. I (will/shall) be (see) you tomorrow to discuss your behaviour, young man.

4. He (will/shall) be (show) us how to do the project next week.

REVISION OF TENSES

Fill in the different tense forms in the grid below.

INFINITIVE	PAST SIMPLE	PRESENT SIMPLE	FUTURE SIMPLE
to run	He ran to the shop.	She runs all the time.	They will be running.
to give	He	She	They
to look	He	She	They
to eat	He	She	They
to take	He	She	They
to gamble	He	She	They
to do	He	She	They
to make	He	She	They
to shop	He	She	They
to visit	He	She	They

INFINITIVE	PAST CONTINUOUS	PRES. CONTINUOUS	FUT. CONTINUOUS
to jump	I was jumping.	I am jumping.	I will be jumping.
to see	I	I	I
to grow	I	I	I
to hop	I	I	I
to avoid	I	I	I
to stumble	I	I	I
to manage	I	I	I
to travel	I	I	I
to worship	I	I	I
to concede	I	I	I

One Saturday Red Rose Drove Through the New Court and Took the Left Road

Are you intelligent enough to use the mnemonic above in the grid below? What links them?

INFINITIVE	PAST SIMPLE	PAST CONTINUOUS	FUT. CONTINUOUS
to win			
to throw			
to leave			

Can you guess the only animal to have a chin besides humans? You're very clever if you do.

USING ASSONANCE: LONG 'O' SOUNDS

Assonance is when the same, or similar, vowel sounds are used in two or more words in a passage of writing. Sometimes this can be a coincidence. More often than not, however, it is a very deliberate technique used by a writer or poet. Assonance is used to affect the mood of a passage. It is easy to remember by the simple mnemonic:

I USE ASSONANCE.

As you can see, all the vowel sounds are represented. In this case, there isn't anything particularly sad or joyful about the sentence. If we were to use this sentence, however, that might change:

"The lonely wind moaned through the cold house of the old man."

There are four sounds that have the exact same sound. This is assonance. Can you pick them out? Do you agree that the Gaelic phrase 'ochon is ochon o' is the saddest phrase in any language? Ochon is pronounced as 'oakown'. It means 'alas' or 'woe'.

There are also two half-sounds. Although they do not rhyme exactly, it is still an example of assonance. Can you pick them out?

THE REMARKABLE POWER OF ASSONANCE

The most remarkable thing about assonance is how different cultures use the long and sad 'o' sound to reflect grief and hardship. Look up the following words and their origin on: **etymonline.com**. You may have to draw the grid in your own portfolio if it is too small.

SAD WORDS	ORIGIN	ORIGIN	OTHERS
doleful	late 13th century from the Latin word '*dolere*'(grief)	c.1300 Old English saying *all ane* (all one)	alone
forlorn			broken
groan			grove
lonely			low
moan			mope
morose			phobia
mournful			shadow
sombre			solo
sorrow			soul
woe (begone)			widow

WHAT IS FLASH FICTION?

The term 'flash fiction' can be dated back to the 6th century B.C. This is when it is believed 'Aesop's Fables' were collected. Flash fiction is when a story is cut down to the bare minimum of words. A lot of competitions on the internet want less than 1,000 words. Others want less than 500.

Most people see it as an art that requires less than 100 words, or sometimes 55. Here is an example from Aesop's Fables that fulfils this requirement:

Driven by hunger, a fox tried to reach some grapes hanging high up on the vine. He couldn't do it, even though he leaped with all his might. Eventually, he gave up. As he walked away, he said: "I didn't want you anyway. You aren't even ripe and I don't need sour grapes."

Did you like this story? What is the moral of the story, in your opinion? Count the words and see how many there are.

The important thing to recognise is that the story has a beginning, middle and an end. It also has a setting, characterization and conflict. Just like any other short story, these features are important. Flash fiction is also known as micro fiction, postcard fiction and short shorts. In China, it is referred to as 'smoke long'. They believe the story should be finished before your cigarette is!

In the 1920's, the writer Ernest Hemingway was in Luchow's restaurant in New York. The accepted story is that he challenged a group of writers that he could start, maintain and finish a story in six words. He put $10 on the table and said he would give them the same amount if they failed. Although they were reluctant at first, they discussed it and said it was impossible. They all put their $10 on the table. He wrote six words on a handkerchief and passed it around. They all paid up when they saw it.

That, apparently, is the start of flash fiction as we know it. It involves stripping away any unnecessary words. However, if you Google **www.quotefinder.com** you may get a different perspective on this event. If you are wondering what Hemingway wrote down, he scribbled:

For sale, never used, baby boots.   Do you find this very sad? Others do.

Do you think you could write a story in either 6 words or less than 55? Try to do it and you will see how it requires a more distilled way of thinking and writing. Underneath are some ideas:
1) Life's a dance. I never learned.
2) Distracted driving. Oak tree. Closed casket.
3) Wake, school, sleep. Resistance is futile.
4) Ship returns, empty slippers, waiting children.
5) She drove away, never to return.
6) Oh no! The parachute is jammed!

Did you know? Humans have only got five tastes: salty, savoury, sour, sweet and bitter. In contrast, we can distinguish between approximately 10,000 smells. A master perfumer can smell a modern perfume with 100 scents, go into a laboratory and write down the 100 different scents it is made of. Similarly, a wine taster can tell the alcohol content, the year, the brand and the area a glass of wine comes from just by sniffing and having a sip.

Humans have only 3 receptor types for colour vision and 2 for sound. Using the senses of taste and smell in your writings is very important as they are linked to our memories. Smell used to be the most important sense in a human being. A prehistoric hunter could smell predators, use his 'spidey-sense' to track animals and find herbs, edible plants and mushrooms.

It's a very important tool to use in a passage of writing. If you mention the word 'rose' in an essay, different readers will extract different colours, smells and memories from it. Some will think of yellow roses at a wedding. Others will think of red roses at a funeral. Similarly, if you say something is 'meringue sweet', it is likely that the reader will remember the last time they ate meringue. Putting taste and smell and the other three senses into your writing will enrich it for the reader. Fill in the grids and look up the challenging words in the dictionary.

Pick out your favourite words also and put them in your magical words grid.

SWEET TASTES	BITTER TASTES	SAVOURY	SALTY TASTES
car_m_l sweet	acr_d	del_c_ous	brac_i_h
can_y sweet	like ba_te_y acid	exqu_s_te	bri_y
conf_ct_on_ry sweet	b_t_ng	extr_v_gant	co_pe_y
gl_c_se sweet	caust_c	into_ica_ing	sali_e
ho_eyco_b sweet	ghouli_h	lavi_h	**HOT LIQUIDS**: tea etc.
mer_ng_e sweet	meta_l_c	lus_io_s	like drinking G_e_k fire (too hot)
noug_t sweet	tan_y	lu_h	as hot as la_a
sh_rb_t sweet	ta_t	scrum_t_ous	like drinking _oo_fla_e (tasty)
s_r_p sweet	tasted of t_o_l	toothso_e	like drinking s_a_light (yummy)
tut_i-fr_i_y taste of	vamp_ri_h	w_ol_some	as hot as s_n_i_e

SWEET SMELLS	BAD SMELLS	CONIFEROUS	DECIDUOUS
al_e Ve_a sweet	feste_ing	am_er aroma of	cl_y-rich
like b_k_d apples	fet_d	glyceri_e smell of	eart_y
bl_ss_m sweet	mus_y	g_mmy scent of	l_amy
jasmi_e sweet	p_ng of	medi_in_l smell of	mus_ro_my
me_d_w sweet	ranc_d	min_y tint of	mulc_y
myr_h sweet	ra_k	p_ne fragrance	o_k_n
nec_a_ine sweet	to_ic	res_n scent	org_n_c
po_l_n sweet	ungo_ly	s_p sweet	p_aty
sac_hari_e sweet	vi_e	star_h sweet	seas_n_d
tre_cle sweet	y_c_y	t_y_e sweet	wo_dy

USING 'PULSE' WORDS

Using the sensations, both physical and spiritual, is also a powerful way for your story to form a bridge to the reader. Phrases like 'skin-tingling' have a dramatic effect because the reader almost shares the sensation with you. He or she becomes teleported into the world you are constructing. This enhances the experience for any reader. After completing the grid, pick out the phrases suited to your ability and put them into a 'pulse words' section.

PHYSICAL GOOD	PHYSICAL BAD	SPIRITUAL GOOD	SPIRITUAL BAD
eye-op_n_ng	bl_d_er-em_t_ing	heart-ha_nting	ego-crus_ing
eye-w_t_ring	blo_d-cu_d_ing	mind-b_o_ing	heart-si_k_ning
eye-wi_e_ing	e_e-po_p_ng	soul-g_o_ing	joy-ki_l_ng
fist-pu_pi_g	h_ir-ra_s_ng	soul-no_ri_hing	mind-m_l_ing
g_o_e/b_m_s	h_nd-wri_ging	soul-ref_e_hing	mind-n_m_ing
he_rt-ra_i_g	he_rt-cl_n_hing	soul-s_ot_ing	nightmare-in_piring
pu_se-quic_e_ing	m_r_ow-fr_e_ing	soul-s_ir_ing	soul-nu_b_ng
s_in-ti_g_ing	sk_n-cra_l_ng	soul-sw_l_ing	soul-fr_e_ing
s_i_e-ti_g_ing	s_i_e-ch_l_ing	spirit-kind_ing	spirit-b_t_ng
j_w-d_op_ing	ve_n-fr_e_ing	spirit-l_f_ing	spirit-k_l_ing

The same applies for phrases that can conjure up a scene. All the adjectives below are examples of onomatopoeia. They are also 'season-specific'. Their job is to build a picture in the reader's mind of a certain time of the year. Pick your favourite ten words and make a story from them. If you include the other senses also, you will be proud of your writing skills.

SOUNDS OF SPRING	SOUNDS OF SUMMER	SOUNDS OF AUTUMN	WINTER WINDS
ble_ting lambs	cha_te_ing starlings	boo_ing thunder	b_t_ering
bu_bling bees	chit_e_ing swallows	c_wing crows	b_w_ing
bur_ling streams	co_ing pigeons	chi_ruping songbirds	be_l_wing
b_z_ing midges	flu_ing songbirds	clip-cl_p_ing hoo_es	bla_ting
c_r_ling dawn chorus	h_ffing breezes	cr_m_ling leaves	cater_auling
c_e_ping chicks	lis_ing rills	d_o_ing dragonflies	fl_ying
chir_ing grasshoppers	lo_ing cows	h_o_ing owls	la_hing
h_m_ing mowers	mu_b_ing bees	kee_ing winds	ma_gling
p_in_ing raindrops	nuz_ling foals	lil_ing tones of	mew_ing
pu_ping heart of	pi_ing robins	mu_f_ed forest sounds	r_a_ing
s_g_ing winds	pur_ing rivers	ph_t-ph_t of nuts	sc_ea_ing
sni_ping shears	qu_v_ring wheat fields	pul_ing soul of	sc_e_ching
spu_te_ing rain	soug_ing winds	s_s_ing rain	sh_i_king
sp_a_hing trout	spri_k_ing hoses	s_uf_ling noses	sl_s_ing
sw_sh_ng cow tails	thr_m_ing heart of	sq_e_ching feet	sn_r_ing
tinti_nab_lation of	tril_ing thrushes	w_e_zing winds	w_i_ing
war_ling songbirds	whit_ling gardeners	whim_e_ing winds	wal_o_ing
whin_ying foals	w_iz_ing falling stars	wh_rl_ng leaves	wh_n_ng
w_ir_ing dragonflies	wo_b_ing ice creams	whi_peing wheat fields	yam_ering
yel_ing fox cubs	zin_ing raindrops	ya_ning winds	yow_ing

ASSOCIATIVE LEARNING

Fill in the blanks by finding the links between the words.   **LINK WORDS**

1. To r_n is to wa_k as to ju_p is to h_p.   infinitives

2. P_o_y is to fu_sh_a as o_ch_d is to ca_am_ne.   flowers

3. T_x_c is to po_g as wa_t is to w_i_f.   smells

4. Zo_b_e is to q_ic_li_e as b_ea_h is to fa_g.   colours

5. I'_l is to yo_'ll as w_'ll is to th_y'll.   contractions

6. B_e_w_x is to f_a_en as mo_n_low is to s_ar_eam.   colours

7. W_e is to so_r_w as l_ne_y is to f_rl_rn.   assonance

8. Wr_n_led is to r_g_se as cr_n_led is to r_m_led.   mountains

9. Ti_e is to p_a_e as m_n_er is to d_gr_e.   types of adverbs

10. D_vi_e is to u_e_rt_ly as g_lac_ic is to st_l_ar.   tastes

11. Pu_c_ing is to p_er_ing as st_b_ing is to sp_a_ing.   mountains

12. A_g_d is to g_l_d as nu_b_ng is to p_er_ing   cold

13. Cl_p_ing is to b_o_ing as r_m_ling is to b_llo_ing   sounds

14. Dr_f_ed is to d_a_ted as g_os_ed is to g_i_ed   smell movements

15. H_at_er is to j_ni_er as o_pi_e is to m_l_erry   colours

16. C_r_i_al is to f_s_i_al as p_i_m is to s_ec_rum.   Find the link

17. F_ee_ing is to pi_c_ing as a_c_ic is to Si_er_an.   Find the link

18. Bl_w is to c_r_ied as st_a_ed is to fl_a_ed.   Find the link

19. Cr_s_ing is to r_a_ing as gr_w_ing is to gr_m_ling.   Find the link

20. Cr_g_y is to cr_m_led as g_ar_ed is to g_iz_led.   Find the link

Did you know? The longest one-syllable word in the English language is screeched. The longest word in the English language is 1,909 letters long and refers to a part of D.N.A.

CLASS IDEAS REVISION GRIDS

The grid below can be filled in as the class is doing a creative page of fill in the blanks. It may also be used at the end of the module for revision purposes. The teacher might also decide to put different headings in the grid. The template for the first two pages is done for you. The rest needs to be filled in by the student.

CHRISTMAS LIGHTS REFLECTING
SOUNDS IN THE HOUSE
IMAGES IN THE HOUSE
MAGICAL WORDS GRID
THE CHRISTMAS FIRE
EMOTIONAL SENSATIONS
SMELL
TASTE

Riddle # 25: A king has no sons, no daughters and no queen. For this reason, he must decide who will take the throne when he dies. To do this, he decides to give every child in the kingdom a single seed. Whichever child grows the biggest, most beautiful plant will earn the throne. He sees this as being a metaphor for the kingdom. At the end of the contest, all of the children come to the palace with their enormous and beautiful plants in hand. After seeing all of the children's pots, he decides that a little girl with an empty pot will be the next queen. Can you figure out why he decided to do this?

MAKE A MOUNTAIN CROSSWORD

Ask your teacher for guidance if you need it. This exercise should be done with a partner.

TRUE OR FALSE?

1. The wren is the smallest bird in Ireland.

2. There are more stars in the universe than grains of sand on earth.

3. There is a species of jellyfish that is immortal.

4. A typical lead pencil can draw a line 35 miles long.

5. The average chocolate bar has 8 insect legs in it.

6. Most humans alive today have never made a phone call.

7. Alcohol kills more people than all the illegal drugs combined.

8. It takes about 63,000 trees to make the average edition of The New York Times.

9. Giraffes can go without water longer than camels.

10. Cancer has only been a human disease since approximately 1,600 B.C.

11. There are more people alive on the planet now than the total that have ever died in Earth's history.

12. The total weight of all ants on Earth is heavier than the total weight of humans.

13. Most mass whale beachings are caused by sonar from big ships and poisoning from chemicals.

14. The largest living thing on Earth is a mushroom 3 and a half miles in diameter.

15. If you hit your skate off the ice you can tell how safe it is. An A note is good, E is bad.

16. Falling coconuts kill more people every year than sharks.

17. There are more mobile phones than toothbrushes in the world.

18. Honey discovered in the Egyptian pyramids is still edible today.

19. Bananas are a berry.

20. Horses cannot breathe through their mouths.

21. The biggest squid ever caught was 33 feet long.

22. An owl's night vision is only 2.7 times greater than ours but his hearing is 10 times better.

23. Humans in peak condition can outrun any animal on earth in a marathon.

24. The average teenager today would beat 98% of the 1910 adult population in an I.Q. test.

25. Shakespeare had only one split infinitive in all his writings.

Date: / /	Title: **DESCRIBING FEMALES: 1ˢᵗ GRID**	Lesson number:

Latin phrase:　　　　Latet enim veritas, sed nihil pretiosius veritate.

Definition:　　　　Tr_th/is/hi_d_n, b_t /no_h_n_/is/m_r_/b_a_t_f_l/t_a_/th_/t_u_h.

Meaning: _____

_____

Spelling revision	New words	Dictionary definitions, corrections, and synonyms.
astr_l	moc_a	
unea_t_ly	st_ll_r	
alg_d	cor_l	
astro_o_ic_l	nym_h	
gel_d	ho_r/gla_s	
ha_d/ta_k	pix_e	
cos_ic	Valkyr_e	

You must describe a female in detail. How many features can you name with an adjective?

1 POINT	2 POINTS	3 POINTS	4 POINTS
moc_a-brown eyes	g_m-green eyes	cor_l-black hair	c_p_er-brown hair
j_w_l-blue eyes	cle_r skin	mer_u_y-red hair	Valkyr_e-gold hair

5 POINTS	6 POINTS	7 POINTS	8 POINTS
a so_gbi_d's voice	kidu_t clothes	a sw_n's neck	p_a_o/k_y teeth
a st_ll_r smile	mo_n/rou_d eyes	s_g_r/pl_m lips	s_a/nym_h ears

9 POINTS	9 POINTS	10 POINTS	10 POINTS
fi_m/st_r fingernails	sp_d_r's-leg eyelashes	a bu_bl_b_e/wa_st	an ho_r/g_a_s figure
a p_x_e's nose	pe_c_l thin eyebrows	glo_ing/co_ple_ion	

super student ideas

0-50 good first try	51-100 well done	100-120 very good	120-148 excellent

RIDDLE # 26: Use your brain or dictionary to find the only two words which start and end in 'he'.

There are only two words that end in 'shion' also. Can you guess them?

FEMALE CHARACTER DESCRIPTION

You met a girl when you were in Spain. She was so beautiful that you jotted down a list of her qualities. Fill them in properly and use a different word or phrase on the right hand side.

(OTHER WORD OR PHRASE)

1. She had j_w_l-blue eyes.   (**gemstone-blue** eyes   )

2. Her hair was c_r_l-black.   (   )

3. She had glowing, c_e_r skin.   (   )

4. She spoke as sweetly as a s_n_b_rd sings. (   )

5. She had a st_l_ar smile.   (   )

6. I noticed she wore ki_u_t clothes.   (   )

7. Her eyes were m_on r_u_d.   (   )

8. She had a s_a_'s neck.   (   )

9. She had s_g_r pl_m lips.   (   )

10. Her teeth were like a line of p_a_o k_ys. (   )

11. She had s_a n_m_h ears.   (   )

12. Her fingernails were as bright as a fi_m s_a_s. (   )

13. She had a p_x_e's nose.   (   )

14. Her sp_d_r's leg eyelashes were s_e_k and gl_s_y. (   )

15. They fluttered under her pe_c_l th_n eyebrows. (   )

16. She had a b_m_l b_e waist.   (   )

17. I loved her glowing c_mp_e_i_n.   (   )

18. She had an h_ur g_a_s figure.   (   )

19. She flashed me a win_i_g smile.   (   )

20. It was heart-m_l_i_g.   (   )

RIDDLE # 27: I wiggle and cannot see, sometimes underground, sometimes on a tree. I really don't want to be on the hook and I become a person when combined with a book. What am I?

Did you know? Most advertisements featuring a clock put the hands at 10 minutes past 10.

Date: __/__/__	Title: **DESCRIBING FEMALES: 2nd GRID**	Lesson number:

Latin phrase: Non opus est follo suspendere tympana collo.

Definition: A/f_o_/d_e_/n_t/n_e_/a_y/b_l_s.

Meaning: _____

_____

Spelling revision	New words	Dictionary definitions, corrections, and synonyms.
moc_a	op_l	
st_ll_r	ber_l	
cor_l	s_l_r	
nym_h	mil_po_d	
ho_r/gla_s	jas_er	
pix_e	mi_t	
Valkyr_e	d_wpond	

instead of said

1 POINT	2 POINTS	3 POINTS	4 POINTS
she ans_e_ed	she re_li_d	she hi_t_d	she in_i_ted
she expla_n_d	she res_o_ded	she de_an_ed	she sug_es_ed

colour of blue eyes

du_k-e_g blue	hea_e_ly-blue	ga_a_y-blue	che_ic_l-blue
r_b_n's-egg blue	d_v_ne-blue	s_l_r-blue	pl_s_a-blue

colour of green eyes

s_a-green	mi_t-green	par_di_e-green	ber_l-green
la_e-green	f_r_st-green	mi_t/v_ll_y-green	jas_er-green

shape of eyes

d_e shaped	sa_c_r shaped	o_b round	d_w pond round
a_mo_d shaped	S_t_rn shaped	op_l round	mil_po_d round

others

vibra_t clothes	b_e/stu_g lips	b_b_ly personality	ele_tr_c personality
ret_o clothes	C_p_d's bow lips	j_y_us personality	ma_ne_ic personality

WRITING A STORY WITH CHARACTER DESCRIPTIONS

You are walking on a beach. You see a woman and you admire her beauty. Then you see a shark's fin behind her and plunge into the sea to help. Use the words and phrases from previous chapters to create a very sensory story. Fill in the blanks to write your version of it.

INTRO: I was on vacation in Florida when it happened. I was walking on the (   ) soft beach and lapping up the sights and smells. The sea was a perfect, (   )-blue and the waves were gently (   ) onto the beach. I could smell the (   ) of hot dogs and burgers in the air. I bought one and it tasted (   ).

PAR 1: I decided to sit down and watch the surfers for a while. Just then the most beautiful woman I have ever seen passed me by. Her eyes pierced right through me. They were a bewitching, (   )-egg blue and (   ) shaped. She had (   ) lips and they were (   )-red. It was a heart (   ) moment when she nodded at me. She seemed to know everyone and had a (   ) personality.

PAR 2: I lay back on the sand with my elbows pr_p_ing me up. They burned like (   ) but I didn't mind. I was going to stay here a while. I drank in all the sights and sounds around me. The hor_z_n was like a long (   ) of (   ). Boats were (   ) up and down in the distance and a flock of (   ) were (   ) far out to sea. The surfers all had (   ) skin and looked (   ). They whooped and ho_ler_d with (   ) when they caught a good wave. I think we all realised we were holidaying in (   ).

PAR 3: Then I blinked. I rubbed my eyes. What was that shape under the water? It looked like a (   ). My eyes were b_ur_y from the sun tan lotion but then I saw it again. It was a (   ) moment when I saw a fin rise slowly out of the water and move towards the surfers. My pulse was (   ) and my blood (   ). I jumped up and down and (   ) at the surfers to get out of the water. They couldn't hear me. I waved my arms (   ) but they still didn't notice. The other people on the beach were staring at me as if I were a (   ). I didn't care. I started to run.

PAR 4: The water was (   ) cold when I plunged into it. My heart felt as if it would (   ) and I didn't know if I wanted to reach the surfers in time or not. Coming between a shark and his pr_y was not very sensible. My head was c_a_h_ng against the waves and I could see the sand below me getting lower and lower. I was well out to sea when I po_ed my head up. To my dism_y, there was no one around me. The surfers had all left! They must have been warned by the other bea_hgo_rs. I was alone. Then a fin rose not fifty yards away me and begin to circle.

CONCLUSION:

Write the conclusion to this story.

Date: __ / __ / __	Title: **DESCRIBING FEMALES: 3RD GRID**	Lesson number:

Latin phrase: Vincil qui patitur.

Definition: H_/w_o/pe_s_v_r_s, c_n_u_rs.

Meaning: _____

_____

Spelling revision	New words	Dictionary definitions, corrections, and synonyms.
op_l	ebo_y	
ber_l	rin_l_ts	
s_l_r	sab_e	
mil_po_d	velo_r	
jas_er	tres_es	
mi_t	noug_t	
d_wpond	glo_s	

instead of said

1 POINT	2 POINTS	3 POINTS	4 POINTS
she ad_ed	she sta_ed	she an_ou_ced	she ob_er_ed
she con_in_ed	she com_en_ed	she de_la_ed	she re_ar_ed

colour of black hair

raven-black	velvet-black	sab_e-black	midnight-black
coral-black	gloss-black	ebo_y-black	panther-black

colour of brown hair

co_o_ut-brown	bis_u_t-brown	wa_nut-brown	ca_a_el-brown
ches_n_t-brown	wa_er-brown	noug_t-brown	cin_am_n-brown

hair movement (over the shoulders)

cra_h_d upon	sw_o_ed over	to_pl_d over	sp_ra_led over
tum_led over	plu_g_d over	ca_c_ded over	plu_me_ed over

other phrases for hair

lu_h hair	tres_es of hair	curt_i_ed her face	ve_v_t soft
lusc_o_s hair	rin_l_ts of hair	wrea_hed her face	velo_r soft

WRITING A HORROR STORY USING A WORD BANK

You are lost in a forest after getting separated from your group. Nightfall is closing in and there are rumours of witches in the forest. You see a beautiful woman on the path in front of you who turns into a witch. How you develop the story is up to you but you may choose to use some of the words in the grid. These are atmospheric words that will improve your story. Try to make up your own word bank of terrifying, dark forest sounds also.

THE DARK FOREST

COLOURS	IMAGERY	ASSONANCE
ab_ss-black	The s_a_less sky spoke of bad things to come.	alone
b_t-black	The s_nless sky covered the forest in gloom.	groan
c_t-black	The j_y_ess moon looked down on me like a sour eye.	grove
ca_e-black	The blood-red moon was co_f_rtless.	lonely
c_ll_r-black	The trees glared at us like silent se_tr_es.	low
co_ra-black	Their bo_ghs reached up like the li_bs of the da_ned.	moan
do_m-black	B_a_ds of moss dripped with ce_t_ries-old hate.	shadow
mi_ni_ht-black	Steam rose from the floor like s_ooky in_en_e.	sorrow
r_v_n-black	In the shadows, spiders clutched their s_are-strings.	soul weary
t_r-black	Their c_bw_bs shimmered like s_eel nets.	woebegone

SMELLS	PUT IN BEAUTIFUL WOMAN DESCRIPTIONS	OTHERS
cl_m_y		bi_te_s_eet
d_nk		ch_er_ess
d_ca_ing		fo_l
mo_ldy		gl_o_y
mus_y		s_oty
r_t_ing		h_wl
sic_ly		li_eless
st_le		m_rky
st_f_y		old wi_lo_s
so_r		h_o_ing/o_ls

PHYSICAL SENSATIONS	SPIRITUAL SENSATIONS	SOUNDS
blood-cur_l_ng	My mind was fl_sh-fro_en to the spot.	
bone-ch_l_ing	heart-sic_e_ing	
knee-kn_c_ing	mind-n_m_ing	
marrow-fr_e_ing	nightmare-ins_i_ing	
rib-r_t_ling	spirit-ki_li_g	

Suspected witches in the 16th and 17th centuries had their right thumb tied to their left toe and their left thumb tied to their right toe. Rope was tied to their waist and if they sank in the lake, they were considered innocent. If they floated, they were considered guilty and put to death. Many 'witches' sank to the bottom, and after a second attempt to double check, were freed.

Date: __/__/__	Title: **DESCRIBING FEMALES: 4th GRID**	Lesson number:

Latin phrase: Scientia non habet inimicum nisi ignorantem.

Definition: K_o_l_d_e /h_s/n_/e_e_ies/b_t/t_e/i_n_r_n_ .

Meaning: _____

_____

Spelling revision	New words	Dictionary definitions, corrections, and synonyms.
ebo_y	willo_y	
rin_l_ts	burni_h_d	
sab_e	oxb_w	
velo_r	meg_w_tt	
tres_es	hen_a	
noug_t	rush_i_ht	
glo_s	pend_nt	

colour of red hair

1 POINT	2 POINTS	3 POINTS	4 POINTS
ru_y-red	w_ne-red	ro_ge-red	hen_a-red
ro_e-red	windf_ll-red	rush_i_ht-red	Titi_n-red

colour of gold hair

sun_i_e-gold	moong_e_m-gold	starf_a_e-gold	flax_n-gold
suns_t-gold	moong_i_t-gold	star_e_m-gold	har_st_ing-gold

figure and waist

a shap_ly figure	a qu_e_ly figure	ch_li_e shaped	wa_p-wa_s_ed
a willo_y figure	a me_m_id's figure	go_l_t shaped	an oxb_w waist

complexion

hea_t_y	fl_w_ess	ap_ic_t complexion	burni_h_d
pe_fe_t	pe_rless	bron_ed complexion	pe_c_es and c_e_m

other phrases

pend_nt-shaped nails	wa_p-wa_st_d	a p_rt nose	lumi_o_s teeth
an aco_n cup chin	a meg_w_tt smile	spel_bi_di_g eyes	st_le_to-shaped nails

THE BEAUTY AND THE BEASTLY

You should have completed your story about a beautiful woman turning into a witch. Now try it again using these words and phrases to help you. You should notice a small improvement in your story.

bl_o_less lips	moonlight-p_le skin	spi_d_y legs like a spider
hi_s_ng voice	wol_ish eyes	b_ck-toothed
d_ad fi_h eyes	s_w-toothed	s_it_ed eyes
po_kma_ked skin	sou_less stare	r_spy voice
she looked b_as_ly	wa_t on her nose	b_t wings and f_ogs' legs
c_sket-black robe	a th_u_and-yard stare	hair like b_ar brist_es
eyes glinted with cr_e_ty	gra_e_ly voice	looked gh_st_y
s_r_w-like hair	a h_ar_less laugh	time-de_a_ed skin
b_e_th like a troll	g_arly hands	teeth like b_o_en glass
fish h_ok eyebrows	f_ded skin	b_e_le-browed
c_t-like eyes	li_e_ess hair	l_ce-infected hair
ha_kish nose	hi_s_ng voice	c_b-nosed
manners of a b_n/f_y	teeth like br_k_n tom_sto_es	face like sna_es_in leather
snag_le-too_hed	h_o_ed nose	b_b_ling cauldron
giml_t eyes	s_c_ly breath	the m_r_ls of a mamba
whee_y voice	sp_d_r cold eyes	looked hi_eo_s
st_le breath	r_v_n's nose	zo_b_e-white skin
eyes gleaming with cu_n_ng	ca_k_ing voice	hair looked ele_t_i_ied

Try to add to the terms given by brainstorming with your class and finishing the grid.

CLASS IDEAS FOR A WITCH

Riddle # 28: A farmer in Australia grows a beautiful pear tree, which he harvests to supply fruit to all the neighbouring grocery stores. One of the store owners calls the farmer to see how much fruit is available to buy. Unfortunately, the farmer is not in the orchard so he has to work it out in his head. He knows that the main trunk of the tree has 5 branches. Each branch has 5 boughs and each bough has 5 twigs. Each one of these twigs bears one piece of fruit, so how many plums can he sell to the store owner? Try to work it out without using a pen or paper.

Date: __/__/__	Title: **DESCRIBING FEMALES: 5th GRID**	Lesson number:

Latin phrase: Ulquibis cum lupis, cum quibis esse cupis.

Definition: W_o/k_ep_/c_m_a_y/wi_h/w_l_es/w_ll/l_a_n/h_w/t_/h_w_.

Meaning: _____

_____

Spelling revision	New words	Dictionary definitions, corrections, and synonyms.
willo_y	dai_ty	
burni_h_d	calc_te	
oxb_w	cres_e_t	
meg_w_tt	div_	
hen_a	cher_b	
rush_i_ht	fin_sp_n	
pend_nt	Bot_x	

instead of said

1 POINT	2 POINTS	3 POINTS	4 POINTS
she cri_d	she draw_ed	she mu_b_ed	she shr_e_ed
she croa_ed	she jo_ed	she ro_r_d	she w_i_p_red

lips   ears

puf_y lips	he_rt/s_a_ed lips	de_ic_te ears	se_s_ell ears
pou_i_g lips	Bot_x/bo_s_ed lips	el_in ears	a cher_b's ears

eyelashes   eyebrows

sil_y eyelashes	fin_sp_n eyelashes	sle_d_r eyebrows	a_c_ed eyebrows
swee_ing eyelashes	ve_v_ty eyelashes	plu_k_d eyebrows	cres_e_t shaped

nose   teeth

a po_nty nose	a b_tt_n nose	b_e_ch-white teeth	u_i_orn-white teeth
a dai_ty nose	a div_'s nose	calc_te-white teeth	wi_a_d-white teeth

others

glos_y skin	ma_icu_ed nails	a nectar_i_e voice	s_g_r-ca_dy lips
an A_a_onian figure	a ter_w_tt smile	cosmopo_it_n clothes	tr_ut/po_t lips

You have nearly completed the module on describing females. How many words can you put in after the categories you have studied? Put in a maximum of 3. The first example is done.

1. Colour of blue eyes: galaxy-blue/solar-blue/chemical-blue

2. Colour of green eyes:

3. Shape of eyes:

4. Colour of black hair:

5. Colour of brown hair:

6. Hair movement:

7. Colour of red hair:

8. Colour of gold hair:

9. Figure:

10. Waist:

11. Complexion:

12. Lips:

13. Ears:

14. Eyelashes:

15. Eyebrows:

16. Nose:

17. Teeth:

Are there other parts of a female character description not included here? Put them into the grid below.

Riddle # 29:   All roses are flowers.

Some flowers fade quickly.

Therefore some roses fade quickly.   True or False?

Did you know? There are an estimated 50 billion chickens in the world. The longest recorded flight for a chicken is 13 seconds and the chicken flew 301.5 feet in that time.

The grid below can be filled in as the class is doing a creative page of fill in the blanks. It may also be used at the end of the module for revision purposes. The teacher might also decide to put different headings in the grid. The template for the first two pages is done for you. The rest needs to be filled in by the student.

COLOUR OF BLUE EYES
COLOUR OF GREEN EYES
SHAPE OF EYES
COLOUR OF BLACK HAIR
COLOUR OF BROWN HAIR
HAIR MOVEMENT

Riddle # 30: Tom's mom had three children. The first was named April and the second was named May. What was the third called?

MAKE A FEMALE CHARACTER DESCRIPTION CROSSWORD

Ask your teacher for guidance if you need it. This exercise should be done with a partner.

Date: __/__/__	Title: **DESCRIBING MALES: 1ˢᵗ GRID**	Lesson number:

Latin phrase: Sapiens dominabitur astris.

Definition: A/w_s_/m_n/w_l_/r_l_/t_e/s_a_s.

Meaning: _____

_____

Spelling revision	New words	Dictionary definitions, corrections, and synonyms.
dai_ty	scro_l_d	
calc_te	dap_er	
cres_e_t	ha_k_sh	
div_	lun_r	
cher_b	ba_s	
fin_sp_n	P_p_ye	
Bot_x	narcis_istic	

You are asked to describe a man. What features do you pick?

1 POINT	2 POINTS	3 POINTS	4 POINTS
colour blue eyes	colour brown eyes	colour black hair	colour red hair
colour green eyes	colour grey eyes	colour brown hair	colour gold hair

5 POINTS	6 POINTS	7 POINTS	8 POINTS
ba_s voice	dap_er clothes	a b_ll's neck	o_st_r-white teeth
wi_n_ng smile	lun_r shaped eyes	pe_p_r_d stubble	scro_l_d ears

9 POINTS	9 POINTS	10 POINTS	10 POINTS
P_p_ye biceps	At_as shoulders	a co_cr_te jaw	an e_rt_y smell
a rapt_r's nose	de_i_ed cheekbones	a das_i_g personality	
			super student ideas

0-50 good first try	51-100 well done	100-120 very good	120-148 excellent

Did you know? The two most handsome men in history were Narcissus and Adonis. Narcissus went for a walk one day and was followed by a mountain nymph. Her name was Echo. Every time he called out "Who's there?" she repeated it. When he refused to embrace her, she was heartbroken. She spent the rest of her life in lonely glens until nothing remained of her but an echo. Narcissus loved his reflection in a pool so he stayed there until he died!

ADDING YOUR OWN IDEAS

Underneath is the list of words from the previous page. Using a dictionary or thesaurus if needed, substitute your own adjectives for the ones already given. The first example is done for you. Can you add five more male traits (i.e. characteristics) at the end?

1. A **bass** voice: a powerful voice.

2. A winning smile:

3. Dapper clothes:

4. Lunar-shaped eyes:

5. A bull's neck:

6. Peppered stubble:

7. Oyster-white teeth:

8. Scrolled ears:

9. Popeye biceps:

10. A raptor's nose:

11. Atlas shoulders:

12. Defined cheekbones:

13. A concrete jaw:

14. A dashing personality:

15. An earthy smell:

16.

17.

18.

19.

20.

Riddle # 30: What is the beginning of eternity,

the end of time and space,

the beginning of every end

and the end of every place?

Date: __ / __ / __	Title: **DESCRIBING MALES: 2nd GRID**	Lesson number:

Latin phrase: Ut amens, amibilis esto.

Definition: B_/am_able, th_n/y_u'l_/b_/l_v_d.

Meaning: _____

_____

Spelling revision	New words	Dictionary definitions, corrections, and synonyms.
scro_l_d	rapt_r	
dap_er	Ac_ill_s	
ha_k_sh	Had_s	
lun_r	Teut_n_c	
ba_s	Ap_l_o	
P_p_ye	Nord_c	
narcis_istic	Ar_an	

long, gold hair

1 POINT	2 POINTS	3 POINTS	4 POINTS
V_k_ng-gold	Nord_c-gold	Ar_an-gold	Ac_ill_s-gold
He_cu_es-gold	Scand_n_v_an-gold	Teut_n_c-gold	Ap_l_o-gold

short hair

1 POINT	2 POINTS	3 POINTS	4 POINTS
a cr_w cut	a Mohi_an	a m_r_ne cut	a b_zz-c_t
clo_e/cro_p_d	a ro_st_r cut	a m_l_t_ry cut	a r_z_r's edge cut

eyebrows

1 POINT	2 POINTS	3 POINTS	4 POINTS
bu_hy	sic_le shaped	b_e_le-browed	Had_s-black
br_st_y	scyt_e shaped	eq_in_x-black	firew_rshi_p_r-black

cheekbones

1 POINT	2 POINTS	3 POINTS	4 POINTS
d_med	half-do_e	ar_h_d	pi_c_ed-in
def_n_d	half-mo_n	ang_lar	promi_e_t

nose

1 POINT	2 POINTS	3 POINTS	4 POINTS
a fal_on's	a Ro_an	a lord_y	an aqu_l_ne
a ha_k_sh	an im_er_al	a king_y	a prom_n_nt

In the land of Fantasia, an Elven army has gathered to fight a bigger army of trolls. Your job is to describe the features of both armies before the battle begins. Then you must write a battle scene describing what happened. The best mix of colours to use for a battle scene is black, red and silver. Try to use these colours in your descriptions. There is a grid to describe the trolls underneath. You may decide to use it or come up with your own ideas. There is also a grid to recreate the sound of missiles flying. This was covered in a previous chapter.

grea_y hair	l_nk hair	ho_k-nosed
bar_ac_da-eyed	a g_b_in's grin	skin as rough as t_ee/b_rk
p_g-nosed	p_ran_a-eyed	j_g ears
teeth like ta_on tips	spi_t_e-flecked lips	lepro_s-yellow teeth
f_o_ty eyes	f_n-shaped canines	co_ra-cold eyes
do_t_oth-yellow fangs	co_p_e-white skin	bu_bous nose
ra_or-thin lips	gl_c_al eyes	pa_ty-white skin
a bu_f_lo's neck	c_uel, cur_ed eyebrows	w_nt_y eyes
b_g-eyed	a s_a_k's teeth	tank_rd-handle ears
ha_c_et-faced	a s_y look	dem_nic power
f_l_ne eyes	jee_ing voices	sca_y skin
a g_r_lla's shoulders	kn_t_y fingers	ma_t_d hair
wi_d-eyed	p_p-eyed	to_b-deep voices

ARROWS THROUGH THE AIR	FAST WORDS WITH DOUBLE LETTERS	
b_z_ing	h_m_ing	his_i_g
f_z_ing	st_u_ming	s_s_i_g
fi_z_ing (for fire arrows)	t_r_m_ing	p_rri_g
si_z_ing	w_ir_ing	wh_o_hi_g
w_iz_ing	zo_m_ng	z_p_ing/z_n_ing

TROLL SOUNDS	TROLL SOUNDS	ELVISH SOUNDS	ELVISH SOUNDS
cla_ging swords	clan_ing army	d_nging swords	chi_king stirrups
cla_gorous axes	c_onking boots	jin_ling saddles	clin_ing chain-mail
g_nging warhammers	clun_ing steel fists	p_nging arrows	p_inking raindrops
jan_ling chain-mail	p_unking maces	rin_ing of steel	t_nkling armour
t_anging bowstrings	t_unking spears		

When you are writing a battle scene, you have a choice whether to write it in 1st person narration (i.e. using the words 'I' or 'we') or 3rd person narration (i.e. using the word 'they'). It may be better to use 3rd person narration while you are still developing your writing skills. Picture yourself on a hill watching the battle. You can see, hear and smell the action taking place. This is your point of view. Describe the sky as sunless to evoke a gloomy atmosphere and put in the sounds of the weather also. Is thunder growling? Is lightning sissing? Writing a great battle scene takes practice and patience and does not come overnight. Above all else, enjoy the pleasure you get from writing effectively.

"We are what we repeatedly do. Excellence, then, is not an act, but a habit." **Aristotle**

Date: __/__/__	Title: **DESCRIBING MALES: 3rd GRID**	Lesson number:

Latin phrase: Sic parius magna.

Definition: Gre_t_e_s/c_m_s/f_om/s_a_l/b_g_n_i_gs.

Meaning: _____

_____

Spelling revision	New words	Dictionary definitions, corrections, and synonyms.
rapt_r	Sa_s_n	
Ac_ill_s	ox-yo_e	
Had_s	Atl_s	
Teut_n_c	bra_ny	
Ap_l_o	fel_ne	
Nord_c	bur_y	
Ar_an	gra_ite	

shoulders

1 POINT	2 POINTS	3 POINTS	4 POINTS
a wre_t_er's	b_ar-like	Atl_s	a ti_an's
a wei_h_lif_ers	ox-yo_e	Sa_s_n	a levi_th_n's

jaw

a co_c_ete jaw	a ma_b_e jaw	an o_ken jaw	a la_te_n jaw
a cr_g_y jaw	a fli_ty jaw	a gra_ite jaw	a Gi_le_te ad jaw

movement

a c_t-like gr_ce	a ti_er-like tre_d	an at_le_ic grace	a fel_ne grace
a le_p_rd-like gr_ce	s_re-fo_ted	a l_on-like po_er	a pa_t_er in sl_w-mo

strength

P_p_ye biceps	bra_ny	a Sp_rt_n's muscles	a g_m/ho_ed body
a gla_ia_or's arms	bur_y	Go_i_th's strength	a g_m/to_ed body

others

ir_n/mus_les	a s_x/pa_k	ca_v_d from ro_k	an Ol_m_ian's chest
cast ir_n/mus_les	a ba_r_l/ch_st	ca_v_d from gra_i_e	a w_shbo_rd stoma_h

164

You may have noticed that a character description takes up a very small piece of a writing passage. The words you are studying inject the maximum amount of impact in the shortest space of time, however. It is a gift to be able to describe a place or a character without having to think. These exercises are designed to improve your vocabulary, your thought processes and your imagination. Bearing that in mind, let us take you to a different environment. You have been lost in the desert for two days. Then a man turns up to rescue you. His character description and who he is are up to you. The desert grid will provide ideas if you need them.

sp_r_t_ess place	shimmering o_s_s	Your blood simmers, your brain stews and your bones smoulder.
stunted cac_i	b_rnt-umber	The sun scorches, the heat swelters and the dust sparkles
empty he_l_ole	a t_ea_re of misery	There's no joy, no movement and no hope.
infla_ed brain	f_rn_ce-hot	I tramped, trudged and tottered across the sand.
b_rnt-c_rk colour	deh_d_ated	The sun blazes, the heat bakes and your skin boils.
stabbed by sun l_n_es	st_rl_t nights	Every barb, hook and thorn ripped us.
ski_te_ing lizards	slit_e_ing snakes	The desert is stark, sterile and savage.
old N_ck's oven	pa_c_ed throat	The desert is a hazy mirror of your own doom.
as hot as a dr_g_n's breath	as cold as a g_o_l's soul	hallucinations
an a_e_a of death	a fo_tsl_g	**DESERT TREES**
scu_t_ing scorpions	sw_l_en tongue	d_te palms
sweat sod_en	like ra_ia_ion in my brain	Jos_ua tree
ar_d wilderness	b_rnt-sienna colour	p_nc_ke cactus
the d_v_l's kitchen	like walking on h_t/coa_s	desert ir_nw_od
pa_c_ed throat	as cold as a ba_s_ee's soul	cha_n fruit

Using words or phrases in clusters of three is an impressive technique to use in your writing. Have one of the sentences above grabbed your attention? If so, it will do the same for the reader. It is called **triplication** and it is an important tool to use in a speech or debate.

CLASS IDEAS ON THE DESERT

"Inspiration is for amateurs. The rest of us just show up and get to work." Chuck Close

Date: __/__/__	Title: **DESCRIBING MALES: 4ᵗʰ GRID**	Lesson number:

Latin phrase: Aegrescit medendo.

Definition: B_r_/n_t/y_u_/h_u_e/t_/r_d/i_/o_/t_e/m_u_e.

Meaning: _____

_____

Spelling revision	New words	Dictionary definitions, corrections, and synonyms.
Sa_s_n	nom_d	
ox-yo_e	galw_y	
Atl_s	naut_c_l	
bra_ny	Socr_t_s	
fel_ne	wayf_r_r	
bur_y	mar_n_r	
gra_ite	Capta_n/Ah_b	

interesting blue eyes

1 POINT	2 POINTS	3 POINTS	4 POINTS
sea rov_r-blue	nom_d-blue	seaf_r_r-blue	trailb_az_r-blue
mar_n_r-blue	naut_c_l-blue	wayf_r_r-blue	Rasp_t_n-blue

beards

a goat_e	a sp_d_ shaped beard	a Mo_es beard	a Socr_t_s beard
a galw_y	a d_v_l's fork beard	an A_e/Li_co_n	a Capta_n/Ah_b

moustaches

bus_y	pen_il thin	a toot_b_u_h	a han_l_bar
brist_y	a mil_t_ry	a sm_g	a w_lr_s

stubble

da_k	gr_i_y	sa_d-rough	mo_ni_g/sh_d_w
coar_e	grit_y	de_i_ner	sa_t and pe_p_r

smiles

son_c	co_m_c	f_l_/st_r	conta_io_s
ang_l_c	ga_a_tic	rav_s_i_g	ele_t_if_ing

WRITING A SPORTS ESSAY

If you want to sprinkle some stardust on your sports essay, try to include some of the terms below. The sights, the sounds and the smells are just as important in this **genre** (i.e. **type** or style of essay) as any other. The main focus should be on demonising your opponents. This adds humour to your story. How did you feel afterwards? Were your opponents too rough? Did you wake up to the cheep-cheep sound of a heart monitor? Add drama to your essay!

demonising your opponent

like ca_e trolls from a f_b_e	f_led-down fangs	p_p eyes and sau_y beards	monsters from a g_re-fest
knu_k_es scraping the ground	b_a_y, glinting eyes	g_ou_s from a horror movie	se_i_l killer mentality

stormy stadium sounds

a to_n_do of sound	a bli_za_d of scores	a c_cl_ne of sound	a t_unami of sound
a hu_ri_ane of noise	a wh_rl_ool of rage	a v_l_ano of noise	a te_p_st of noise

creating atmosphere with onomatopoeia

ba_g_rs exploded	fi_e_orks whizzed	r_c_ets whooshed	thun_erlashes hissed
c_ac_ers popped	f_a_es sizzled	sq_i_s sissed	dr_m-rolls of d_om

your team was

cut to ri_b_ns	sh_ed_ed like tissue paper	like la_bs against rave_o_s wolves	like B_m_i on ice
like a_ts walking in trea_le	guilty of p_w_er-puff defending	smashed to smi_he_eens	tackling like B_r_ie d_l_s

your opponents were

sl_g slow	le_d_n footed	j_t heeled	Con_o_de-heeled
slo_h slow	l_w_mo_er slow	qu_c_si_ver fast	w_ll-o'-the-w_sp fast

dressing room smells

st_le air/old smells	ban_a_es and b_o_d	ar_pi_s/body odour	b_e_ch/disin_ect_nt
o_d/soc_s and s_eat	smelly boot ton_u_s	vo_it and u_i_e	cheap a_t_r/s_a_e

"Gold medals aren't really made of gold. They're made of sweat, determination and a hard-to-find alloy called guts."

Dan Gable

167

Date: __/__/__	Title: **DESCRIBING MALES: 5th GRID**	Lesson number:

Latin phrase: Dum spiro, spero.

Definition: Wh_le/I/bre_t_e, I/h_p_.

Meaning: _____

_____

Spelling revision	New words	Dictionary definitions, corrections, and synonyms.
nom_d	ub_r	
galw_y	swashb_c_ling	
naut_c_l	port_ls	
Socr_t_s	tous_ed	
wayf_r_r	trom_one	
mar_n_r	der_ing-do	
Capta_n/Ah_b	smoul_ering	

archaic words for eyes

1 POINT	2 POINTS	3 POINTS	4 POINTS
a-fi_e	a-g_ow	a-g_e_m	a-sp_r_le
a-fli_k_r	a-gli_m_r	a-l_g_t	a-t_i_k_e

deep voice

de_p	a ba_s voice	a tro_b_ne voice	a gr_t and g_a_y voice
bo_m_ng	ru_b_ing	a vol_a_ic voice	like bo_t_ed/th_n_er

personality

bal_n_ed	cha_m_ng	da_h_ng	d_v_l-may-ca_e
go_d-nat_r_d	win_i_g	d_na_ic	der_ing-do

clothes   what eyes are

snaz_y clothes	g_p/ye_r clothes	wi_d_ws to the soul	gat_w_ys to the soul
rit_y clothes	M_a_i/V_ce clothes	m_rr_rs of the soul	port_ls to the soul

others

ub_r-tanned	wind-tu_b_ed hair	smo_ld_ring eyes	f_ve o'c_o_k shadow
swashb_c_ling	wind-to_sl_d hair	expr_ss_ve eyes	mou_ta_n/pe_k cheekbones

Blue-Sky Thinking

The purpose of this exercise is to find the adjectives in the grid. When you have finished that, write them into the empty box below **with the noun they come before**. For example, if the words **pouting** (going down) and **sweeping** (going across) are in the grid, write them in thus:

pouting **lips**	sweeping **eyelashes**

FEMALE ADJECTIVES WORDSEARCH

e	r	i	d	o	c	o	r	a	l
k	b	f	i	n	e	s	p	u	n
l	m	r	v	m	o	i	t	p	e
s	o	m	a	g	n	e	t	i	c
f	c	h	e	r	u	b	a	x	t
l	h	v	o	a	k	m	r	i	a
a	a	k	x	j	a	s	p	e	r
x	m	a	b	b	r	o	e	a	i
e	g	l	o	s	s	y	r	s	n
n	b	u	w	i	n	p	t	r	e
a	n	s	l	s	w	a	n	p	d
c	e	h	s	t	e	l	l	a	r

MALE ADJECTIVES WORDSEARCH

w	e	n	j	k	i	n	g	l	y
r	a	p	t	o	r	s	r	o	c
d	l	a	n	g	u	l	a	r	l
j	r	b	u	r	l	y	i	d	a
d	o	m	e	d	u	f	n	l	n
a	o	k	a	t	p	a	y	y	t
p	s	a	p	m	a	r	b	l	e
p	t	c	o	s	m	i	c	h	r
e	e	b	l	o	h	t	a	l	n
r	r	a	l	n	c	z	w	t	a
u	f	s	o	i	g	y	q	c	s
a	c	s	e	c	r	a	g	g	y

FEMALE ACROSS	FEMALE DOWN	MALE ACROSS	MALE DOWN

WHAT'S UP WITH POETRY?

"We should run glittering like a brook in the open sunshine, or we are unblest."

William Wordsworth

Do you want to know what the greatest poem ever written is? The greatest poem ever written is the one *you* think is the greatest. Poetry is a great module for a student to enjoy (i.e. because you can never be wrong!) If you think a poem is excellent, then it is excellent. If you think a poem is terrible, then it is terrible. After a while, you might find yourself saying: "Well, it doesn't do anything for me, but I understand what the poet was trying to do….."

Congratulations. You are now a critic.

It is interesting that the word 'criticise' originally meant 'to evaluate' (i.e. to weigh up the merits of). When you are criticising a poem, try to see both the demerits and merits of it.

Some writers think that the meaning of a poem is its most important feature. Others think its mood should be explored first. This would include how it makes you feel. Quite a few consider that the techniques the poet used deserve a mention. This is important also. All of the above can be pared down to three simple questions.

1. What is the central message (i.e. **theme**) of the poem?

2. How does it make me feel (i.e. **tone**)?

3. How did the poet get his/her message across (i.e. **techniques**)?

These are the three most important questions in poetry. Three is the magic number when it comes to studying a poem. There is a formula to help you understand poetry later in the book.

Some poems can be epics. This means that they are very long. The classic example of this is 'The Rime of the Ancient Mariner' by Samuel Taylor Coleridge. Others can be very short and simple but still leave an impression. We shall look at 'Invitation' by Shel Silverstein as our first poem. It is a short poem. In the meantime, why not write down what you think of poetry? What is poetry? Use these metaphors if you wish and try to think of some more.

1. Poetry is a window to a hidden world.
2. Poetry is the mood music of English.
3. Poetry is what sad people with too much time on their hands do when they are lonely.
4. Poetry is dragonblood for the heart.
5. Poetry is what made Eminem, Shakira, The Beatles, and even The Spice Girls, zillionaires.
6. Poetry is the language of the soul and caviar for the mind.
7. Poetry is simply lyrics without the music.
8. Poetry is the sigh of the sea, the cry of the me, the dying of the bee.
9. Poetry is manna for the soul.
10. Poetry is wild, sad, funny, energetic, thoughtful, loud, fragile and zesty and has something everyone can enjoy.

'Invitation' by Shel Silverstein

"If you are a dreamer come in.
If you are a dreamer, a wisher, a liar,
A hope-er, a pray-er, a magic-bean-buyer…
If you're a pretender come sit by my fire,
For we have some flax golden tales to spin.
Come in!
Come in!"

Did you like this poem? Read it again and write down the first words that come into your head.

Now read it again and try to get into the rhythm of it by waving a finger in the air like a composer. Treat it like a song rather than a poem. Can you sing it to yourself? If you can, you have a high degree of musical intelligence.

Do you agree that it has got the rhythm of a child rocking in its cot for the first 4 lines? Then the rhythm takes on a serious, I-am-your-friend-now tone for the 5th line. For the final two lines you can almost see someone beckoning you in to his/her house. There, the two of you can spin "flax golden" tales and probably lie to each other about your adventures! Make up an adventure you would tell to someone who loves listening to stories and read it to the class.

Did you find that there is a special type of magic in the lines of this poem?

'Invitation' by Shel Silverstein

"If you are a dreamer come in.
If you are a dreamer, a wisher, a liar,
A hope-er, a pray-er, a magic-bean-buyer…
If you're a pretender come sit by my fire,
For we have some flax golden tales to spin.
Come in, come in, come in!"

Do you think the poem is improved by rewriting the last two lines? Say why or why not.

Count up how many times words are repeated. We know that this is called repetition and that it is a very effective technique. Can we add 'The Rule of Three' to repetition? This means that saying something three times (or in groups of three) is the perfect technique in a speech or poem. It makes the poem more memorable and it is the classic mnemonic device. How many times does Shel Silverstein use 'The Rule of Three' in his poem? Do lines two and three qualify for this rule?

Did you know? Psychologists believe that you can be seen to be a good listener by facing your feet towards the person talking. As they are making their point, nod your head three times slowly. They will then think highly of you because you value their opinion.

THE OLDEST SURVIVING POEM

The oldest surviving poem has not been discovered yet. It is locked away underground in a dusty vault waiting for someone to discover it. Maybe, one day, that someone will be you. Until then, the oldest, known surviving poem is called 'The Tale of the Shipwrecked Sailor'. It comes from the Middle Egyptian period and it is approx. 4,200 years old, giving it a date of 2,200 B.C.

The oldest known writing is a source of dispute. Many cultures used symbols. Even cave art, which is approx. 35,000 years old, had 26 separate symbols and they were used for 20,000 years! It is interesting that our English alphabet today contains 26 letters also. Contenders for the earliest form of writing include:

1. Chinese dating to 7,000 B.C.

2. Writing from Pakistan dating to 3,000 B.C.

3. Writing from Mexico dating from 3,000 B.C.

Most experts believe that writing dated from the use of farming, however, and comes from Sumer in Mesopotamia (i.e. the borders of Iraq, Iran and Syria) around 3,400 B.C. Counting tokens dating to 9,000 years old are probably the oldest form of symbol discovered and came from this area also. The Akkadian language from Sumer is considered the oldest at the moment but that may change. When grain began to be harvested and converted into bread (and beer!), many different cultures around the world gave up their hunter-gatherer ways. They needed a system to count animals, their plots of land and bushels of grain. Symbols written on small, clay tablets were used and then language began to be written down.

Poetry then developed as a form of mnemonic device so that people could remember stories of their ancestors and entertain each other with tales of courage and sorrow. When we began to domesticate animals, this became more important. Everyone had more time on their hands as there was a constant supply of food. Artists such as painters, poets, writers and skilled craftsmen were in high demand and could get paid for their work. Underneath is the reason why 'leisure time' overtook hunting and gathering and why people could settle in one place.

These are all approximate dates for when the animals were domesticated:

1. Dog-20,000 B.C.   Man and dog lethal at clearing areas of predators and protecting homes. Still vital for lions/tigers/wolves etc. in rural areas today as an early warning system.

2. Sheep-11,000 B.C.   Enabled bigger communities to prosper with woollen clothing.

3. Pig-9,000 B.C.   A very important source of food and led humans to mushrooms etc.

4. Goat-8,000 B.C.   A valuable source of milk and cheese and a permanent food source.

5. Cattle-8,000 B.C.   Humans could now plough fields and get cattle to carry large items.

6. Cat-8,000 B.C.   Great for keeping rodent numbers down if you were storing food.

7. Chicken-6,000 B.C.   An estimated 50 billion chickens alive today tells its own story.

8. Donkey-5,000 B.C.   Became a very adaptable beast of burden. Survives hostile climates.

9. Horse-4,000 B.C.   *The domestication of the horse probably coincided with the start of writing as we know it today. Humans could travel vast distances overland and trade their goods, both grain and luxury items. Writing started to become a crucial means of communication, first with math symbols, then with a common language. Art takes off.

10. Silkmoth-3,000 B.C.   The export of silk from China led to major international trading.

11. Pigeon-3,000 B.C.   Written messages could now be carried vast distances.

12. Turkey-180 A.D.   Christmas could be invented and celebrated properly!

This is considered the first poem written to be in existence today. It is 'The Tale of the Shipwrecked Sailor'. It is a story about a sailor who is announcing his return from a failed expedition. He is nervous of meeting his king, so the sailor's servant tells of how he (i.e. the servant) had overcome a previous disaster and that all will be well.

The Tale of the Shipwrecked Sailor

May your heart prosper, my master.

Behold, we have reached home.

The mallet having been taken, the mooring post is driven in.

The bow-rope having been placed on land, thanksgiving and praise to God are given.

Everyone is embracing his companions.

Our crew returned safely;

there was no loss to our army.

We have reached the end of Wawat;

we have passed Senmut.

Do you like this poem? Write down your first impressions of the poem in a few words. Do you like the fact that internet technology makes all these poems available at our fingertips?

Look up the words you don't understand on Google and see if the place names in the last two lines still exist today. The full text of the poem can be read at: **ancient.eu.com**.

The first epic tale written is thought to be 'The Epic of Gilgamesh'. It was written approx. 2,600 B.C. This is an extract from it and the author is describing Gilgamesh, king of Uruk. Although it is older than 'The Tale of the Shipwrecked Sailor', it is more of a tale than a poem. Therefore, 'The Tale of the Shipwrecked Sailor' is considered the oldest poem.

The Epic of Gilgamesh

Supreme over other kings, lordly in appearance

he is the hero, born of Uruk, the goring wild bull.

He walks out in front, the leader

and walks at the rear, trusted by his companions.

Mighty net, protector of his people,

raging flood-wave who destroys even walls of stone!

Offspring of Lugalbanda, Gilgamesh, is strong to perfection,

son of the august cow, Rimat-Ninsun.......Gilgamesh is awesome to perfection.

It was he who opened the mountain passes,

who dug wells on the flank of the mountain.

It is he who crossed the ocean, the vast seas, to the rising son,

who explored the world regions, seeking life.

Write down the first words that come to mind after the first reading.

Do you think this is a better poem than 'The Tale of the Shipwrecked Sailor'?

Who do you think Gilgamesh is? Is he a man, a god or something else?

Are you surprised at the quality of language from poems 4,000 years old? Do you think you would enjoy listening to these poems and tales if they were accompanied by music?

Of course, there is no evidence that these poems would have been accompanied by music. The earliest evidence of a poem accompanied to music dates from 1,400 B.C. Remarkably, you can listen to it on YouTube. It is called 'The Hurrian Hymn no.6' and it was discovered in Syria in the 1950's as part of a collection of clay tablets. Musical instructions came with the song and it would have been accompanied by a lyre, a stringed instrument used before the guitar. It is well worth listening to and the finish to the song may surprise you.

Did you know? The earliest message in a bottle comes from 1784. A man called Chunosuke Matsuyama asked for rescue after he was shipwrecked. Alas for him, it was found in 1935.

Extract from The Poem Voted the Best Song of all Time in Ireland

'Hallelujah' by Jeff Buckley

"Well I heard there was a secret chord

that David played and it pleased the Lord

But you don't really care for music, do you?

Well it goes like this:

The Fourth, The Fifth,

The minor fall and the major lift

The baffled king composing Hallelujah.

Hallelujah, hallelujah, hallelujah

Hallelujah......

Your faith was strong but you needed proof

You saw her bathing on the roof

Her beauty and the moonlight overthrew you.

She tied you to her kitchen chair

She broke your throne and she cut your hair

And from your lips she drew the Hallelujah.

Hallelujah, hallelujah, hallelujah

Hallelujah......

Just like all poems, this song is better listened to rather than read on your own. You should write out the rest of the lyrics and then listen to the full song on YouTube.

You might find it interesting that the lines of the song are written out in groups of 3. This makes it a very mnemonic poem for the listener. Similarly, the refrain (i.e. chorus) of Hallelujah is sung 3 times. Then it is repeated once in a much longer way. The repetition of the word is catchy and this helps the listener to absorb the song. The next page has a diagram that shows how 'The Rule of Three' can make poetry very easy to understand and appreciate.

THE SECRET TO GREAT POETRY: THE RULE OF THREE

FIGURATIVE LANGUAGE

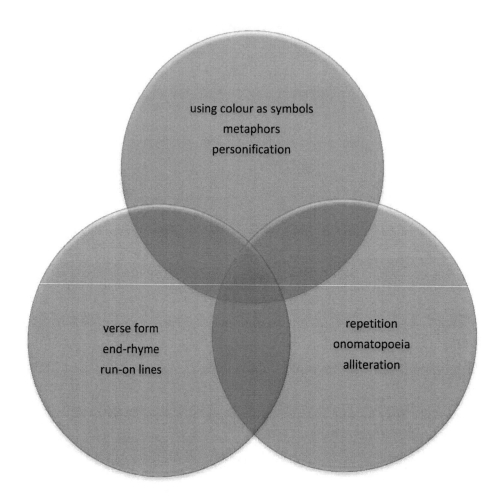

using colour as symbols
metaphors
personification

verse form
end-rhyme
run-on lines

repetition
onomatopoeia
alliteration

MECHANICAL DEVICES   **MNEMONIC TECHNIQUES**

The only question is to figure out where to put the following:

a) imagery

b) rhythm

c) theme

d) tone.

Put the most important of the three into the centre circle. Then put the other three carefully into the intersecting circles.

We've already discussed what the greatest poem ever written was. It is the one you think is the greatest. The most *successful* poems of all time are easier to talk about. The third most successful poem of all time is called 'Auld Lang Syne'. It was written by the poet Robert Burns in 1788. It is usually sung on New Year's Eve and at funerals and graduations. The title means 'For Old Times (Sake)'.

Interestingly, Robert Burns said the following of his poem:

"The following song is an old song of the olden times, and which had never been in print, nor even in a manuscript, until I took it down from an old man."

This means the poem was probably in existence for hundreds of years before Burns got it from the old man. The chorus also follows 'The Rule of Three', making it easier to remember as a poem. These are the words, although Burns admits he changed them slightly:

"Should Old Acquaintance be forgot,

and never thought upon;

The flames of Love extinguished,

and fully past and gone;

Is thy sweet Heart now grown so cold,

that loving Breast of thine;

That thou canst never once reflect

On Old long syne.

Chorus:

> *On Old long syne my Jo,*
>
> *On Old long syne,*
>
> *That thou canst never once reflect,*
>
> *On Old long syne.*

You should look up the song on YouTube and listen to the melody. Although it is a catchy song, the secret of its success is simpler. The chorus (i.e. the words *Old long syne*) is repeated three times. This would have made it a very mnemonic song for different generations of Scots people to remember. The old man and his people before him would have had the words burned into their minds before ironically Robert Burns came along and wrote it down. You should see how long it takes to learn the poem by singing it to yourself.

The second most popular poem in history is called 'For He's a Jolly Good Fellow'. It was written the night after the Battle of Malplaquet in France in 1709. Marie Antoinette then made it popular after she heard a maid singing it. By the 1850's it was being sung in the United Kingdom and it reached America in 1862. Like 'Auld Lang Syne', its genius lies in its simplicity and the rule of three.

These are the words used in the United Kingdom:

For he's a jolly good fellow, for he's a jolly good fellow

For he's a jolly good fellow (pause), and so say all of us

And so say all of us, and so say all of us

For he's a jolly good fellow, for he's a jolly good fellow

For he's a jolly good fellow (pause), and so say all of us

As you can see, it is a simple poem. The same two phrases are repeated three times and the poem finishes with an extra repetition of: "and so say all of us." This balances the lines very well. The question students may ask is if the last two examples are poems, melodies or songs? The answer is that they are all three.

Music and poetry have been best friends since man first sang. If you are singing, you need something to sing about. The lines must be written in verse form or else the poem/song will lack rhythm. Most musicians write the lyrics before composing the song. This means that musicians are poets before they become singers.

In order to understand poetry fully, it should be seen from the point of view of music first. This brings us to the most successful poem of all time. It was written in 1893 by two sisters who were teaching in Lexington, America. Everyone knows the lyrics and they go like this:

Happy Birthday to you.

Happy Birthday to you.

Happy Birthday dear………….

Happy Birthday to you.

Once again, the line 'Happy Birthday to you" is repeated three times. The 3rd line balances the rhythm beautifully in between. Looking at poetry from the point of view of having three basic parts is a good start. After that, it gets a bit more complicated! Did you know that Warner-Chappell Music Ltd. own the copyright to Happy Birthday? Technically, you should be paying them a fee whenever you sing it. As it is, the song brings in $5,000 a day for them in royalties. Every time it is used in a film, they charge the producers up to $50,000.

NURSERY RHYMES

The link between music and poetry is at its most obvious with nursery rhymes. Nursery rhymes are the most successful, long-lasting poems ever written.

They lasted hundreds of years without being written down and became even more popular when they *were* written down. Even in this computer age, children still learn them easily and remember them.

Is it because they are mnemonic poems? That is the main reason but there are others also. Let's test our formula for great poetry on one of the more famous: Ring-a-ring o' Roses.

Ring-a-ring o' roses

A pocket full of posies,

A-tishoo! A-tishoo!

We all fall down!

Figurative language:

Using colour as symbols: The rose-coloured rings on line 1are the bright red circles people used to get from the Black Death in England. The white handkerchiefs (or posies) on line 2 may refer to the scented handkerchiefs rich people tied around their mouths to hide the smell of death. Poor people also carried sweet-smelling flowers in their pockets to mask the smell.
Red: A symbol of d_a_h.
White: A symbol of in_oc_n_e.

Metaphors: The nursery rhyme is a metaphor for the Black Death. It is possible that peasants believed sneezing was a symptom of the disease. The 3rd/ 4th lines mean that if you sneezed, you were going to get the disease and "fall down" dead. "Fall down" is a metaphor for death.

Personification: Personification is giving things human terms. By singing about death as a constant companion, people were trying to cope with the horror of the 17th century. Death and disease are personified as something that could strike at any time. In modern times, a funeral mass and a burial give people a lot of comfort. Unfortunately, people back then didn't have that luxury. The bodies were burned or just left there in many villages if there weren't enough people left to bury them. That's why death is personified as an imaginary friend in this rhyme.

We can see that all three figurative devices are present in this nursery rhyme. The use of colour as symbols, the use of metaphors and the use of personification helped to make the poem memorable. Let us look at the other two circles in the formula next.

Mechanical techniques:

A simple verse form: The verse form chosen is as simple as it can get.

End-rhyme: Children sing it as 'rosies' instead of 'roses'. This makes it rhyme perfectly with 'posies'. This in turn adds to the mnemonic effect.

Run-on lines: The lines run into each other fluently. It gives the rhyme its breathless and energetic effect.

All three mechanical techniques are present. Poems that have end-rhyme and run-on lines are catchier than those that don't. That is one reason why nursery rhymes survived for so long.

Mnemonic techniques:

Repetition: It is used twice. The word 'ring' is repeated, as is 'A-tishoo'. This makes it simpler for children to remember.

Onomatopoeia: It is used with the words 'a-tishoo'. This helps the children to act out the sneezing. In this case, it is a form of 'active learning' where a child can act out the event.

Alliteration: The 3 r's, the 2 p's and the 2 t's make this the ultimate mnemonic rhyme for a child. There is nothing complicated to this nursery rhyme.

All three mnemonic devices are present. These make this rhyme a pumping, pulsing mnemonic poem. It proves the old adage: "In simplicity lies genius."

'Ring-a-ring o' Roses' has a timeless appeal that has survived disease, war, famine, drought and floods. There is a debate ongoing about whether it is actually about the Black Death or not. Occam's razor would lead most people to conclude that it is. It first appeared in written form in Kate Greenaway's book of nursery rhymes in 1881. To this day, children love its sense of rhythm, its simple structure and its plain language. Does all great poetry have to use the techniques shown here? The answer is no. All *memorable* poetry does, however. Most of the poems we would consider classics use these simple devices and many others besides. It makes sense that a poem you find easy to recite will be favoured over one you don't find easy.

A lot of great poems may not use all of these techniques. They rely instead on a powerful theme or message which brings meaning to peoples' lives. Before we look at a poem like that, try to apply the formula of great poetry to the nursery rhyme 'Baa-baa black sheep'. The rhyme was invented as a protest against woollen taxes by Edward 1 of England in 1275. This makes it nearly 1,000 years old. Edward put a tax of 66% on all wool and the original verse had the little boy down the lane crying! The crying boy was a metaphor for the sheep farmers.

Baa-baa black sheep

Baa-baa black sheep,

Have you any wool?

Yes sir, yes sir,

Three bags full.

One for the master

And one for the dame

And one for the little boy

Crying down the lane.

Figurative language:

Using colour as symbols:

Metaphors:

Personification:

Mechanical techniques:

A simple verse form:

End-rhyme:

Run-on lines:

Mnemonic techniques:

Repetition:

Onomatopoeia:

Alliteration:

In simplicity lies genius. The answer is that it uses all of the 9 techniques that mega-successful poems have in common. It also has a regular rhythm. In fact, if you think about it carefully, it has the same tune as two other highly successful mnemonics.

These are 'Twinkle Twinkle Little Star' and 'The Alphabet song'. Can you spot the similarities by humming out the two nursery rhymes?

Twinkle, twinkle, little star,

How I wonder what you are.

Up above the world so high,

Like a diamond in the sky.

Now try it for 'The Alphabet song'.

A-B-C-D-E-F-G

H-I-J-K-LMNO-P

Q-R-S; T-U-V,

W; X, Y and Z.

Now I know my ABC;

Next time won't you sing with me?!

Hopefully, you can now see that all great poems may have something in common with each other. They have a regular rhythm, they use end-rhyme and they use the techniques in the circle. Sometimes, a poem of genius can spring up without using these techniques, however...

'THE FOG' by Carl Sandburg (1878-1967)

The fog comes

on little cat feet.

It sits looking

over harbour and city

on silent haunches

and then moves on.

Read this poem once. Write out the first word or phrase that springs to mind after reading it.

Now read it again aloud. Are there any other words or phrases that spring to mind?

The poem has a magical quality that seems to affect everyone who reads it. It is a very simple poem but it may have layers of meaning. Answer the following questions in your copybook once you have read it three times.

1. Do you like this poem? Why? Why not?

2. Is there a message in this poem? What do you think it might be?

3. What do you think the cat in the poem represents?

4. Do you think this poem is about fog or something else? What might the fog represent?

5. Write down, or draw if you are able, the main image that this poem gives you.

This poem is an example of 'free verse'. It does not rhyme and does not have a regular rhythm. Write a poem called 'The fog cat' in free verse or rhyme. Try to do it in 50 words or less. If you find yourself stuck for a rhyming word, look up **rhymer.com**.

Figurative language: Finish the sentences in the grids. A symbol is an object that can represent something else like an idea, an emotion or a quality. Fill in the blank grids where necessary.

Example: The dove is a symbol of peace.

Using colour as symbols: The grey fog is a symbol of m_s_e_y and d_n_er.

Metaphors: The fog is a metaphor for how qu_c_ly our l_v_s start and end.

Personification: The fog is personified because it is given "li_t_e cat f_et."

Mechanical language:

A simple verse form: It is written in a simple, free v_r_e form.

End-rhyme:

Run on lines: There are 6 run on lines as there are only two f_ll st_ps but there are six l_n_s.

Mnemonic language:

Repetition:

Onomatopoeia:

Alliteration:

Count up how many of the above techniques Carl Sandburg used. Are you impressed with the skill it takes to write a simple poem like this? Make a list of the 6 assonance words and see if the 'o's' rhyme or if they are half-rhymes. You may be surprised at the result!

Assonance

WRITING A POEM

Writing a poem is great fun. The simplest form of poetry is called a haiku (pronounced high-kuu). This is a Japanese term meaning 'amusement'. Haikus are usually written about nature or the seasons but they are also written as jokes. Most modern haikus have a structure of 5-7-5. This means there are 5 syllables on the first line, 7 syllables on the second line and 5 syllables on the third line. This is not a golden rule, however. Do you think the haiku underneath has a 5-7-5 structure?

Haiku's are easy

Don't even have to make sense

Hippopotamus

Write down one reason why you liked this haiku. Did it make you smile or laugh?

Here are some of the most famous haikus:

An old silent pond....

A frog jumps into the pond

Splash! Silence again.　　　Basho Matsuo

Do you like this haiku? Does it conjure up a specific image in your mind? Write down, or draw if you can, the image given to you by this poem. Then write down some reasons why you did or did not like the haiku. Would you prefer a haiku like these?

Over the wintry

forest, winds howl in rage

with no leaves to blow.　　　Natsume Soseki

I kill an ant

and realise my three children

have been watching.　　　Kato Shuson

Which was the best haiku, in your opinion? Write down why you feel it is the best and explain whether it gives you a certain image or feeling, or both.

Hai	ku's	are	ea	sy

Don't	ev	en	have	to	make	sense

Hipp	o	pot	a	mus

If you were to take a photograph of your back garden every day of the year, you would have a lot of photographs. That is how the brain works also. Every image we see is put away into a bundle for storage. What if you were to select only one photograph to represent each season, however? This is what we might call a 'snapshot' of the season. That is what a haiku is; a snapshot of a season or nature. Follow these easy steps to build your haiku's for the seasons:

1. Pick the best **word-bundle** (i.e. word-grid) from your brain that represents spring. Write out the entire list. It may include lambs, frog spawn, daffodils, nesting birds etc.

2. Pick two nouns that you think represent spring the best. Then pick two verbs to link your images to each other. These may be lambs **leaping**, daffodils **growing** etc.

3. Try to create a scene where the two nouns and verbs have a link to each other. Practise until you're happy the syllable structure of 5-7-5 will fit into the grids. Read it to a classmate.

SPRING

SUMMER

AUTUMN

WINTER

HOW TO MAKE YOUR OWN POEM

Making up your own poem is both easy and enjoyable. It helps if you can think of one phrase/metaphor or short sentence that is unique to you. The whole poem should then spring up around this one, meaningful phrase. **Observe** the world around you and it will provide it!

Then try to get your end-rhyme words if you want to make it a mnemonic poem. Make a list of 8-10 words that fit in with the theme of your poem. Type in **'Word Families'** to: **enchantedlearning.com** for the best sets of end-rhymes.

Finally, try experimenting with the length of the sentences until they seem right to you. You may decide to have a poem that has balance and rhythm. If so, use the syllable grid below to help you. Try to keep the poem simple at first with a maximum of 12 syllables.

As you develop your craft as a poet, you will find yourself delighted with your ability to write great poetry. If you want to make a sad poem, look at the assonance words in this book.

SYLLABLE GRID FOR AN 8-LINE POEM

END-RHYME GRID

attack	bad	ail	brain	blame	bright	bin	fog	core	bump
back	clad	fail	chain	fame	delight	din	bog	fore	clump
black	dad	hail	grain	flame	fight	fin	flog	gore	dump
crack	glad	mail	main	frame	fright	gin	grog	lore	grump
knack	had	nail	pain	game	height	grin	hog	ore	jump
lack	lad	pail	plain	lame	light	kin	jog	pore	lump
pack	mad	rail	rain	name	night	pin	log	score	slump
sack	pad	sail	slain	same	sight	sin	slog	shore	stump
stack	sad	tail	strain	shame	slight	thin	smog	wore	thump
whack	tad	wail	train	tame	tonight	win	tog	yore	trump

MAKE YOUR OWN RHYMING GRID

'THE EAGLE' by Alfred Lord Tennyson (1809-1892)

He clasps the crag with crooked hands;

close to the sun in lonely lands,

ring'd with the azure world he stands.

The wrinkled sea beneath him crawls;

he watches from his mountain walls,

and like a thunderbolt he falls.

,

* A crag is a rocky ledge.

* Azure is a deep sea-blue.

Read this poem once. Write out the first word or phrase that springs to mind after reading it.

Now read it again aloud. Are there any other words or phrases that spring to mind?

CREATIVE WRITING QUESTIONS

1. Did you like this poem? Say why/why not giving examples from the poem.

2. What do you think is the theme (i.e. central message) of the poem? Are there sub-themes in it as well, in your opinion? A sub-theme is not the main theme but it is still important.

3. Try to write a 6-line poem with the same title.

4. What are the best images in the poem, in your opinion? Give examples from the poem.

5. Write a short descriptive passage on what the eagle sees from the mountain top. Include as much micro-detail as possible. He has eagle-vision, after all!

6. What is the mood of the poem, in your opinion?

You are the world's greatest poetry detective. Find one example for each technique.

Figurative language:

Using colour as symbols:

Metaphors:

Personification:

Mechanical language:

Verse form:

End-rhyme:

Run on lines:

Mnemonic language:

Repetition:

Onomatopoeia:

Alliteration:

'THE SPLENDOUR FALLS' by Alfred Lord Tennyson (1809-1892)

The splendour falls on castle walls

And snowy summits old in story:

The long light shakes across the lakes,

And the wild cataract leaps in glory.

Blow, bugle, blow, set the wild echoes flying.

Blow, bugle; answer, echoes, dying, dying, dying.

O hark, O hear! how thin and clear,

And thinner, clearer, farther going!

O sweet and far from cliff and scar

The horns of Elfland faintly blowing!

Blow, let us hear the purple glens replying!

Blow, bugle; answer, echoes, dying, dying, dying.

O love, they die in yon rich sky,

They faint on hill or field or river.

Our echoes roll from soul to soul,

And grow for ever and for ever.

Blow, bugle, blow, set the wild echoes flying.

Blow, bugle; answer, echoes, dying, dying, dying.

Read this poem once. Write out the first word or phrase that springs to mind after reading it.

Now read it again aloud. Are there any other words or phrases that spring to mind?

CREATIVE WRITING QUESTIONS

1. Did you like this poem? Say why/why not giving examples from the poem.

2. What do you think is the theme of the poem? Are there sub-themes in it as well, in your opinion? Write down what you think they may be.

3. Try to write a 6-line poem with the same title.

4. What are the best images in the poem, in your opinion? Give examples from the poem.

5. Write a description of the waterfall and lake using the images the poet has provided.

6. What is the mood of the poem, in your opinion? Can this poem be sung instead of read?

POSITIVE MOODS/TONES IN A POEM

carefree	energetic	tranquil	lively	gushy
light-hearted	tender	excited	humorous	peaceful
relaxed	chipper	relaxed	dream-like	gleeful
joyous	playful	bouncy	optimistic	musical
sentimental	welcoming	joyous	funny	refreshing
mellow	passionate	empowering	liberating	ecstatic

NEGATIVE MOODS/TONES IN A POEM

angry	haunting	bossy	lonely	hopeless
cold	grave	worried	tense	sombre
bitter	brooding	suspenseful	outraged	frantic
mocking	envious	sad	gloomy	harsh
ominous	painful	direct	sinister	gloomy
despairing	heartbroken	terrifying	foreboding	nightmarish

ADD IN MORE MOOD WORDS

You are the world's greatest poetry detective. Find one example for each technique.

Figurative language:

Using colour as symbols:

Metaphors:

Personification:

Mechanical language:

Verse form:

End-rhyme:

Run on lines:

Mnemonic language:

Repetition:

Onomatopoeia:

Alliteration:

'THE STOLEN CHILD' by W.B. Yeats (1865-1939)

Where dips the rocky highland

Of Sleuth Wood in the lake

There lies a leafy island

Where flapping herons wake

The drowsy water rats;

There we've hid our faery vats

Full of berries

And of reddest stolen cherries.

REFRAIN: *Come away, O human child!*

To the waters and the wild

With a faery hand in hand.

For the world's more full of weeping than you can understand.

Where the wave of moonlight glosses

The dim gray sands with light

Far off by furthest Rosses

We foot it all the night,

Weaving olden dances

Mingling hands and mingling glances

Till the moon has taken flight;

To and fro we leap

And chase the frothy bubbles,

When the world is full of troubles

And is anxious in its sleep

REFRAIN: *Come away, O human child! etc.*

Where the wandering water gushes

From the hills above Glencar,

In pools among the rushes

That scarce could bathe a star,

We seek for slumbering trout

And whispering in their ears

Give them unquiet dreams;

Leaning softly out

From ferns that drop their tears

Over the young streams.

REFRAIN: *Come away, O human child! etc.*

Away with us he's going,

The solemn-eyed:

He'll hear no more the lowing

Of the calves on the warm hillside

Or the kettle on the hob

Sing peace into his breast,

Or see the brown mice bob

Round and round the oatmeal chest.

For he comes, the human child!

To the waters and the wild

With a faery hand in hand.

For the world's more full of weeping than you can understand.

Read this poem once. Write out the first word or phrase that springs to mind after reading it.

Now read it again aloud. Are there any other words or phrases that spring to mind?

CREATIVE WRITING QUESTIONS

1. Did you like this poem? Say why/why not giving examples from the poem.

2. What do you think is the theme of the poem? Are there sub-themes in it as well, in your opinion? Write down what you think they may be.

3. Try to write a 6-line poem with the same title.

4. What are the best images in the poem, in your opinion? Give examples from the poem.

5. If you were asked to rewrite one word or line from the poem, which would it be?

6. What is the mood of the poem, in your opinion?

7. Ask your teacher to play the YouTube video on the poem. Type in: 'The Waterboys The Stolen Child by Mick Wilbury'. It flashes up images of an Ireland long gone.

8. Has your opinion of the poem changed after watching the video? Do you like the poem more or less after watching it?

9. Learn off any verse from the poem. Some have 8 lines, some have 11. Pick the one you like the most. You may find it easier to act out the lines while you are learning it. For example, verse one gives you the opportunity to do the following:

1. ….."dips the rocky highland." Make a hand motion from shoulder height to knee height when you are reciting the word "dips".

2. ….."lies a leafy island." Make a swirling motion with your hand when you are reciting the word "leafy". You can lie on the desk for the word "lies" if you are confident enough!

3. ….."flapping." You can clap or you can make a flapping motion.

4. ….."drowsy water rats." Put two hands to your cheek in the universal sign of sleeping.

These are just examples. The teacher can agree with the class which movements are the best for each line. Active learning helps you to remember poetry in a fun and long-term way. You'll be able to recite the lines many years from now. You'll also smile at the memory of this class when you do.

You are the world's greatest poetry detective. Find one example for each technique.

Figurative language:

> Using colour as symbols:

> Metaphors:

> Personification:

Mechanical language:

> Verse form:

> End-rhyme:

> Run on lines:

Mnemonic language:

> Repetition:

> Onomatopoeia:

> Alliteration:

'THE LAKE ISLE OF INNISFREE' by W.B. Yeats (1865-1939)

I will arise and go now, and go to Innisfree,

And a small cabin build there, of clay and wattles made;

Nine bean rows will I have there, a hive for the honey bee,

And live alone in the bee-loud glade.

And I shall have some peace there, for peace comes dropping slow,

Dropping from the veils of the morning to where the cricket sings;

There midnight's all a-glimmer, and noon a purple glow,

And evening full of the linnet's wings.

I will arise and go now, for always night and day

I hear lake water lapping with low sounds by the shore;

While I stand on the roadway, or on pavements gray,

I hear it in the deep heart's core.

Read this poem once. Write out the first word or phrase that springs to mind after reading it.

Now read it again aloud. Are there any other words or phrases that spring to mind?

CREATIVE WRITING QUESTIONS

1. Did you like this poem? Say why/why not giving examples from the poem.

2. What do you think is the theme of the poem? Are there sub-themes in it as well, in your opinion? Write down what you think they may be.

3. Try to write a 6-line poem with the same title.

4. What are the best images in the poem, in your opinion? Give examples from the poem.

5. If you were asked to rewrite one word or line from the poem, which would it be? Write out the word or line.

6. What is the mood of the poem, in your opinion?

7. Write a description of the island and the lake (Lough Gill) using the images the poet has provided.

ABOUT THE POEM

STANZA 1: This is a poem written in 1893 about escaping from city life. Yeats says he will build a small cabin on the uninhabited island of Innisfree in Co. Sligo. He will make it from mud and sticks and he will grow beans to live on. He will also keep bees and live a simple existence. In his mind, it is a form of heaven to live off the land. It is obvious he does not want to depend on anyone and would prefer to live alone. He shows that he is a dreamer because it is not a very realistic plan. The tone of the first stanza is both dreamy and musical. The repetition of the 'b' sound in "bean/bee/bee" gives it a humming quality also. The repetition of the lilting and soft 'i' sound in "nine/I/hive/live" adds to the musical effect.

STANZA 2: This stanza gives us both colour and the suggestion of colour. He starts with the metaphor for mist, the "veils of the morning". You are given an image of grey lake-mist just above the water and creeping over to the island. On the island the green grasshopper "sings" by rubbing his legs. "Midnight's all a-glimmer" tell us that parts of the island are dark and mysterious. It gives us a sense of how wild and lonely this island with black shadows is. "Noon a purple glow" shows how deep the colours are around this island. It suggests that they are lodged deep in his memory also. Finally, the fawn-coloured linnet flaps his wings. The only sounds so far are the bees, the cricket and the linnet on this island. These are all soft sounds and emphasise how isolated the island is.

STANZA 3: The last stanza has a very mellow and sad tone in the first two lines. The 5 words with 'l' in them (will/always/lake/lapping/low) try to recreate the sound of lake water lapping against the shore. The long 'o' sounds (go/now/low/shore) ensure that the lines have to be read slowly. Yeats is trying to show how the lake island has a grip on his mind, his memory and his soul. He calls it the "deep heart's core." Even when he is on the "pavement" of big cities like London, the water laps slowly like a heartbeat. Someday he will go back.

You are the world's greatest poetry detective. Find one example for each technique.

Figurative language:

Using colour as symbols:

Metaphors:

Personification:

Mechanical language:

Verse form:

End-rhyme:

Run on lines:

Mnemonic language:

Repetition:

Onomatopoeia:

Alliteration:

'THE ROAD NOT TAKEN' by Robert Frost (1874-1963)

Two roads diverged in a yellow wood,

And sorry I could not travel both

And be one traveller, long I stood

And looked down one as far as I could

To where it bent in the undergrowth;

Then took the other, as just as fair

And having perhaps the better claim,

Because it was grassy and wanted wear;

Though as for that the passing there

Had worn them really about the same.

And both that morning equally lay

In leaves no step had trodden black.

Oh, I kept the first for another day!

Yet knowing how way leads on to way,

I doubted if I should ever come back.

I shall be telling this with a sigh

Somewhere ages and ages hence:

Two words diverged in a yellow wood, and I-

I took the one less travelled by,

And that has made all the difference.

Read this poem once. Write out the first word or phrase that springs to mind after reading it.

Now read it again aloud. Are there any other words or phrases that spring to mind?

CREATIVE WRITING QUESTIONS

1. Did you like this poem? Say why/why not giving examples from the poem.

2. What do you think is the theme of the poem? Are there sub-themes in it as well, in your opinion? Write down what you think they may be.

3. Try to write a 6-line poem with the same title.

4. What are the best images in the poem, in your opinion? Give examples from the poem.

5. If you were asked to rewrite one word or line from the poem, which would it be? Write out the word or line.

6. What is the mood of the poem, in your opinion?

7. Look up the comments and how it is rated on the net by typing in: 'The Road Not Taken' to **poemhunter.com**

ABOUT THE POEM

This is what is known as a cryptic poem. A cryptic poem can be difficult to understand at first. It has a simple theme for everyone once you consider it carefully.

Everyone has two paths in life they can travel on. You can 'go with the herd' or you can strike out by yourself. If you decide to achieve all the things in life that you dream of, you are a rare person. You are taking the road less travelled. It is difficult to 'break the mould' and be yourself. Frost has the same dilemma.

He sees two roads in the forest. One looks less well-worn because very few people have travelled on it. This is a metaphor for the choices we all face in life. Do we take the road everyone else takes even when we know it is wrong for us?

Frost decides to take the road less travelled. He doesn't say whether it was a success or not. The good news is that if you take the road less travelled, you will meet other extraordinary people along the way. Whether you want to be a poet, a pilot, a politician or a pop star-do it!

'STOPPING BY WOODS ON A SNOWY EVENING' by Robert Frost (1874-1963)

Whose woods these are I think I know.

His house is in the village though;

He will not see me stopping here

To watch his woods fill up with snow.

My little horse must think it queer

To stop without a farmhouse near

Between the woods and frozen lake

The darkest evening of the year.

He gives his harness bells a shake

To ask if there is some mistake.

The only other sound's the sweep

Of easy wind and downy flake.

The woods are lovely, dark and deep,

But I have promises to keep.

And miles to go before I sleep,

And miles to go before I sleep.

Read this poem once. Write out the first word or phrase that springs to mind after reading it.

'STOPPING BY WOODS ON A SNOWY EVENING' by Robert Frost (1874-1963)

Now read it again aloud. Are there any other words or phrases that spring to mind?

CREATIVE WRITING QUESTIONS

1. Did you like this poem? Say why/why not giving examples from the poem.

2. What do you think is the theme of the poem? Are there sub-themes in it as well, in your opinion? Write down what you think they may be.

3. Try to write a 6-line poem with the same title.

4. What are the best images in the poem, in your opinion? Give examples from the poem.

5. If you were asked to rewrite one word or line from the poem, which would it be? Write out the word or line.

6. What is the mood of the poem, in your opinion?

ABOUT THE POEM

This poem is based on a real incident in Robert Frost's life. He was returning home one evening from a failed business trip to the market. It was snowing heavily in New Hampshire, America. New Hampshire is 212 miles from New York and is close to the border with Canada.

Frost could not sell his goods and it occurred to him that he could not buy Christmas presents for his children. He had a sleigh attached to the horse in order to transport his goods. He came to a bend in the road and stopped the horse. Then he began to cry uncontrollably. After a few minutes, the horse shook his harness. The bells on the harness had an effect on Frost. He snapped out of his depression. Then he moved towards home even though he had bad news for his family. He wrote this poem in one night at a later date.

Frost himself said that this poem is over-analysed. Its genius lies in the simple language, its simple rhythm and its simple message. It has a universal theme that everyone can relate to. Sometimes in life we are going to face great challenges. We can bow down to them or we can rise to meet them. In this poem, Frost uses the woods as a symbol of his depression. He struggled with it a lot in life.

Like depression, they are "dark and deep" and want to lure him in. That is why he calls them "lovely" also. Depression can creep up on adults without them being aware of it. In this case, he sees it as a choice. He decides to beat his depression by going home and facing up to his responsibilities. This time Frost wins. He has "many miles to go" before he sleeps. In this case, sleep is probably a metaphor for death or suicide. It is a very powerful poem.

'THE RIME OF THE ANCIENT MARINER' by Samuel Coleridge (1772-1834)

The fair breeze blew, the white foam flew,

The furrow followed free;

We were the first that ever burst

Into that silent sea.

Down dropt the breeze, the sails dropt down,

'Twas sad as sad could be;

And we did speak only to break

The silence of the sea!

All in a hot and copper sky,

The bloody sun, at noon,

Right up above the mast did stand,

No bigger than the moon.

Day after day, day after day,

We stuck, nor breath nor motion;

As idle as a painted ship

Upon a painted ocean.

Water, water, everywhere,

And all the boards did shrink;

Water, water, everywhere,

Nor any drop to drink.

Read this poem once. Write out the first word or phrase that springs to mind after reading it.

Now read it again aloud. Are there any other words or phrases that spring to mind?

CREATIVE WRITING QUESTIONS

1. Did you like this poem? Say why/why not giving examples from the poem.

2. What do you think is the theme of the poem? Are there sub-themes in it as well, in your opinion? Write down what you think they may be.

3. Try to write a 6-line poem with the same title.

4. What are the best images in the poem, in your opinion? Give examples from the poem.

5. What is the mood of the poem, in your opinion?

ABOUT THE POEM

In the spring of 1798, three people were walking in the hills of Somerset. One of them was Samuel Taylor Coleridge, who was an up-and-coming poet. William Wordsworth and his sister Dorothy were the others. The conversation turned to a book that Wordsworth was reading, 'A Voyage Round the World by Way of the Great South Sea'. It was written in 1726 by Captain George Shelvocke. In the book, a sailor shot an albatross and the ship suffered bad luck afterwards.

Coleridge had also read James Cook's second voyage of exploration (1772-1775). Coleridge's tutor had served on Cook's ship and he was fascinated by the tales of trying to break through the ice. These were probably the biggest influence on Coleridge's poem. The plot is this:

It starts with a mariner who meets someone on the way to a wedding party. The mariner is cursed to forever roam the earth telling his story. He was on board a ship in Antarctica which hit a storm. An albatross leads them out of the storm but for no reason the mariner shoots it. The weather improves at first and the crew praise him. Then the ship sails to a place where there is no wind and the sun burns them terribly. The crew force the mariner to wear the dead albatross around his neck. One by one, they all die, leaving the mariner alone. After many adventures, the mariner's curse is lifted when the albatross falls off his neck. As his penance, the mariner is forced to wander the earth telling his tale of woe.

You are the world's greatest poetry detective. Find one example for each technique.

Figurative language:

Using colour as symbols:

Metaphors:

Personification:

Mechanical language:

Verse form:

End-rhyme:

Run on lines:

Mnemonic language:

Repetition:

Onomatopoeia:

Alliteration:

'IF' by Rudyard Kipling (1865-1936)

If you can keep your head when all about you

Are losing theirs and blaming it on you;

If you can trust yourself when all men doubt you,

But make allowance for their doubting too:

If you can wait and not be tired of waiting,

Or, being lied about, don't deal in lies,

Or being hated don't give way to hating

And yet don't look too good, nor talk too wise;

If you can dream-and not make dreams your master;

If you can think-and not make thoughts your aim,

If you can meet with Triumph and Disaster

And treat those two impostors just the same:

If you can bear to hear the truth you've spoken

Twisted by knaves to make a trap for fools,

Or watch the things you gave your life to, broken,

And stoop and build 'em up with worn-out tools;

If you can make one heap of all your winnings

And risk it on one turn of pitch-and-toss,

And lose, and start again at your beginnings,

And never breathe a word about your loss:

If you can force your heart and nerve and sinew

To serve your turn long after they have gone,

And so hold on when there is nothing in you

Except the will which says to them: "Hold on!"

If you can talk with crowds and keep your virtue,

Or walk with Kings-nor lose the common touch,

If neither foes nor loving friends can hurt you,

If all men count with you, but none too much:

If you can fill the unforgiving minute

With sixty seconds' worth of distance done,

Yours is the Earth and everything that's in it,

And-which is more-you'll be a Man, my son!

Read this poem once. Write out the first word or phrase that springs to mind after reading it.

Now read it again aloud. Are there any other words or phrases that spring to mind?

CREATIVE WRITING QUESTIONS

1. Did you like this poem? Say why/why not giving examples from the poem.

2. What do you think is the theme of the poem? Are there sub-themes in it as well, in your opinion? Write down what you think they may be.

3. Try to write a 6-line poem with the same title.

4. What is the best advice given in the poem, in your opinion? Give an example from the poem.

5. If you were asked to rewrite one word or line from the poem, which would it be? Write out the word or line.

6. What is the mood of the poem, in your opinion?

7. What do you think are the main differences between this poem and the ones earlier in the book?

'THE COTTAGE IN THE GROVE' by Liam O' Flynn (Still alive)

The building's now a widow,

grown old with ivy veil;

and small things creep and shadows grow

among the broken shale.

How the sunlight sweetly burns

the walls with broken eyes;

and lime-tears stretch towards the urns

with silent, crumbling cries.

No robins sing, no song is heard,

the cottage is forlorn.

The Titian-breasted Jesus bird

will not announce the morn.

How the moonlight harpstring lanced

inside the kitchen door;

where songs were heard and children danced

upon the flagstone floor.

How the starflame freely spilled

upon the wellworn path;

before the fields now untilled

were wrinkle-clapped with wrath.

Whiskey flowed and candles glowed

stout bonds of kinship made.

The fire danced low and turfy slow

burning the path to jade.

Laughter rang and children sang

with mouths raised to the thatch.

And how the starfire freely spilled

upon the sumptuous grass.

No crack of snail, no thrush refined,

shall this place ever hear.

Small birds know all about bloodlines;

and why they disappear.

How the sunlight awful burns

the cottage in the grove;

where children laughed away concerns

swirling in carefree cloaks.

Now the sunlight awful peeps

where moonlight once shone hale;

and shadows creep and half-things weep

among the broken shale.

Read this poem once. Write out the first word or phrase that springs to mind after reading it.

Now read it again aloud. Are there any other words or phrases that spring to mind?

CREATIVE WRITING QUESTIONS

1. Did you like this poem? Say why/why not giving examples from the poem.

2. What do you think is the theme of the poem? Are there sub-themes in it as well, in your opinion? Write down what you think they may be.

3. Try to write a 6-line poem with the same title.

4. What are the best images in the poem, in your opinion? Give examples from the poem.

5. If you were asked to rewrite one word or line from the poem, which would it be? Write out the word or line.

6. What is the mood of the poem, in your opinion?

WRITE A 10-LINE POEM ON ANY SUBJECT OF YOUR CHOICE

_____

_____

_____

_____

_____

_____

_____

_____

_____

_____

'DO NOT STAND AT MY GRAVE AND WEEP' by Mary Elizabeth Frye (1905-2004)

Do not stand at my grave and weep:

I am not there; I do not sleep.

I am a thousand winds that blow,

I am the diamond glints on snow,

I am the sun on ripened grain,

I am the gentle autumn rain.

When you awaken in the morning's hush

I am the swiftly uplifting rush

Of quiet birds in circling flight

I am the soft starshine at night.

Do not stand at my grave and cry:

I am not there; I did not die.

Read this poem once. Write out the first word or phrase that springs to mind after reading it.

Now read it again aloud. Are there any other words or phrases that spring to mind?

CREATIVE WRITING QUESTIONS

1. Did you like this poem? Say why/why not giving examples from the poem.

2. What do you think is the theme of the poem? Are there sub-themes in it as well, in your opinion? Write down what you think they may be.

3. Try to write a 6-line poem with the same title.

4. What are the best images in the poem, in your opinion? Give examples from the poem.

5. If you were asked to rewrite one word or line from the poem, which would it be? Write out the word or line.

6. What is the mood of the poem, in your opinion?

THE EXTRAORDINARY STORY OF THIS POEM

For over 60 years, nobody knew who wrote this poem. It was used at funerals and it was written on bereavement card for all that time in America. Nobody came forward to claim ownership of it. This was surprising as it would have made the poet a lot of money.

In 1995, the father of a British soldier killed in Northern Ireland read it on BBC radio. His son had it among his personal effects. That was the first time it had been introduced to the general public in Britain.

Later that year, 'The Bookworm' television programme decided to conduct a poll of Britain's favourite poems. Even though this poem wasn't even on the list of poems, it won hands down! Thirty thousand votes later, it was now officially Britain's favourite poem.

In 1998, the world's most famous female journalist was Abigail van Buren. She was the first global 'agony aunt' and had 110 million readers. She discovered who wrote the poem and the story went like this:

In 1932, Mary Frye and her husband kept a female lodger in their house. This lodger, named Margaret, was German. She was very upset that she could not visit her mother who was ill in Germany. Hitler was coming to power and there was a lot of unrest in Germany. When her mother died, Margaret was heartbroken. She said she never had the chance to "stand by my mother's grave and shed a tear."

Almost immediately, Mary Frye wrote out the poem on a brown shopping bag. She wrote it out in one quick movement exactly as it is seen today. Remarkably, she had never written a poem before. She said the words "just came to her." She gave it to some friends as a gesture of comfort but never sought publicity for it. It was so impactful that it gained in popularity over the next 60 years. In all that time, Mary Frye never claimed to own it. When she eventually did, she did not put a copyright on it. Because of that, it is free for anyone to use. That was her final gift before she died in 2005.

This poem, just like Robert Frost's and Rudyard Kipling's, proves one point. Although a lot of great poems use the rule of three, not all do. Just like painting and music, sometimes the message is enough to have an effect on people. When you are writing a poem, think of the message you want to convey first. If after that, you decide to add in onomatopoeia, metaphors and alliteration, well and good. They help, but they can never define a poem.

Spare grids which may be used for any poem.

Figurative language:

Using colour as symbols:

Metaphors:

Personification:

Mechanical language:

Verse form:

End-rhyme:

Run on lines:

Mnemonic language:

Repetition:

Onomatopoeia:

Alliteration:

Spare grids which may be used for any poem.

Figurative language:

Using colour as symbols:

Metaphors:

Personification:

Mechanical language:

Verse form:

End-rhyme:

Run on lines:

Mnemonic language:

Repetition:

Onomatopoeia:

Alliteration:

Spare grids which may be used for any poem.

Figurative language:

Using colour as symbols:

Metaphors:

Personification:

Mechanical language:

Verse form:

End-rhyme:

Run on lines:

Mnemonic language:

Repetition:

Onomatopoeia:

Alliteration:

DIFFICULT SPELLING WORDS AND PRONUNCIATIONS

Most of the words in the grid have a mixture of two difficulty ratings. They are difficult to spell *and* they are difficult to pronounce. A lot of them also break the spelling rules in different ways. Your job is to pick one word and make up a simple mnemonic. You can then spell it and help your classmates by sharing the mnemonic with them. Here are some ex's. :

1) There are two **seas** (i.e. '**c**''s) in the Ar**c**ti**c**.

2) I went to Loch Ness. It was the busi Ness!

3) 'I' before 'e' except after 'c' for bel**ie**ves.

4) De**ss**erts have **two sugars** but a desert only has one **s**on.

5) The princi**pal** is my **pal** and a princi**ple** is a ru**le** I follow.

LEVEL 3

TOUGH WORDS	TOUGHER WORDS	TOUGHEST WORDS
pronounce	February	jewellery
pronunciation	interpret	Alzheimer's disease
utmost	business	deterioration
perspire	mayonnaise	in parentheses
library	vocabulary	refrigerator
sneaked	Mississippi	remuneration
lease	parliament	entrepreneur
Arctic	Antarctic	dementia
mauve	espresso	psychiatrist
probably	triathlon	cacophony
rarely	unfortunately	utolaryngology
Australia	foliage	diphtheria
relevant	candidate	conscience
believes	particularly	vulture
January	et cetera	composition
sherbet	literature	principal
federal	hierarchy	mosquito
sixth	nuclear	rhododendron
little	regardless	physician
thoroughly	miniature	conscious
hospital	prescription	punctuation
athletic	fiscal	orchid
situation	calendar	stationery
barbed wire	medicine	principle
cavalry	poison	cauliflower
truth	paralysed	prophet
helicopter	yacht	cocoa
clothes	retrieve	rhubarb
rhythm	punctual	conjunction

EXTRA LESSONS: ONOMATOPOEIA

You are walking in the city. The sounds all around you can be described in three different ways. The first one is given to you. Can you fill in the rest? Add in 5 more at the end.

cars	honking	blaring	hooting
tyres	screeching		
people	chattering		
buses	growling		
feet	stamping		
music/stereos	blaring		
drills	pounding		
traffic	whizzing		
dogs	snapping		
alarms/sirens	whining		
planes	humming		
breaking glass	tinkling		
doors	slamming		
paper/flags in wind	flapping		
rain	sissing		

If you are very clever and have finished before everyone else, listen to the sounds of the classroom. Are the students making noise as they work? Fill in the grid below with the sounds you hear. The first example is done for you. Try to get two sounds for every action.

chairs	scraping	rasping

When you are finished, write a story on walking through the city. Use only the words you have filled in. Do not use the other senses of sight, sensation, touch and taste. You will find you have written a very powerful passage. Then write a story entitled: 'The classroom is so annoying today!' Try to make it as humorous as possible by presenting yourself as a victim.

MNEMONIC GRAMMAR POEM

Every name is called a **noun**

As field and fountain, street and town.

In place of noun the **pronoun** stands

As he and she can clap their hands.

An **adjective** describes a thing

As magic wand and golden ring.

The **verb** means action, something done-

To read, to write, to jump, to run.

How things are done, the **adverbs** tell

As quickly, slowly, there and here.

The **preposition** shows relation

As *in* the street or *at* the station.

Conjunctions join in many ways

Sentences, words, clause or phrase.

The **interjection** cries out "Hark"

I need an **exclamation mark**!

Through poetry, we learn how each

Of these make up the **parts of speech**!

INTELLIGENCE A	Y/N/S	INTELLIGENCE B	Y/N/S
Do you:		**Do you:**	
have very good balance and ride a bicycle easily?		love groups of people and crowds?	
use hand gestures a lot when talking to friends?		enjoy teaching things to others?	
have problems sitting still for long periods?		have a lot of friends?	
love to run and exercise whenever you can?		enjoy team sports?	
like to try out new sports and find them easy?		like to give others advice?	
move, tap or fidget when seated for a long time?		love meeting new people?	
like to touch something rather than just look at it?		like to take part in group activities?	
mimic other people sometimes with your voice and actions?		like to win over other people?	
have different physical sensations when thinking or working?		like to solve other peoples' problems?	
like to make or build things?		have a talent for judging the mood of other people?	
	Score		**Score**

INTELLIGENCE C	Y/N/S	INTELLIGENCE D	Y/N/S
Do you:		**Do you:**	
like to work alone?		like word games?	
like to write in diaries or journals?		like puns and riddles?	
think you are a perfectionist?		enjoy writing more than most?	
think you are very independent?		love English class?	
like to think about where life will lead you?		enjoy the sounds and words of foreign languages?	
see yourself working for yourself in the future?		like to read about and use famous quotes and sayings?	
like to spend time thinking and reflecting?		like the sound and rhythm of words?	
like to discover new things about yourself and your personality?		notice spelling and grammar mistakes better than others?	
like to set personal targets and goals?		like to talk about the things you read?	
know your own strengths and weaknesses as a person?		like to use words that others think are fancy?	
	Score		**Score**

Y=Yes   N=No   S=Sometimes

INTELLIGENCE E	Y/N/S	INTELLIGENCE F	Y/N/S
Do you:		**Do you:**	
easily do maths in your head?		easily memorise songs?	
like science experiments?		have a good sense of rhythm?	
like strategy games?		often hum or sing?	
wonder how things work?		love Music class?	
enjoy working with numbers?		notice and enjoy different sounds?	
organise things by category?		feel you have a talent for singing?	
love Maths class?		feel you have a talent or love for a musical instrument?	
have a mind like a computer?		like to tap out the rhythm of a song?	
look for rational explanations for things?		often have a song running through your head?	
see connections that maybe others don't?		easily notice when a note is off-key?	
	Score		**Score**

INTELLIGENCE G	Y/N/S	INTELLIGENCE H	Y/N/S
love the idea of having pets?		love to solve visual puzzles?	
like to learn about nature?		enjoy geometry at school?	
enjoy the idea of gardening?		remember places vividly?	
appreciate beautiful, scenic places?		enjoy photography?	
think about pollution and get angry?		have a great sense of direction?	
feel more alive and at peace when you are in contact with nature?		love to look at books with pictures or photographs?	
like to camp outdoors, go for long nature walks and climb?		think in 3-dimensional terms sometimes?	
notice nature above all other things?		notice shapes, colours and textures more than most people?	
love to read National Geographic and nature books?		think you are above average at drawing?	
like to classify and categorise things and models of things?		like to visualise pictures in your head quite often?	
	Score		**Score**

It may be more accurate to approach the scoring system above with 5 points from 1-5.

1= Never
2= Rarely
3= Sometimes
4= A lot
5= Always

DESCRIBING THE RAIN

SPRING	SUMMER	AUTUMN	WINTER
airy rain	beads of rain	**hissing** rain	Amazonian showers
drizzling rain	dewdrops of rain	**saturating** rain	a biblical **deluge**
evanescent rain	droplets of rain	**seething** rain	monsoon rains
mist-like rain	pearls of rain	**shredding** rain	Noah's-Ark-lavish
mizzling rain	*****ploppy** drops of	**sibilant** rain	**sluicing** rains
pitter-patter of rain	plump drops of	**sissing** rain	**torrential** rainfall
showering rain	pregnant drops of	**sizzling** rain	silver icicles of rain
spraying rain	**splattering** rain	**soaking** rain	silver nails of rain
sprinkling sound of rain	the **susurration** of rain	**spitting** rain	upside-down rain (so heavy it bounces upwards)
tinkling rain	teardrops of rain	stinging rain	the billion-fold **ping**

The rain is the white noise of nature. Of course, some people love white noise and others find it off-putting. Maybe it is because we all have a memory buried deep down in our psyches. This memory is of the billion-fold plip and plop of rain dripping just outside of a cave. It is a memory of moss and wet cave floors, the musty smell of bears and the Jurassic-green of ferns. It is also a memory of crackling fires, sooty faces, laughter and safety. Depending on which memory you choose to believe in, you will either love or hate the rain.

The words that are highlighted in bold above are onomatopoeic words. The word *'ploppy' is technically not a word, but it sounds so right for raindrops I just had to put it in! Now that you have your word banks for the seasonal nature of rain, it is time to concentrate more on its sound. All the onomatopoeic words you need to describe rain falling are on the next page.

SOFT RAIN SOUNDS	**HEAVY RAIN SOUNDS**
The rain was:	The rain was:

burbling (gurgling) into the drains.	**boiling** the surface of the river.
dripping from the flowers.	**buzzing** incessantly with noise.
chinking off the windows.	**dinging** furiously off the tin roof.
clinking off the cars.	**drumming** off the tarmacadam.
making a lovely, **lilting** sound.	**fizzing** against the top of the bus.
murmuring like white noise.	**hammering** off their leather jackets.
plinking off the puddles.	**ker-plunking** off the swollen pools.
strumming against the roof tops.	**pinging** angrily against the glass.
suspiring (sighing) through the air.	**plunking** onto the muddy earth.
swishing off my skin.	**smashing** onto the heads of the crowd.
thrumming off the cobble stones.	***swooshing** onto the flooded fields.
weaving (moving side to side) with the wind.	**tapping** madly off the door.
whirring (a rapid buzz) off the leaves.	**thunking** the tops of the trees.
gently **whisking** (stirring) the lake's surface.	**whizzing** from the sky.
whispering in the air.	**whooshing** as the heavens opened.

'Swooshing' is not a word either, although it should be! The next step is to think up of a scene or situation where you can use the words and sentences above. A simple example might look like the paragraphs on the next page.

LEVEL 1

I looked out the window. The sky was tar-black and the large clouds were moving towards me. I heard a tapping on the window and then it became a pitter-patter. People ran for cover outside and umbrellas were opened as the clouds spat out their beads of water. Puddles began plinking as the rainfall became heavier. The roofs of the cars danced with spray and I could hear the murmuring of the rain through the window. It sounded like the buzzing of angry bees.

For a Level 2 assignment, more detail should be added. Imagine the effect of the rain on the trees and include more detail on the sky and clouds. At the end of the paragraph, try to write something about the sun coming out. This will vary your writing style.

LEVEL 2

I quickened my pace as the clouds began to gather in the sky. Up to now, the sky had been postcard-perfect, but it was changing. The beautiful cocktail-blue shade was beginning to darken into gravel-grey. Large pillows of cloud were forming, blotting out the old-gold colour of the sun.

I got the first splatter of rain when I was halfway across the meadow. I took shelter under an old oak, hoping that I could see out the shower. Droplets of moisture began to drip from the leaves. They were sprinkling onto the grass like a gardener's hose. Then the rainfall became more intense. A wall of rain moved over the oak and the drops were drumming against the canopy. So much rain was falling that the sound blurred into one long, whirring noise. It reminded me of the rotor blades on a helicopter. Eventually, the noise lessened and the drops faded into a musical chime.

The sun came out again, casting slanted beams of light across the meadow. Steam rose slowly from the grass. It rose up eerily and drifted mist-like towards the molten-gold sun. The image was so vivid that it stayed with me all the way home.

Level 3 should conjure up a scene where the rain's effect can be explored in more detail. The words should get more complex also. An idea might be to visualise a forest scene in autumn, for example. Transport yourself there and describe the colours, the sensations and the sounds of the rain.

LEVEL 3

It began as a whispering in the air. The day had been beautiful and the sky was like a dome of plasma-blue. The clouds had looked like airy anvils drifting under the gleaming disc of sun.

We had put our tent up just before the Reaper's moon of autumn appeared over the trees. The moon seemed to turn the leaves into a flaming patchwork of colours: scorching-yellows, lava-reds and burnished-browns. It added an alien glamour to a perfect scene. We heard a greedy thrush, snail a-tapping on rock; he finished his supper before fluttering into the owl-light of the forest. The mournful cry of a lonely fox echoed through the vault-still silence of the trees.

A huffing wind rose up then, stirring the flaps of our tent. A tinkling sound came to our ears as the first pearls of rain dropped onto the leaves. The sound was like the glassy clinking of a champagne flute, lilting and clear. A sheet of rain passed over us and the sound intensified. The noise on the tent was like the phut-phut-phut that ripened nuts make when they hit the ground. It wasn't the soft, sodden, swollen drops of spring we were hearing; it was like ball-bearings were hitting the canvas roof with force. We could also hear an occasional ker-plunking sound. It was caused by the rainwater gathered on the tent falling to the ground in a great swash of release.

The thermometer plunged as we huddled together and shivered in the tent. For a brief moment, we thought that we might be doomed adventurers, destined to get swept away in a mighty flood. We needn't have worried. The curtain of rain passed over by the time dawn arrived. An explosion of birdsong erupted from the dripping trees and it was if the rain had never been.

DESCRIBING THE SUN

When describing the sun, there are 5 simple ways to do it. These are: the shape using *a metaphor*, *the reflection*, *the colour*, *weapons* and *water*. Then you are using an 'artist's eye' in order to portray the sun and its beams in a different way. We will start with 10 metaphors for the shape.

10 *metaphors* for the shape:

1. … a fiery ball in the sky.

2. … a glowing medallion in the sky.

3. … a golden globe in the sky.

4. … God's morning star (i.e. the sunrise).

5. … the celestial fireball in the sky.

6. … a heavenly orb.

7. … Titan's fiery wheel.

8. … the God-goldened disc in the sky.

9. … God's golden eye.

10. … God's luminous daystar.

These are just some examples of possible metaphors to be used. The next step is to apply the *reflection* of the sun to the metaphors. The best 5 are probably:

| blazing | flaming | glowing | shining | scorching |

You can also use *archaic words* which will lend a sense of age and antiquity to the sentence. 5 examples of this are:

| a-gleam | a-dazzle | a-glint | a-glitter | a-shine |

Now 10 *colours* relating to yellow or gold may be used. Some interesting ones are:

honeycomb-yellow	saffron-yellow	waxmelt-yellow	molten-gold	gloriole-gold
ore gold-yellow	yolk-yellow	ingot-gold	motherlode-gold	auriole-gold

The final step is to link all of these into a sentence using terms to do with *weapons* and *water*. For example, underneath are 5 terms of each for you to use.

1. *Arrows* of sunlight *bathed* the meadow.

2. *Hafts* of sunlight *drowned* the valley.

3. *Lances* of sunlight *splashed* the forest's floor.

4. *Shafts* of light *poured* onto the lake.

5. *Spears* of light *showered* the lonely moor.

All the techniques can then be joined into a short paragraph in order to make your writing more effective. Underneath is the finished product:

I walked through the forest. The sun above me was blazing like Titan's fiery wheel in the sky. It was a-dazzle with splendour and it was a soul-swelling experience. Between gaps in the forest's canopy, lances of its molten-gold beams splashed onto the floor. In places, the dead leaves seemed to be a-fire with an inner glow.

That is just one example of how to give your writing a more interesting slant. Using a different grouping of words, you can write the following:

I sat down by a glass-clear lake. The sun was like a celestial fireball in the sky. Its beams were scorching the land and sent the lake a-glitter with golden sparkles. In the afternoon, it began to get cloudy. The sun was a muted, waxmelt-yellow but shafts of light still poured through patches of cloud and onto the lake. Speckled trout arced into the air and plopped onto the water's surface, seeking to grab a fly from the platoons of them hanging over the lake.

DESCRIBING THE MOON

	American Indian	Medieval English	Colonial American	Others
January	wolf	wolf	winter's	Ice moon **(neo pagan)**
February	snow	storm	trapper's	Budding moon **(Chinese)**
March	worm	chaste	fish	Death moon **(neo pagan)**
April	pink	seed	planter's	moon of Awakening **(Celtic)**
May	flower	hair	milk	Dragon moon **(Chinese)**
June	strawberry	dyad	rose	moon of Horses **(Celtic)**
July	blood	mead	summer	Hungry Ghost **(Chinese)**
August	sturgeon	wort	dog day's	Lightning moon **(neo pagan)**
September	corn	barley	harvest	Singing moon **(Celtic)**
October	hunter's	blood	hunter's	Blood moon **(neo pagan)**
November	beaver	fog	beaver	Dark moon **(Celtic)**
December	cold	oak	Christmas	Long Night **(neo pagan)**

The wolves howl mournfully outside the village, slinking between shadows and the dark shape of the tents. A bitter, winter-white moon hangs in the sky and the smoke from dying fires still lingers in the air. A pile of buffalo bones lie to one side, gleaming silver and attracting the ravenous wolves. It is January 16, 1621. In exactly two months to the day, an Indian named Samoset will walk into an encampment at Maine, New England with the words: "Welcome, Englishmen!" They give him a coat and he will trade furs and fish with the pilgrims of the Mayflower. Life for the Indians will never be the same again.

The similarity between the moon-names of the pilgrims from Plymouth fleeing persecution and the native Indians is fascinating. One can trace the development of their traditions, culture and hunting/farming habits from the terms applied. Underneath are some explanations of the most difficult:

1. **Worm moon**: so called because the worms used to leave trails in the melting snow.

2. **Dyad moon**: from the word duo, meaning two, when the sun and moon appeared in the sky together.

3. **Mead moon**: named after a drink of honey and ale used for celebrations. Hunting for honey sounds dangerous!

4. **Harvest moon**: named after the medieval word 'haerfest', meaning autumn. A celebration usually occurred around September 23rd after the last 'mell' or sheaf of corn was brought in. Hence the term 'pell-mell', meaning crazy! Playing 'hooky', meaning absent, comes from this era also.

5. **Wort moon**: named after healing plants such as butterwort and woundwort which grew at this time.

6. **Sturgeon moon**: Indians around the Great Lakes were able to catch the huge fish, the sturgeon, which were active at this time.

7. **Dog day's moon**: The Roman's named it thus originally after Sirius, the Dog Star. It was traditionally the hottest time of the year and dogs either went mad or collapsed with fatigue.

8. **Blood moon**: so named because the moon can appear red at certain times.

9. **Blue moon**: It became popular as a term after an article was published in the 'Sky and Telescope' in March 1946. I'm inclined to believe the theory that it comes from the word 'belewe', however, an old Saxon word meaning 'beware' (as in beware the false moon). A blue moon does occur once every 2-3 years. This is because the **lunar month** is 11 days shorter than the calendar month (**29.53 days** in a month). Hence, every two and a half years or so, there is an 'extra' moon. There are 13 moons instead of 12. Monks used to have to convince the populace on the occurrence of a 'bewere' moon that they had to fast for another month for Lent! Monks also caused the extinction of the beaver moon term. Beaver and turtle were classed as aquatic animals in England so that the monks could eat them on Fridays. Blue moons **can** exist to the naked eye. In 1950 and 1951, forest fires in Sweden and Canada scattered the red and yellow light particles, turning the moon blue for those watching it. The same happened after the Krakatoa volcano in 1883.

10. **Dark moon**: There is no such thing as the dark side of the moon. Dark spots on the moon can be seen from earth, however. These are caused by old lava beds and meteor impacts, which are grey on the moon but appear as dark spots to us.

For the purposes of descriptive writing, being able to put in a term like a wolf moon adds a touch of exotica and spice to a passage. I love the Reaper's moon, personally, when the corn or wheat was brought in by the reapers. The section on OTHERS in the grid has capital letters because the choice is up to the writer to decide if they should be capitalised or not.

The moon is perhaps the 'magic pill' of imagery when you want to create an evocative scene. Everyone has their own idea on what makes for a great moon image. It could be a shimmering, globe-gold moon. It could be the eerie, blood-red harvest moon of autumn, the dreaded death moon of March or a silver sea-moon. If you want evoke a beautiful image, the sea-moon is the best. There are no rules to descriptive writing. However, there are some useful hints that you might take on board. For example, it is easier to divide the moon into the following categories: *shape, colour, reflection, metaphors for the moonbeams and similes.*

Suggested *shapes* are the following:

an orb	a disc	a halo	a ring	a salver

The *colours* are completely up to you but some nice silvers are to be found with metals.

alloy-silver	argent-silver	nickel-silver	orris-silver	zinc-silver

You could be more creative and try using ghostly silvers for an eerie scene:

1. ghostly-silver or dewgleam-silver

2. phantom-silver or diamond-flame silver

3. spectre-silver or hoarfrost-silver

4. spooky-silver or solar-silver

5. wraith-silver or sequin-silver

The best 5 *reflective* verbs for the moon are:

gleaming	glinting	glowing	shimmering	glimmering

Then it is just a simple case of using creative ***metaphors for the moonbeams***. Here are 5 of the best:

1. chords of moonlight

2. harpstrings of moonlight

3. ribbons of moonlight

4. strands of moonlight

5. tendrils of moonlight

The final stage of the process is to use ***similes*** that contain these words or similar words. It is important to note that, as always, this process is only a ***guide to developing an 'artist's eye'***. I don't claim to know it all by any means. However, the hints given should inspire the readers to think about their own creativity and attempt to better the sentences below. Underneath are some nice expressions for a sea-moon using the formula.

1. The moon was like a ghostly-silver orb in the sky. Its beams spilled across the sea ***like lines of glittering fire***. It was an alluring scene.

2. The moon was like a phantom-silver disc in the sky. Chords of moonlight lasered across the sea ***like lines of glimmering fire***. It was a captivating scene.

3. The moon was like a spectre-silver halo in the sky. Ribbons of light rebounded off the mirrored surface of the sea ***like silver tracers of fire***. It was soul-enriching.

4. The moon was like a spook-silver ring in the sky. Its ghostly light shimmered on the water, silvering the sea ***like rippling aluminium***. It was an entrancing sight.

5. ***The moon was like a wraith-silver salver hanging in the lonely sky. Tendrils of moonlight, as bright as diamond-flame, turned the sea a-glow like melted platinum. It was as if I was watching a scene from an old fable stepping off the page and I was beguiled by its beauty. The Chinese called the May moon the dragon moon and I could see why. The waves were a-glitter like curved scales and I became lost in the haunting lullaby of their swell and sigh.***

DESCRIBING THE STARS

For the stars, you should again focus on four main aspects: the *colour*, the *reflection*, the *shape* and using an effective *simile*. This comes back to the concept of looking at the world with an 'artist's eye'.

A child loves the way the stars are twinkling like little pulses of light. They also love drawing stars as there is symmetry to the five sides that other shapes don't have. As well as this, it is the first shape they will draw which gives them a sense of achievement because of its complexity. If you think of it, a square, circle or triangle is relatively easy. Drawing a star, however, exercises parts of the brain that haven't been used before. Starting at the bottom left, they have to go up, down, up and across, across, then down and across. I often wonder how many teachers actually show them how to do this. I'm pretty certain that it would save a child a lot of time were they to be shown how to trace a star properly from first day. If not, then a lot of stars would have to be drawn in ignorance before achieving success.

These posts I'm uploading hope to achieve the same. Make your students *think of the different components* that make up descriptive writing. Whether it be the branch of a tree that is compared to a similar shape or the texture of flowers, nearly everything in nature has a colour, shape, action (or inaction, like a womb-still lake) and sensation/smell associated with it. Every English student should be able to grasp that essential fact. It then makes it so much easier to evoke a sensory piece of descriptive writing for the reader. If they are not taught that, they may end up like the child trying to draw a star while other children in the class are moving on to complex octagons.

5 different colours for the stars:

birthstone-blue	molten-gold	solar-yellow	sequin-silver	polar-white

The reflection of the stars:

flashing and flickering	gleaming and glittering	sparkling and shimmering	twinkling and dazzling	glistering and pulsing

The stars are similar in shape to:

snowflakes	pinpricks	asters	petals	pentagrams

5 *creative similes for the stars. The stars looked:*

1. …like scattered moondust in the sky.

2. …like a large hand had tossed diamond dust into the sky.

3. …like beacons of hope for all the lost souls of the world.

4. … like bejewelled grains of sand allowed to sparkle in silence.

5. …like the glittering sparks from angelfire.

The final step is to pick out which words and phrases you like the best and put them together into a sentence. Also try to pick a remote location for your setting where the stars would be most vividly seen. We will give you an example using the ocean. You are lost at sea. Are the stars comforting and a sign of hope or are they making you pine for civilisation? Are they the streetlamps of nature or are they a flashing reminder of your own fleeting mortality? The story is up to you, but by using our formulas you should come up with something like this:

The waves glopped and slashed off the wooden raft. Then the full moon came out and the wave-motion died down. It was an eerie, spectre-silver moon. Its ghostly lustre sent beams of argent-silver spilling across the sea. The wraith-like light flooded the sea, making it glow like silvered mercury.

Stars winked at me from the endless arch of void-black beyond the moon's corona. In places they were birthstone-blue and beautiful, all a-glitter in their heavenly finery. The ones furthest away, almost outside the span of human comprehension, were like flashing pinpricks in a veil of darkness. They had a faint, silver tint and they looked like they were the distant, glittering sparks from angel fire. All of them were beacons of hope for all the lost souls of the world, or so I thought. It seemed to me that there was a snowfall sparkling in outer space and I felt privileged to witness it.

A QUICK REFERENCE GUIDE

SPRING

FIELD COLOURS	SOFT SOUNDS	FLOWERY SMELLS	SPIRITUAL SENSATIONS	HEAVENLY TASTES
A_a_on-green	the baa-baa of l_m_s	al_e V_ra sweet	soul embra_ing	ambrosi_l
aph_d-green	the ba_b_ing of brooks	balsam_c sweet	soul bolste_ing	angel_c
car_iv_l-green	the bumb_ing of bees	bl_ss_m sweet	soul cheri_hing	Arcadi_n
chartre_se-green	the bur_ling of streams	cala_ine sweet	soul com_orting	celesti_l
garl_nd-green	the buz_ing of mi_ges	ho_e_suckle sweet	soul cultiv_ting	cherub_c
jasp_r-green	the c_rol_ing of the dawn chorus	jasmi_e sweet	soul lul_ing	divi_e
p_a-green	the ch_eping of chic_s	me_d_w sweet	soul nour_shing	empyre_l
pa_sl_y-green	the chim_ng of catara_ts	myr_h sweet	soul nurtu_ing	godlik_
s_p-green	the chir_ing of gr_ss_o_pers	p_ll_n sweet	soul refre_hing	seraph_c
wate_c_ess-green	the dri_z_ing of raindrops	rose_ater sweet	soul stok_ng	supern_l

An excellent site can be accessed by typing in: Alphabetical list of fragrances to: **anovelideaco.com**. It gives pictures and images to go with the foods and fragrances on offer.

Note: The words in the 'Heavenly Tastes' column are included for Senior Cycle students.

SPRING

MEADOW COLOURS	SOFT SOUNDS	SUGARY SMELLS	SPIRITUAL SENSATIONS	TASTE ADJECTIVES
broch_re-green	the ex_a_ing of the wi_d	bak_d ap_le	spirit boo_ting	app_tizing
fab_e-green	the hu_ming of law_mo_ers	candi_d	spirit enha_cing	del_ctable
fanta_y-green	the intone_g of bumb_e bees	confection_ry	spirit enkindl_ng	deli_ious
fai_yla_d-green	the mizz_ing of the ra_n	d_wy	spirit ennobl_ng	exqui_ite
fai_y_ale-green	the plin_ing of wat_r_alls	hon_y_d	spirit enri_hing	extravag_nt
fantas_a-green	the pran_ing of l_m_s	lemo_y	spirit fill_ng	fuls_me
Jur_ss_c-green	the puf_i_g of the wi_d	nectar_ne	spirit lif_ing	into_icating
pos_ca_d-green	the orinas_l hum of be_s	saccha_ine	spirit rai_ing	lav_sh
sto_y_ook-green	the rust_ing of grass	syru_y	spirit refres_ing	lusci_us
wo_derla_d-green	the sh_sh over the l_nd	tut_i-frui_y	spirit rene_ing	lu_h

Try to make a story using any combination of the words above. Pick 10-15 words you are comfortable with first. Then look up 5 more of the words that strike you as unusual and look them up in the dictionary. You will then be able to write a very evocative story based on the 4 senses used above. You can also write a spring story using only the onomatopoeic words if you wish.

SPRING

HEAVENLY VALLEYS	SOFT SOUNDS	SWEET SMELLS	PHYSICAL SENSATIONS	TASTE ADJECTIVES
Arca_ian-green	the sig_ing of zephyrs	blancma_ge sweet	eye-ope_ing	luxury_nt
Ba_yl_n-green	the snip_ing of shears	car_m_l sweet	eye-wi_ening	mouth wa_ering
E_en-green	the sob_ing of streams	gelat_n sweet	goose bu_p-inducing	opule_t
Ely_ium-green	the splos_ing of trout	gluco_e sweet	hair-rai_ing	ravis_ing
Jer_sal_m-green	the swis_ing of horsetails	man_a sweet	heart-clenc_ing	savou_y
par_d_se-green	the trem_ling of leaves	march pa_e sweet	heart-clam_ing	scrumpti_us
Shangri-La green	the whinn_ing of foals	marzip_n sweet	heart-pum_ing	sumptuo_s
utopian-green	the whir_ing of dragonflies	mering_e sweet	heart-thum_ing	tantali_ing
Valhalla-green	the whit_ling of gardeners	noug_t sweet	skin-tin_ling	tooths_me
Zion-green	the yel_ing of fox cubs	treac_e sweet	jaw-drop_ing	wh_lesome

SUMMER

SEA-BLUE RIVERS	SOFT SOUNDS	LOUD SOUNDS	COSMIC SMELLS	MOVEMENT OF SMELLS
aqua_ium-blue	the chit_ering of swallows	cl_p-clop_ing horses	astr_l	bl_w
Atlan_ic-blue	the chu_ging of rivers	cha_tering starlings	astrono_ical	car_ied
Atla_tis-blue	the co_ing of pigeons	champ_ng cows	cosm_c	draft_d
Balt_c-blue	the cro_ning of songbirds	crop_ing sheep	galact_c	dri_ted
Carib_ean-blue	the dren_hing of showers	glop_ing raindrops	otherworl_ly	floa_ed
Mediter_anean-blue	the drif_ing of clouds	gurg_ing rivers	out-of-this-wor_d	gli_ed
Neptu_e-blue	the fluti_g of blackbirds	mastica_ing cows	out-of-this-uni_erse	ghos_ed
Paci_ic-blue	the huf_ing of the breeze	munc_ing sheep	stell_r	rus_ed
Sarga_so-blue	the hu_h of the land	neig_ing horses	transcendent_l	sai_ed
ripari_n-blue	the linge_ing moon	nicke_ing foals	unearth_y	stra_ed

SUMMER

SKY BLUES	SOFT SOUNDS	LOUD SOUNDS	A MIX OF SMELLS	VERBS FOR SMELLS
auro_a-blue skies	the lisp_ng of rills	plun_ing fish	a barbe_ue of smells	languis_ed in
birthst_ne-blue skies	the lol_ing of lake boats	pum_ing heart of summer	a br_w of smells	leisu_ed in
chemi_al-blue skies	the low_ng of cows	quive_ing wheat fields	a bro_h of smells	linge_ed in
cockta_l-blue skies	the mum_ling of bees	scrun_hing leaves	a buff_t of smells	loiter_ed in
constella_ion-blue skies	a murmu_ing of the wind	siz_ling summers	a burg_o of smells	loun_ed in
electr_c-blue skies	murmura_ions of water	slos_ing fish	a chow_er of smells	pas_ed through
halog_n-blue skies	the nuz_ling of foals	splos_ing salmon	a goula_h of smells	percola_ed through
halcy_n-blue skies	the pi_ing of blackbirds	splut_ering streams	a me_u of smells	phantom_ed through
lodest_r-blue skies	the purli_g of rivulets	sput_ering rain	a st_w of smells	pilfer_d through
polar_s-blue skies	the pur_ing of runnels	tintinna_ulation of water	a so_p of smells	puf_ed through

SUMMER

BLUE WATERFALLS	SOFT SOUNDS	LOUD SOUNDS	A MIX OF SMELLS	WORDS FOR SMELLS
cerule_n-blue	the skim_ing of swallows	warb_ing songbirds	a carni_al of smells	the aro_a of
plas_a-blue	the soug_ing of the wind	whit_ling gardeners	a carous_l of smells	the bouqu_t of
si_k-blue	the sprin_ling of hoses	whirrupi_g waterfalls	a cornucop_a of smells	the colo_ne of
sat_n-blue	the swir_ing of wheat fields	whiz_ing falling stars	a cir_us of smells	the fragr_nce of
starbla_e-blue	the trick_ing of rills	whoo_hing comets	a fun_air of smells	the olfact_ry overload of
starfla_e-blue	the throb_ing heart of	wob_ling ice creams	a pagea_t of smells	perfu_e of
sol_r-blue	thrum_ing hooves of foals	yip_ing foxes	a ri_t of smells	the redolen_e of
sue_e-blue	the tril_ing of thrushes	zing_ng waterfalls	a smorgasb_rd of smells	the sce_t of
vel_et-blue	the twe_ting of chicks	zip_ing hawks	a tape_try of smells	the wa_t of
velo_r-blue	the wh_sking of wheat ears	zo_ming falcons	a theat_e of smells	the whi_f of

AUTUMN

AUTUMN REDS	AUTUMN GOLDS	SOFT SOUNDS	LOUD SOUNDS	DECIDUOUS SMELLS
barbe_ue-reds	glea_ing-golds	the care_sing of the wind	bat_ering winds	cl_y-rich
bon_ire-reds	glin_ing-golds	the chir_uping of songbirds	blas_ing storms	eart_y
conflagr_tion-reds	glit_ering-golds	the crin_ling of leaves	boi_ing skies	loa_y
cremat_rium-reds	glo_ing-golds	the cr_sping of flaky leaves	boo_ing thunder	mushroo_y
em_er-reds	light_ing-golds	the crum_ling of vegetation	buf_eting squalls	mulc_y
inciner_tor-reds	lumin_us-golds	the dro_ing of the dragonflies	caterwa_ling windstorms	oak_n
infer_o-reds	lustro_s-golds	the hoo_ing of owls	ca_ing ravens	orga_ic
la_a-reds	molt_n-golds	the la_ping of water	chur_ing clouds	pe_ty
mag_a-reds	sunbur_t-golds	the lil_ing tones of autumn	cla_ing warlocks	seaso_ed
py_e-reds	waxm_lt-golds	the muf_led forest sounds	cree_ing crawlies	woo__y

AUTUMN

AUTUMN REDS	AUTUMN ORANGES	SOFT SOUNDS	LOUD SOUNDS	CONIFEROUS SMELLS
clar_t-reds	fie_y-oranges	the ph_t-ph_t of falling nuts	cr_nching cannibals	the amber whi_f of
haemog_obin-reds	fl_ming-oranges	the pulsi_g soul of autumn	droo_ing ogres	the glycerine aro_a of
oxblo_d-reds	bla_ing-oranges	the puli_g of the soft winds	ech_ing sounds	the gummy fragran_e of
marr_w-reds	broil_ng-oranges	the quave_ing of wrens' wings	explo_ing toadstools	the medicinal sce_t of
rushli_ht-reds	bur_ing-oranges	the rus_ling of leaves	gu_zling gorgons	the minty t_nt of
Ti_ian-reds	incandes_ent-oranges	the shud_ering of trees	heav_ng seas	the pine sweet colo_ne of
verme_l-reds	scorc_ing-oranges	the shuff_ing of forest walkers	how_ing wolves	the resin sweet pot pou_ri of
vermil_on-reds	smoulder_ing-oranges	the silen_e of the dawn	keeni_g north winds	the sap sweet redolen_e of
vinaceo_s-reds	swelte_ing-oranges	the snuf_ling of whiskey-noses	pro_ling ghosts	the starch sweet hotchpot_ch of
windf_ll-reds	volca_ic-oranges	the squel_hing of feet	rag_ng rivers	the thyme sweet per_ume of

AUTUMN

AUTUMN REDS	AUTUMN YELLOWS	SOFT SOUNDS	LOUD SOUNDS	FRUITY SMELLS
balefi_e-reds	brimst_ne-yellows	the slum_ering of hedgehogs	scraw_ing goblins	citr_s sharp
brazi_r-reds	candle fla_e-yellows	the tin_ling of waterfalls	skit_ering animals	fruitca_e heavy
devil bl_od-reds	feveri_h-yellows	the twir_ing of leaves	sis_ing rain	full b_died
dr_gon f_ame-reds	flas_ing-yellows	the twit_ering of songbirds	slob_ering trolls	me_d sweet
firebra_d-reds	flic_ering-yellows	the whee_ing of the wind	slur_ing vampires	mel_n ripe
firedra_e-reds	h_t-yellows	the whir_ing of leaves	splin_ering boughs	orch_rd sweet
firef_y-reds	incendia_y-yellows	the whim_ering of the wind	suppura_ing floods	peac_y
glowwo_m-reds	moonfla_e-yellows	the whis_ering of wheat fields	wai_ing witches	pe_r ripe
hellhou_d-reds	sulph_r-yellows	the yaw_ing of the wind	yow_ing banshees	plum_y
phone_x-reds	sult_y-yellows	the yaw_ of fog horns	zin_ing raindrops	windf_ll sweet

The most beautiful word in the English language is **'cellar door'**, according to Tokien and Poe. A lot of internet surveys also have the words in the grid in common.

serendipity	languorous	rapture
_he	cinnamon	vivacious
_hany	phosphorescence	Elysium/elysian

Blue-Sky Thinking

Printed in Great Britain
by Amazon.co.uk, Ltd.,
Marston Gate.